P9-EDP-104

Nancy Astor and Her Friends

Nancy Astor and Her Friends

Elizabeth Langhorne

PRAEGER PUBLISHERS
New York • Washington

Published in the United States of America in 1974
by Praeger Publishers, Inc.
111 Fourth Avenue, New York, N.Y. 10003

Library of Congress Cataloging in Publication Data
Langhorne, Elizabeth.
Nancy Astor and her friends.
Includes bibliographical references.
1. Astor, Nancy Witcher (Langhorne) Viscountess.
I. Title.
DA574.A8L36 942.082'092'4 [B] 72-83006

Printed in the United States of America

To John, Elizabeth, and Harry

Contents

Sections of photographs follow pages 86 *and* 150.

Acknowledgments

In addition to providing notes on sources, which appear at the end of this book, I should like to make some special acknowledgment to those who have encouraged as well as helped me. I am grateful to my editor at Praeger, Gladys Topkis, for her close reading and always helpful suggestions for revision. The Langhorne family as a whole has been very kind, and none more helpful than NA's youngest nephew, Douglas Langhorne. I am especially grateful to David Astor for a general discussion of his parents' views and foreign-policy attitudes in the unhappy "appeasement" period. My interpretation is entirely my own, but Mr. Astor greatly strengthened my sense of the importance of this book and my conviction that it should be written without any attempt to gloss over the tragic miscalculations of that time.

Additional thanks go to the most sympathetic of all typists, Edith Good. I will close with a note of gratitude to the staff of the Alderman Library at the University of Virginia, who have most kindly extended to me the full use of their facilities, and to the Fellows and management of the MacDowell Colony, where most of this book was written.

Prologue

WHY write about Nancy Astor? Because she was the first woman Member of Parliament; because she knew everyone and, if she did not go everywhere, everyone came to her; because she was an ebullient, aggressive woman, married to one of the richest men in the world; and because she worked tirelessly for social reform and for world peace and her work for these things affected the world she lived in. All this makes us want to know her. But Nancy Astor did not want to have her biography written. She believed that only those who have given the world a new idea are worth writing about. She knew her own limitations. She was not an original thinker, and she never pretended to be one. But Nancy Astor did create something new. Just by living, just by being herself, she created an existential image of the woman in public life on her own terms, not as a pale copy of the male. When she entered the House of Commons she was a woman alone among 614 men, "none of whom wanted me there." It took fortitude to be the pioneer, and a religious belief in oneself.

For the friends, great and obscure, who surrounded her she had a magic quality. How can one define it? Among Nancy's close friends, Lloyd George and T. E. Lawrence had it; Philip Lothian and Bernard Shaw, for all their brilliance, did not. It is a mysterious quality, a sort of electric-power factor. One hopes that something of its nature will come clear in the course of this book about Nancy Astor and her friends.

1

Nancy in Virginia

Across the rather dull skies of Britain between the wars Nancy Astor—born Nancy Langhorne in Danville, Virginia—flashed like a shooting star. "A legend in her own time" is a nice phrase, and in this case an accurate one. But Nancy did not create the legend; she brought it with her. Her father, Colonel Chiswell Dabney Langhorne, was the prototype. Every Langhorne after him felt that he or she had to be larger than life, loaded with charm, and twice as funny as anyone else. To produce the unique phenomenon that was Nancy Astor it was only necessary to add high seriousness of purpose to the family type, shake vigorously, and turn loose upon an astonished, amused, and sometimes resentful world.

The Langhornes, like every Southern family, were ruined by the Civil War. The first Langhorne had emigrated from Laugharne in South Wales around 1670, and generations of

Virginia life failed to suppress a Celtic strain in the family character. The Langhornes were shrewd and imaginative, fantastic and resourceful, all at the same time. At the beginning of the war they were one of the "old" families of Lynchburg; they owned mills and warehouses and were popular and leading citizens of that town.

Chiswell Dabney, known as Chillie (pronounced "Shilly"), joined the Army of the Confederacy at the age of seventeen. At the end of of the war he was mustered out, penniless, just twenty-one, and with a new young wife to support into the bargain. Chillie had married Nancy Witcher Keene, a Danville girl of good family, in December, 1864. He described his start after the war with "nothing but a wife, a ragged seat to my pants, and a barrel of whiskey."

He earned a livelihood as best he could in Danville, principally as a tobacco auctioneer. This profession gave scope for the ready wit and good fellowship with which Chillie was abundantly endowed, but it by no means met his plans for his own future. He was out to restore the Langhorne fortunes, and in fact he eventually did that and more, increasing them many times over.

Almost no one believed, in those years, that material success was possible for a Southerner, particularly for one who, like Chillie, had not even had an education before disaster fell. From 1865 to 1885 he struggled through the grim years of Reconstruction in Danville. All but one of his eight children who survived infancy were born there. First came Keene, born within a year of his marriage, then Elizabeth, Irene, and Harry. Nancy, named after her mother and, like her mother, always called Nannie by family and friends, was born on May 19, 1879. The next youngest Langhorne, the closest to Nannie in affection as well as age, was Phyllis. Then came another brother, William Henry, always known as Buck.

During the years in Danville a cluster of dependent relatives clung to Chillie. In 1885 he shook himself loose from the cloying poverty of Danville and moved his immediate family to Richmond. The youngest child, Nora, was born shortly after this move. Chillie had gone in pursuit of a dawning recovery, which he must have sniffed in the air; it was certainly not offered to him on a silver platter on his arrival in the state capital. For five more years the Langhornes remained as poor in Richmond as they had been in Danville.

Richmond in the 1880s was a quiet town. During the short, mild winters and through the long, hot summer days its energies were given over to dream. This people of a defeated land created an image, more perfect than the original, of the vanished South. Leisure and charm were its essential ingredients; the illusion of leisure, the effect of charm were therefore produced.

The social life of a town where money, being nonexistent, did not count fit the Langhornes to perfection. The dignified mammies, dressed in black with spotless white aprons, would promenade with their charges up and down Franklin Street, an unpaved thoroughfare between wooden houses. It was a great treat to turn uphill to Broad Street to watch the "cyars" on the railroad tracks that at that time ran through the city. On the other side of Broad lay the great world—the crowded, vulgar, enticing world of the penny arcades, where no nice child of Franklin Street was allowed to set foot. One day little Nannie Langhorne broke away from her mammy and ducked between two huge black "cyars" to reach the other side of Broad. A nice man gave her two pennies. She spent them on candies and brought one back to baby Buck, then in his carriage. Mammy Lisa did not betray her to Chillie, who would have spanked Nannie and roared at them both.

It was at about this time that Nannie, aged eight, returned to Danville on a visit. She was offered a ride on a cousin's pony. The pony threw her, taking several kicks at the fallen rider before trotting off. Nannie was next seen pursuing the pony, launching vigorous kicks of her own at its fat posterior.

Although sheltered, life in Richmond was not entirely isolated. Members of a nondescript population known generically as "tramps" occasionally appeared at the door and were always given milk and biscuits and stopped at the back porch for a chat. Nannie, venturing out alone, would meet "Blind Willie" on the corner. This little colored boy was a Richmond fixture; he would do a sort of breakdown dance known locally as "eefing." Sometimes he was given pennies, sometimes not. When Nannie and he met they danced together. Nannie loved it. Indeed, throughout her life, Nannie was apt to break into a little dance step distinctly reminiscent of Blind Willie and the streets of Richmond.

Only Chillie refused to slip gently and unresisting into this peaceful life, so like the life of a quiet country town. He could not forget that Richmond had once been the capital of the Confederacy. He loved this land; he had fought for it as patriotically as any man alive. He could not accept its decline; he persisted in wanting a future as well as a past. While his womenfolk sat at home, happily sewing and gossiping about parties and beaux and more than half believing that the war had never been, Chillie roamed abroad. He was searching for a plain, honest-to-God, non-Confederate dollar.

Success, however, continued to elude him. By 1890 even Chillie's courage had failed him. He was preparing to send his family to the home of Cousin Charley Price, a hospitable relative who owned a farm in Albemarle County. Mrs. Langhorne was already packed, sitting among children and boxes in the hall of her dismantled home, when Chillie came bursting in. "Dammit, Nannie! Stop everything. I've got a job!" And indeed he had. Through the good offices of his friend and former commander, Colonel Henry Douglas, he had been given a contract for work on the new Chesapeake and Ohio Railroad. He had never been hired as a contractor before, but there was no trick, as he confidently remarked, to rounding up Negroes and mules. The trick had been to get one foot on the bandwagon. A whole nation was about to go on iron wheels, and Chillie Langhorne was all set to help it roll.

Success had little effect on Chillie's naturally rambunctious temperament and manners, which sometimes recalled the army camp and the auction ring rather than the drawing room. The young married friends of Nannie's older sister Irene found him trying. In self-defense they were forced to provide cuspidors when Mr. Langhorne came to visit, although the vulgar receptacle no longer appeared in polite society. Their anxiety may have been unfounded. When some years later, in a more exalted sphere, Nancy Astor was asked if her father was a good shot, she is reputed to have replied, "Oh, yes, he hits the fireplace every time." What became an amusing eccentricity at Cliveden irritated house-proud young matrons in Richmond in the 1890s, as did Chillie's inveterate habit of hollering,

"Dammit, shut the door," before the most well-brought-up young lady had had a chance to cross the threshold.

To the younger children Chillie was like Jove, formidable but the object of unstinted admiration. The hazards of this relationship seem to have been stimulating rather than terrifying, at least to Nannie. "He would often spank us and send us to bed for some remark he did not consider suitable, though as often as not we had no idea why." There was the visit to the stable to inspect the new horse, by the stallion Prosper. Chillie asked the children to suggest a name, which should begin with the first syllable of Prosper. Nannie felt inspired: "Why not call him Prostitute?"

"Go to your room," thundered Chillie.

"But why?" Nannie asked tearfully. "Why?"

Chillie was reduced to saying, "Your mother will explain," but as it turned out Mrs. Langhorne could not explain either.

There was nothing mean, no subtle urge to dominate in Chillie. He was simply a slightly larger than life version of the typical paterfamilias. If one could survive the first jars and jolts of life with Chillie, one found him a delightful companion and a loyal, warm-hearted friend. Men in particular liked him. He was a superb story teller and never told the same tale twice. He could have made a living at poker—but he gave up the game after nearly killing a man who had accused him of cheating. It seemed that, after Chillie had knocked him down, the fellow proceeded to fall the entire length of a flight of stairs! On another occasion a friend apologized to his wife for arriving home with tobacco-juice stains on his shirt front. He explained that he had "stayed up all night playing poker with Chillie Langhorne and had not had time to turn his head away from the table in order to spit." This excuse was considered quite adequate. Chillie's sister, the respected Aunt Lizzie Lewis, described her brother as "kind, and tremendously honest. He was irascible, yes, impetuous, impulsive; but big." The fight over the poker game and its aftermath seems to show that, like his daughter in later life, he would often go to reckless lengths, yet could somehow manage to call a halt before matters were out of hand.

In business Chillie was the ideal front man, the persuasive winner of contracts over a bottle of bourbon. But stacks of accounts, contracts, and business letters, all in his own hand, and even plans of Pullman cars show that, when he worked, he worked hard. For Chillie one railroad contract led to another, and on every one he turned a handsome profit.

During the next few years it was not Chillie's success but Irene's that loomed largest in Nannie's eyes. No time and no place has ever idealized feminine beauty as the South did after the war. Having lost all else, they felt that this one asset, at least, remained to them; it was the period *par excellence* of Southern womanhood, and Irene was, to perfection, the Southern belle. Before the war the landowner, lacking in the very nature of the economy a capital city of his own, had made the Virginia Springs a common meeting ground. The therapeutic waters had been the ostensible drawing card. Now the waters quite frankly took second place to the girls. Every Southern family with any pretensions at all sent its daughters to the great, rambling wooden hotels, showcases of charm and beauty for the whole area. If parents were too poor to afford the trip themselves, the girls went in parties under a single chaperone. Every year one or two would be singled out from the crowd to lead the cotillions; Irene Langhorne was the last, and the most famous, of all the reigning belles.

In the 1890's Irene's glory was unchallenged. There was no disapproval or envy of gilded youth, no fear of standing out from the crowd. Her fame was not limited to the springs. Propelled by Chillie's growing railroad money, she leaped the Mason-Dixon line and conquered the North as well. Her triumphs have the ring of regimental battle honors: led cotillions, the Philadelphia Assembly, 1893; the Carnival German, New Orleans, 1894; the Patriarch's Ball, New York 1894; and, of course, the crowning accolade, sixty-six proposals of marriage. In 1895 she accepted the sixty-seventh and became Mrs. Charles Dana Gibson, wife of a fashionable young artist. Back in Virginia she had already made famous the upward tilt of chin, the fascinating forward thrust of chest that, interpreted in her husband's drawings, were to sweep the nation. As the Gibson girl, Irene became the symbol of an era. Every girl wanted to be her.

At home the main thing was that Chillie adored her. After the long, lean years in Danville he basked in her success. Irene's was the sort of life, he felt, that every Langhorne had been born to enjoy. But he had no idea of transporting his family to the scene of Irene's Yankee triumphs; such disloyalty to the South would have been repugnant to every Langhorne instinct. Instead, in 1892 he bought Mirador, a fine brick house near the Blue Ridge Mountains in Albemarle County. It was an ironical satisfaction that this new home was near the humbler abode of Cousin Charley Price, once so nearly the scene of ignominious retreat.

Chillie had never been an ante-bellum planter, but the Langhornes were near enough to the old life to slip back into it with ease—all the more easily perhaps since master and mistress no longer had to wrest a living from the land. The family could not wait for spring and the yearly migration to Mirador. Here, surrounded by Negroes, horses, dogs, and friends and relatives of every description, they lived a life of patriarchal abundance, supported by crowds of colorful if not very efficient servants. There was "Aunt Liza" Pratt, Nannie's nurse, who smoked a pipe and told her children stories about "Mr. Jesus." The black people on the place would "seek sometimes for two or three weeks for God and not find Him. And then all of a sudden they would cry 'Oh, God came to me last night' and they would go around shaking hands and say, 'Mr. Jesus, he say to me, "Don't you go for to do any washing this day—you go right to your prayers" ' "—a statement that was taken, as it was given, with perfect seriousness. Nannie loved Aunt Liza dearly. She was also fond of Sam, a sporting character who waited on table, and sometimes borrowed Chillie's gun and even his gold cufflinks when the master of Mirador was not around. Nannie, who later in life was to say, "I never lie unless I have to," often lied to protect Sam.

It was not possible to expect correctness from what may very loosely be called the domestic staff at Mirador, but Chillie had an unerring eye for the right man for any job. He knew everyone, black or white, for miles around. On one occasion, needing a butler, he had ridden his horse Blackbird up to a remote cabin to find a certain Jim Brown. Jim was away, but Chillie left word that he would pay the whole family two hundred dollars a year and give it a house and "findings" if it would move in. The next day he had his butler, and was not a bit dismayed at the number of children who came with him.

Langhorne emotions were on the same scale as Langhorne

hospitality. Chillie would let out tremendous roars; there would be quarrels, tears, reconciliations; then in the end everyone usually dissolved in laughter. "I stayed there once," a rather untypical guest complained, "and I couldn't sleep. That house *boiled*." Parties sprang up around the gregarious Chillie as though by spontaneous combustion. Nannie, like the rest of them, adored it all. It was a sink-or-swim sort of household, but, if she did not look like Irene and was never to be so adept as her sister at handling their rambunctious parent, there were nevertheless compensations. She learned to hold her end up in a fight and as often as not to win with a laugh. If Mirador sometimes made the rough and tumble of political life look tame, it had tremendous drawing power. It made one demand a great deal of one's future life, but it was not an unhappy place for a child.

Nannie was too much like Chillie for comfort. If one can imagine Chillie's spirit housed first in the skinny child, then in the enchanting young girl, and at last in the beautiful woman, one will have gone far toward understanding the nature of Nancy Astor. It was this inherited nature that was to cause her many a later struggle with herself as well as, more obviously, with family and friends.

At home at Mirador, Irene had been content with appropriate triumphs of a strictly feminine nature, but as a child Nannie was already given to unexpected eruptions at inconvenient times and places. There was, for instance, the trip to the Chicago Exhibition, where Chillie had taken them for a family treat. All had gone smoothly until the Yankee band broke into the strains, intolerable to a Southerner, of "Marching Through Georgia." The Langhornes sat in frozen outrage, but it would have been silent outrage had it not been for Nannie. Leaping to her feet she cried lustily, "Three cheers for Robert E. Lee!" The crowd took it up, "Hurrah, hurrah, for Robert E. Lee!" For this early demonstration of successful rabble-rousing Nannie got a good spanking. This was hardly fair; Chillie would have done the same thing if he had thought of it first.

Before 1895 the pleasures of family life had been balanced by Irene's successes in society. After her marriage Chillie found himself at least temporarily without a glamorous daughter. He had been accustomed to drawing about him a little knot of reporters, pencils in hand, and when another colorful story about the "beautiful Langhorne sisters" hit the society pages he would ask innocently, "Where do they get all that stuff about the girls?" Nothing would do now but that Nannie should climb aboard the same bandwagon. This was impossible. Irene always did the conventional thing, Nannie never did; Irene was tall and statuesque, Nannie was petite and lively. She looked then, as she was always to look, freshly turned out and sparkling with life. The reporters ransacked their vocabularies and came up with "piquant." In the age of queenliness it was a second-class word; Nannie's looks were not the current style—which had been set by Irene. However, she was not depressed. At Maria Ward Williams's coming-out party in Richmond, Nannie stood under the chandelier with more boys around her than any other girl. She was telling funny stories. It was a line of her own; Nannie was not about to hide behind the image of the Southern belle.

Whenever Nannie felt in need of encouragement, she found it at school. She was, as they said around Richmond, "one of Miss Jennie's girls." Virginia Randolph Ellett was that rare thing, a truly great teacher. This modest proprietor of a small school for the daughters of Richmond's better families spent her summers studying at Harvard or working privately at home under such tutors as William Allen Nielson. Nannie, with instant empathy, found Miss Jennie's intellectual enthusiasm contagious. Before long she not only wanted to go to college herself but had also become a convinced feminist. In one of her summer papers Miss Jennie had quoted a passage from Tennyson's *Princess Ida* that painted a highly inflammatory picture of her sex:

> Live chattels, enemies of each other's fame,
> Full of weak passion, turnspits for the clown,
> The drunkard's football, laughing stock of Time,
> Whose brains are in their hands and in their heels,
> Forever slaves at home and fools abroad.

Nannie need never have read the actual words. It was enough that Miss Jennie thought that way. She could absorb the idea by simple osmosis.

Nannie was to say all her life, "I like the company of my

betters." She meant her moral, spiritual and intellectual betters. Miss Jennie Ellett was the first of these to cross her horizon, and Miss Jennie remained her loved and admired friend for the rest of her life. As was true of all of Nancy's close friends, Miss Jennie had a deeply religious vein in her nature, but Nannie remembered that "She never preached at us . . . she used to put me on my honor." Little Nannie Langhorne once exclaimed, "Oh, Miss Jennie, you've worn my honor out!"

Nannie's desire to go to college was not fulfilled; indeed, it was not even discussed. There was never any chance of it. To Chillie, formal education for women was out of the question, and of course he was not alone in this attitude. Victorian opinion had, if anything, taken a less rather than a more liberal view of the position of women since Samuel Johnson's famous remark about a woman's preaching: "Like a bear dancing, it need not be done well, it is remarkable that it is done at all." Chillie's attitude was a reflection of his time, and his daughters would not have dared to question it. Clothes, parties, horses, a trip to Newport, anything the girls wanted—but a trained mind! What in God's name could a girl do with that? In the case of Nannie Langhorne, later Nancy Astor, it is rather intriguing to wonder what, indeed, she might have done had she been able to add a formal education to her formidable natural gifts.

Fortunately for Chillie's daughters, such restriction did not apply to trained bodies. One of the joys of the move to Mirador was that now they all had horses and ponies of their own. Irene had long since given up horses for men, but Nannie, six years her junior, and Phyllis were exactly the right age and were soon addicted to the sport. They followed Chillie on long rides through the countryside; he taught them to hunt, to jump the big natural fences of the day, and to school their own young horses. When a big three-year-old reared with Phyllis on his back, Chillie yelled, "Dammit, give him his head!" It was Mrs. Langhorne who suffered the more usual parental reaction of tortured anxiety. She used to say, "One of these days I shall die." In the village there was an idiot boy, an amiable creature who stayed quietly at home with his mother, and Mrs. Langhorne would often sigh and say, "I wish I had an idiot child." Once, after a bad fall, Nannie was carried into the house half-conscious.

Her mother bent over the victim, who looked up and murmured, "Mother, you've now got your idiot child."

Nannie's loss of a college career—and she did feel it as a real loss—was softened by another and even more potent outlet for her energies. At about the age of fourteen, she discovered her own brand of religion. She had not, of course, been a heathen up to that time. Mrs. Langhorne had taken her to church at a very early age, assuring her, rather rashly, that God answered prayer. Nannie had a little dog called Curly, who was, she felt, cruelly handicapped by the shape of his tail. At the first convenient point in the service she shut her eyes, took a deep breath, and loudly and clearly petitioned God to correct his handiwork. Not only did God fail to answer, but Nannie was given the first of many spankings. It had rather taken the edge off her religious zeal, but later, in the little Episcopal church at Ivy, near Greenwood, she discovered that she was not alone in her convictions. Their new rector, Mr. Neve, believed in the same sort of God, one who would have found it quite possible to straighten Curly's tail. Mr. Neve was the only human being Nannie knew who was not perfectly content with the life of the neo-squires of Albemarle. She herself had enjoyed it all uncritically; now, at times, at least, she began to see through the eyes of Mr. Neve.

The rolling land around Ivy was in the heart of Mr. Jefferson's country. The best of Virginia had flourished here. Memories of three Presidents still shed an aura of past greatness and a gentlemanly sort of culture upon the surrounding hills. It was still possible for the Negro and the poor white to live in minimal comfort, if not prosperity, off the land. It was, in fact, a charming backwater, well out of the currents of contemporary life; anything resembling a social conscience might slumber undisturbed. Mr. Neve was an Englishman. He had heard Dr. Pusey preach at Oxford; he had worked among the industrial poor. In his little church, for the first time, Nannie breathed air from the world outside.

Even in Ivy Mr. Neve found work to do. This formidable young man was not handsome in the ordinary way; he was tall and rugged and slightly walleyed. The wags of the parish declared that he kept one eye on the congregation and the other on the mountains. It was certainly true that he was well aware of the mountain folk. Not far from Ivy as the crow flies were cabins inhabited by families who had never seen a doctor or medicine, read a book, or heard the word of God. Feeling spiritually isolated among the fleshpots of Ivy, the young priest fell into the habit of going every day at noon to ring his church bell and to pray a little while alone. One day he received a vision. Christ appeared to him, "as though visibly present," and His words were impressed upon Neve's mind: "As Captain of the Lord's Host am I now come." On that day it became clear to Frederick Neve that the work he saw waiting for him in the mountains was not his but the Lord's. He harnessed his horse and set himself to follow to its end one of the remote mountain tracks. It was the beginning of his great work; he was to bring the outside world to the whole vast and previously inaccessible region of the Blue Ridge.

As passionately as she had once desired college, Nannie now wanted to be one of the missionaries whom Mr. Neve was sending into the mountains. From the time she was fourteen she went riding with him in the old buggy that carried him into the hills. But the not altogether unworldly Mr. Neve knew well how to deploy the Lord's Host. Chillie's daughter was not likely to become a missionary; when he had her with him he turned, not toward the mountains, but to the Sheltering Arms Home. Here she discovered her gift with the ill and suffering. No one not actually dead and buried could resist her quips; she was, literally, a howling success with the aged poor. On Sunday when she heard Mr. Neve pray for the thousand-fold strength of the spirit, she knew, she could see, that it was given him in his work in the mountains. He was unrolling before her observant eyes the pattern of the dedicated life.

They did, in fact, have a good deal of a quite human nature in common. Mr. Neve was in the habit of taking clothes and medicine from his Ivy parish to the mountains. One day a woman had come down from the hills to thank her benefactor in Ivy. The lady told her, "You mustn't thank me, you must thank the Almighty." "Oh yes," the woman agreed readily. "He was at our house the other day. He sure is a fine gentleman." Nannie loved this tale. It tickled her sense of the ridiculous without really lowering Mr. Neve in her eyes. She would not have understood, much less admired, a milk-and-water saint.

Chillie was not a man who put much stock in the power of

the spirit. He was a conventional but an independent churchgoer. Everyone of his class and type went to church in those days, but for a long time he did not become a confirmed member, a step that carried a far greater commitment than attendance. His insistence that, not exactly a cuspidor, but some such convenience be placed beside his pew met resistance from Mr. Neve and for a time interrupted the harmonious relations between Chillie and the Church. He was not going to yield to clerical despotism!

Mr. Neve, during Nannie's time at home, served both the Ivy and the Greenwood churches. It was not until much later, after the advent of a new young rector at Greenwood, that Chillie, after a fashion, got religion. This most extraordinary event occurred after one of his hunting dogs had killed a neighbor's sheep and the neighbor had shot the dog. The next Sunday in church the young rector, Russell Bowie, who later rose to some eminence as a preacher, made his first convert in the unlikely person of Mr. Langhorne. Quite by chance his sermon that morning had been on forgiveness. The dog killer and the sheep killer were both in church, and there was lively, if silent, speculation as to what would happen when they met during the extended period of conversation that always took place after the service. Mr. Johnson, the dog shooter, apparently left the church first and was standing among a group of men when Chillie walked up to him, red in the face and breathing hard. All conversation ceased; everyone waited to see what Mr. Langhorne would do. In a voice that could be heard all over the churchyard Chillie roared: "Johnson, you shot my dog. But damn you, I forgive you." Never one for half-measures, Chillie then became, rather tardily, a member of the Church.

But these events had not taken place when Nannie was a girl at Mirador. Chillie declared only half-jokingly that she was in love with Mr. Neve and when she was seventeen he decided that it was time she found a more suitable object.

For Chillie, to think was to act. Irene had been to a New York finishing school, so Nannie must go to the same one. Nannie, with so many undirected talents boiling inside her, was far less mature than Irene had been when she had gone away to school. She soon succumbed to homesickness and had to be sent home. Chillie next sent her to visit Irene and Dana in Newport, where the Gibsons were in the very heart of the social whirl, and where Nannie proved to be as great a success with the youthful rich as she had once been with the aged poor.

Almost at once she made a conquest; the richest, most dashing, most eligible young man in the Gibsons' set wanted to marry her. Not only was Robert Gould Shaw a son of the very proper Bostonian Shaws; he was also, even according to Irene's sophisticated friends, "as attractive as he could stick." Naturally Nannie was flattered. It was, inevitably, just the sort of match that Chillie had in mind. Even Mrs. Langhorne, who never had any instinct for social climbing, was in favor of it.

As this episode is recounted by Christopher Sykes in an earlier biography, Chillie and Mrs. Langhorne were both opposed to Nannie's engagement and advised against it. Family tradition in Virginia is against this version. At least two of Nannie's friends, present in the neighborhood at the time of her engagement, have assured me that Chillie encouraged the match. Nannie often displeased her parents but always impulsively, without conscious defiance. It would seem entirely out of character for her to defy their expressed wishes in so serious a matter, while Chillie's perhaps naïve urge "to see the girls marry well" was fairly obvious at the time. Chillie had heard that Bob drank a bit too much, but Mr. Shaw was easily able to allay his suspicions. The elder Shaws themselves had fallen in love with Nannie; they were sure she would be the influence their high-flying young Bob needed. She hardly had time to draw a deep breath before the engagement was announced.

At any rate, as the wedding date approached Nannie hesitated. Running out for the last time with old playmates in Richmond, she punched the point of her parasol into a younger girl's stomach. "Little Trigg, never marry until you are seventy." But hesitation had come too late. On October 27, 1897, Nancy Langhorne, aged eighteen, was married at Mirador to Robert Gould Shaw. It was rather a small wedding, not the bang-up affair Irene's had been. Most dampening of all, the bride had poison ivy. The couple took a honeymoon trip to the Homestead Hotel at Hot Springs, scene of Irene's earlier triumph. After two days Nannie knew for certain that she did not love Bob and that sex was one of the more regrettable aspects of human existence. She ran away, back to Chillie and Mirador. Chillie was not consciously cruel, but after all Bob was not a monster;

there was nothing to do but persuade Nannie to go back to him.

Shortly after Nannie's marriage to Shaw her son Bobbie was born. For three years she struggled to make a go of this increasingly disastrous union. Drink was indeed Bob's problem. It got worse rather than better during these difficult years. In describing her first marriage in later life Nancy wrote, "Like many another young girl I fought for a long time against acknowledging the mistake I had made." But by 1900 she felt obliged to return to live at Mirador with her young son.

To most people at that time, divorce was an almost unthinkable course. Nannie, in fact, refused to consider it, although even Mr. Neve advised her to face the situation and put this disastrous marriage once and for all behind her. Instead she signed a deed of separation in 1902, a document that would have prevented her remarriage and, in effect, meant cutting herself off from life—at least as life was then understood—at age twenty-three.

In the end something entirely unexpected happened to solve this apparently unsolvable problem. The Shaws themselves came down to Virginia and begged her to divorce Bob. It seemed that he had gone through a marriage ceremony with another woman and was now seriously in danger of being sent to prison for the crime of bigamy unless Nannie would agree to divorce. Thus Nannie's scruples were released at last. The Shaws hoped that the grounds cited in court might be incompatibility, but Nannie took a firm stand on the Bible: divorce should be on the grounds of adultery or it should not take place at all. This adherence to purely moral conviction was to stand her in good political stead later on.

The divorce became final in 1903. By now it was an old story, and the final action, as Nannie remembered it, caused astonishingly little fuss. Chillie, who had been at least partly responsible for this sorry state of affairs, now made up for it handsomely. With his most earnest expression he took her in his arms and told her: "As long as you have me you need never fear anyone's doing you any real harm. I'll shoot Bob and the whole Shaw family if necessary!" Even better than the promised shooting, he released Mrs. Langhorne from constant attendance to his own needs and sent her off with Nannie for a rousing holiday abroad.

Irene and Dana were now in England, and of course a visit

to them was the high point of Nancy's trip. The Gibsons again produced introductions, this time with happier results. Nannie felt at home in England and thoroughly enjoyed this glimpse of a society that she was later to know so well. Among the new friends that Nannie and her mother made on this trip was Ava Astor, the estranged wife of Colonel John Jacob Astor IV. This charming woman, born Ava Willing of Philadelphia, was a leader of the new Anglo-American set. She took a fancy to Nannie and was to be a great help to the Langhorne girls in their continuing forays into transatlantic society.

On Nancy's return from this trip she announced to Chillie, "Your beautiful daughter is back again, unwanted, unsought and part widowed for life." She became, once again, involved in family life at Mirador. Older brothers and sisters returned frequently with their families. The oldest girl, Lizzie (Mrs. Moncure Perkins), seems to have gone down in family history with the unfortunate character of being "terribly bossy." The one witty remark ever attributed to her stemmed from her disappointment at having married and left the family home before Chillie's railroad fortune had precipitated his daughters into a world of wealth and fashion. She described herself with a certain grim humor as Mrs. "Obscure" Perkins.

Chillie got along reasonably well with his grown daughters but gave his grown sons a hard time. Chillie was strict and he was possessive; the avenue of escape taken by his two older sons was often by way of the bottle. The pattern of life for young men in the South of that day was an uncertain one, suspended midway between the plantation ideal and an industrial future that had not yet arrived. Chillie's career was atypical, almost suspect. He had, of course, railroad jobs to offer the boys, but to work for their father was next to impossible. The eldest son, Keene, solved the problem in a manner so lordly, so absolutely incredible, that the whole system of finance must have been shaken to its foundations. He was sent to supervise one of his father's work gangs in a small Virginia town. Perhaps it could better be described as a small place, for it contained only a store, a railroad station, and one house. Here Keene, in a single week, managed to spend five thousand dollars of the company's money. When asked how he did it, he explained that a circus had stopped in the neighborhood, and that he had sent to Washington for the best drink and the best caterers and had entertained lavishly until his money ran out. Such an episode would have been impossible in New England, frowned upon in Pennsylvania, but in Virginia among the Langhornes it was received with a certain acclaim. Keene lost his job, but he was neither prosecuted by the law nor was he any less welcome at home.

The bottle affected Harry, the brother who Nannie felt might have become a bishop if he had lived, less happily. He once threatened his wife, Genevieve, with a loaded pistol. Nannie walked up to him quite fearlessly and removed the weapon. Her later aversion to drink surely had a solid foundation in such episodes in her own family, not to speak of her experience with Bob Shaw.

One must not conclude from these stories that Keene and Harry were always drunk, or that life at Mirador was clouded by their outbursts. When sober they were attractive young men, they brought their friends and added to the gaiety of life at Mirador. One friend in particular, Angus McDonnell, had come from his native Antrim to the States to learn railroading and for some time worked for Chillie. He soon became a close friend of the boys. Nannie had met him as she and her mother were about to leave for England, and had invited him to visit Mirador on her return. One weekend appears to have conquered Angus for good and all. He fell hopelessly in love with Nannie. Unfortunately he made himself a doormat. She was not in love with him. Still sore from her failure in the serious business of marriage, she was not kindly disposed toward falling in love with anyone, much less, it appeared, with Angus. Nannie never spared anyone's feelings, and in this situation Angus's feelings were so conspicuous as to be hard to spare.

Horses, not love, diverted Nannie more than anything else in this trying period after the end of her marriage. She and Chillie shared this pleasure. He drove a team of matched brown mares to a four-in-hand, and Nannie rode one of them, her mare, Queen Bee, over five-foot fences at all the shows. On a small mare, ridden sidesaddle, this was a feat of real horsemanship, but Nannie readily admitted that Phyllis was a better horsewoman than she. She certainly was in the hunting field; Nannie called her "the best in the world." Nannie herself loved the show ring and that brief moment of glory in which one gives of one's best alone at stage center. Part of the appeal was a feminist one; here, if anywhere, women competed on equal terms with men.

Chillie, naturally, was not content with being a mere spectator. He and his four-in-hand, complete with the long brass coaching horn, blown by a man standing in the back, were the *pièce de résistance* of the local shows. After the events were over he and his rival, a Yankee, would circle the ring in brilliant figure eights. The Yankee would try to cut off Chillie's lead horses, and Chillie, so it was said, would try to cut off the Yankee's head. Everyone waited until the end of the show in order not to miss Chillie and his four-in-hand. A few years later Nancy, watching her son Bobbie perform in the same ring, leapt up from her seat and called out, "You damn fool, Bobbie, don't ride that horse that way." This, too, has been preserved in local memory. Ladies of the period might perform prodigious feats of skill and daring in the ring, but they were not expected to swear.

Ironically, it was at a horse show that the blow fell which severed Nannie's life in two, finally writing *finis* to her days at home in Mirador. Mr. and Mrs. Langhorne, Keene, and Nannie had set off by train for the Lynchburg Horse Show. Mrs. Langhorne complained of headache, but the family thought nothing of it, attributing it to the motion of the train or to the nervousness she always felt when Nannie was jumping those five-foot fences. They were staying at a cousin's house in Lynchburg. At dinner that night before the opening session, Chillie looked down the long table at his wife; he noticed something special, some sudden, arresting loveliness in her face. "You are looking very beautiful tonight, Mrs. Langhorne." She gave him a smile and said that she was very glad to hear it. But just as they were ready to leave she asked for some black coffee. Nannie and Keene, impatient to be off, went on ahead, expecting their parents to follow. But Mr. and Mrs. Langhorne never came. Nannie, struck by an inexplicable foreboding, left the show and went home, to find the house in darkness and her mother dead of a heart attack. "One of these days I shall die," her mother had said. It was Nannie's only comfort that she had not been jumping that night.

2

England: A New Beginning

THE death of a beloved parent, especially at so young an age (Mrs. Langhorne was only fifty-six), is always a blow, but for most people it is softened by the sense that the parent's life offers a pattern, which one may not wish to follow in detail but which is nevertheless generally serviceable in one's own struggle with life. Nannie had always sought examples, and from a very early age she had recognized in her mother a quality that remained of the utmost importance to her all her life. Her mother had "the right values." The young Nannie had observed that her mother had a finer sense of values and a stronger character than her father. Yet Chillie had the power. He held the purse strings. "Where is the man," Nancy asked rhetorically, "who is not difficult about money?" But now, at this moment of all moments, when she faced life alone and would have wished to follow her mother's example, she could find nothing in her own aspirations or in her own nature that could fit happily into her mother's pattern.

Mrs. Langhorne belonged to an earlier age, one that had passed for Nannie as surely as for her two older brothers. As a young bride during the last year of the war, the older Nannie had gone to stay with Chillie in camp, as did many wives when their husbands were not in the field. At Mirador she had looked after children and servants in much the same way as the Southern woman had always done. It is not necessary to sentimentalize this image to find behind it a very fine woman indeed. The women on the Southern plantations had always led busy and useful lives, responsible as they were for the order and well-being of all the inhabitants, black and white, and indeed very often running the plantation itself when their husbands were away. Many were well read, most were deeply religious in a way that supported the values of forbearance, charity, and self-discipline. That this could coexist with the institution of slavery seems strange to us, and perhaps it could exist only because the women could and did feel that they were not responsible for the evils they saw around them. The great advantage of the position of the Southern women was that, privately, they could lay this responsibility upon the shoulders of their men.

Humor was no stranger to some of these bygone ladies. It was certainly not strange to Mrs. Langhorne, who one day told her family of a "queer dream." She dreamed that she was dead and that another lady came along and announced that she was now going to marry Col. Langhorne. She asked Mrs. Langhorne's advice about what she should wear for the wedding. Mrs. Langhorne had replied promptly, "Knowing the gentleman, I should say sackcloth and ashes."

At Mirador Chillie's sporting weekends with his friends were unadulterated pleasure for everyone but the housekeeper. Nannie wrote in her memoir, "He loved Mother . . . yet after the strange manner of men, he was often unfair to her." He expected one dollar to do the work of two, and when it did not he was angry. He could be difficult in the most unforeseen ways. One day at Mirador Mrs. Langhorne had exclaimed innocently, "Oh, Dab, [a name she alone used] watch out, there's a bee on your plate." No one was going to tell Chillie what to do—he had wrapped the offending insect in a piece of bread and swallowed it in one triumphant gulp.

Nannie saw, and drew her own feminist conclusions. The life of women on the plantation at least had been an integral part of the economy; at Mirador it appeared to Nannie that her mother's life and energies had been exhausted in the service of little more than family pleasures. She saw what her mother had achieved, and she was always greatful. "No life," she wrote in her memoir, "could ever be quite as lovely as what we had had, those early years at home." But at what expense! Women "had no kind of independence. It seemed to me wrong then," and, writing in 1951, "I think it is wrong still."

After her mother's death she consciously tried very hard to follow the old pattern of service to the needs of her men and to the ideal of plantation life. But the ideal was outworn and hollow, gutted by the war and the destruction of the plantation economy. In later life Nannie was to describe herself at that time: "I dreamed great dreams, but I was always the center of those dreams." Miss Jennie had opened the world to her, Mr. Neve had shown her that there were ways of shaping it. The young men around her, if they were ambitious for a larger life, were leaving the South in droves. Nannie could not have foreseen her later career in any clear outline at that time, but she already knew that it must be more than the life the ruined South could offer. Mrs. Langhorne had understood Nannie's plight, perhaps better than Nannie herself. At the time of her daughter's return "part widowed for life," her mother had said, "The world has not heard the last of Nannie yet."

In the days after Mrs. Langhorne's shocking death, all of Nannie's loyalty and devotion to her mother turned her back toward the old ways. Temperamentally she was no gardener, yet the beauty of a garden was the creative achievement traditionally open to the Southern woman. Her mother had knelt weeding the flower beds at Mirador; Nannie knelt there as an act of filial piety. She was determined to keep the beds just as her mother would have liked them. When William, the colored gardener, saw her kneeling there he left his own job and came to work opposite her on the same bed. Looking up through tears that she could not control, she found comfort in that kind, black face. "He knew how I was feeling," she said, "I was ill with misery."

The misery did not lift, because it was rooted in a conflict within herself, between her love of the old life and an undefined longing for the new. The result was attacks of nervous headache alternating with overstimulated activity. Nannie now had the care of Nora, still a teenager, as well as of her own small son Bobbie. She was already a capable housekeeper and intensely proud of her work, and when Chillie roared at some imaginary fault she would stamp her foot and declare: "I thank God every day that I am not married to you." Chillie would fervently agree.

This could have been an explosive situation, Nannie and Chillie together on more or less equal terms, but actually they drew closer together during this unhappy year. Chillie was sensitive enough to see that she should get away from Mirador; he saw, in fact, that she would not recover her health and happiness until she did get away. He suggested that she and Phyllis, then in the process of freeing herself from an unhappy marriage to Reginald Brooks, should go to England together, complete with children and nurses, for a season's hunting in Market Harborough. Nannie leaped at the idea, then hesitated. Would her mother have wanted her to go? Chillie thought that yes, she would have. With this trip, the second part of Nannie's life began.

In England the Nannie Langhorne of Virginia became Nancy Shaw, but she naturally carried much of Nannie's psychological baggage with her. In Boston she had never cared for the fast "horsey" set she had known with Bob Shaw. At Market Harborough she made some warm personal friends, but here, as in Boston, she resisted becoming a dyed-in-the-wool member of the ingrown group that is commonly called "horsey." She liked to ride, that was all; the mores and outward trappings of foxhunting meant little to her. Alas (from the true foxhunter's point of view), she was one of those who "hunt to ride" rather than one of the elect who "ride to hunt." By her own admission, she was no good at finding her way across country, but she was very good indeed at her true interest, finding her way among people. It was here, untrammelled in what was to her a new world, that she set about creating for herself a very new and independent image.

Some of the wives in the hunting set were alarmed. Was little Mrs. Shaw, with her dashing style and her trim figure, immaculately turned out, was she perhaps really hunting their husbands? One of them, Mrs. Gordon Cunard, came straight out with it: "I suppose you have come here to get my husband." Nancy replied, "If you knew the trouble I had in getting rid of mine, you would know I don't want yours." This exchange with Mrs. Cunard was the beginning of a lifelong friendship.

There are always predatory males in every society, but as Nancy said, "One is protected by oneself." She wondered later what Market Harborough really thought of her. "I did not play cards. I went to church. I drank nothing but barley water." She had carried this puritanism straight from Virginia, and, like so much else of her Virginian heritage, it was to survive in its original condition despite the assaults of years. The society of Market Harborough accepted her finally on her own terms. Even the local rake, Sir Humphrey de Trafford, known as the "Wicked Squire," became quite tame. Nancy described him as "always most good and kind to me."

Those who did not accept her proceeded at their own risk. Once, having fallen from her mount into a ditch, she called for help. The only person within earshot was a notorious snob. He pulled up his horse and asked cautiously, "Who is it?" "The Duchess of ———," answered Nancy. "After he pulled me out and saw who it was," she declared, "he longed to drop me back in again." Another man assured her that his family never married beneath them. "I knew they couldn't," she told him, "but I never knew that they realized it."

Not all the gentlemen were so ungallant. Several proposed marriage, offering the protection of their names and of more conventional establishments, but Nancy stuck to her independence. "I came to England," she said, "to chase a fox, not a husband." Those who assumed otherwise were quickly set straight. "I think that you should realize, Mrs. Shaw," warned one disappointed suitor, "that it is a very serious matter to refuse a Peer." She was an implacable opponent of snobbery but, ironically enough, it was with a Peer that Nancy at last fell in love.

Her son Michael once said that his mother had never given herself time for sex—that is, for sex regarded as anything really central to her own development as a person. But for one suitor, Lord Revelstoke, Nancy felt a strong physical attraction. "For a time," she said, "I was deliriously happy, the way young people in love are happy." His presence made the sun shine and the birds sing; for the first, and, we must conclude, the last, time she was "in love." At this time Revelstoke was forty-one, a senior partner in his family firm of Baring Brothers, and one of the most successful bankers in Europe. He cut a brilliant figure in society. The police cleared a way for his carriage as he drove from his home to Baring Brothers or to the House of Lords. His dinner parties were "exquisite"; the beautiful and famous Rosa Lewis, who later had her own restaurant and was to become a London landmark, was Revelstoke's cook. "He was bald," Nancy said, "but I thought him Apollo." For Revelstoke Nancy was the love of his life. Nevertheless, in spite of its promise and its glamour, this affair came to nothing in the end.

Nancy discovered that "he had not the right values." She attributed their breakup quite simply to his snobbery. ("I cannot bear a snob.") Disillusion came when Revelstoke asked her, "Do you really think you could fill the position that would be required of my wife? You would have to meet kings and queens and entertain ambassadors. Do you think you could do it?" Mr. Sykes views this as only Revelstoke's attempt to warn his prospective bride of the possibly irksome demands his banking career might make upon her and not to any doubting of her social gifts or standing, but if so the lover phrased his question rather ineptly. Surely Revelstoke did have doubts. He might well have wondered if Nancy's forthright and explosive manner would advance his career.

For Nancy to have attributed the whole problem to his "snobbery" may have been self-protective, but she was right in her instinct that "he had not the right values." His personal values were those of the "simple English gentleman," but nevertheless, as his career made imperative, they were material values. In a world where she already saw so much materialism, Mr. Neve's protégée could not accept purely worldly benchmarks and goals. In the long run, they would not have met her expectations for herself. What is worse, they would have bored her.

The interference of other people, as so often happens, contributed its share to the debacle of this affair. Lord Revelstoke had long entertained a romantic attachment to an older woman, Lady Desborough. Whether or not she was actually his mistress is not clear, but Nancy believed that she was and that it was she who had lodged the "snobbish" doubts in her lover's mind.

In addition there was the weighty factor of Chillie's disapproval. He had joined his daughters in England for Christmas and had met Revelstoke—to whom he had taken, it appears, an instant dislike. After Nancy's return to Virginia, Chillie's criticisms of Revelstoke probably clinched her doubts and put a final end to the romance. Perhaps in this case he was right, but it should be observed that Chillie was never in favor of any suitor to whom his daughters appeared to be physically attracted. In our own post-Freudian era such a motive would stand out for all to see, but in 1904 Nancy felt that her father "saw through" Revelstoke. In any case, although he pursued her with letters and begged her to see him again, the affair languished and came to nothing in the end.

Nancy and Phyllis had left England with many invitations and promises to return the following year. Unkind gossip maintained that Chillie knew when young Waldorf Astor was due to cross the Atlantic and that he hustled Nancy aboard the same boat. Be that as it may, on Nancy's third crossing, Waldorf was a fellow passenger. By an odd coincidence, the heir to the British house of Astor had been born on May 19, 1879, the same day of the same year that had seen the arrival of little Nannie Langhorne, fifth surviving child of the tobacco auctioneer. No two childhoods can have been less alike; Nannie's among the cheerful, extroverted hubbub of Langhorne family life, Waldorf's lonely and austere in a mansion shadowed by the eccentric personality of his father.

Ever since the founder, John Jacob Astor I, had amassed the greatest single American fortune, the Astor wealth had laid a heavy hand upon his descendants. In the early years of the Republic the first Astor had obtained a start by trading in furs and had gone on to make a considerable fortune in the China trade. He had soon outgrown both of these activities, for there were limits to the market's capacity to absorb furs, silks, and tea, but to Astor's ambition there were no limits at all. His vast appetite for real estate was whetted by a chance to despoil the old established church, disestablished after the American Revolution. Aaron Burr, then Vice President, had obtained very cheaply one of the rich leases in lower Manhattan formerly held by Trinity Church. Burr, in need of ready cash, sold the lease to Astor. Astor next acquired the Eden farm, a tract running roughly from what is now Broadway to the Hudson River, extending from the present Forty-second Street to Forty-sixth. After this the family had only to sit like hens brooding over their real estate. The wealth of Croesus, as the newspapers put it, was assured. The spark of genius which had made John Jacob's method interesting, if not appealing, could and did lie dormant for several generations without checking the phenomenal growth of the Astor fortune.

It was not until the fourth generation that an Astor again attempted, if in vain, to blaze a new path. Waldorf's father, William Waldorf, decided to try his hand at politics, but unfortunately his effort came at the worst possible time. He ran for governor of New York in 1881, a time when the man of wealth, once a universal American folk hero, had fallen to an all-time low in the public esteem. Humiliated by defeat at the polls and by the abuse of "muckrakers" in the press, this Astor heir had fled with his vast fortune to England, where gentlemen, he felt, could be gentlemen without attracting the vulgar rage. By the time he arrived in England, in 1890, no nation in the modern world could have satisfied William Waldorf Astor's sense of his own importance. Cliveden, the great house he acquired on the Thames, became a sort of golden carapace within which the exiled prince lived a fantasy life. Guests, of whom, naturally, there were few, conformed to a rigid schedule laid down by a remote and dictatorial host. After the death of his wife, his children were subjected to the same sort of routine, even more constantly applied. Cliveden was a greater Renishaw, where William Waldorf out-Sitwelled Sir George. Like the Sitwells, the Astor children suffered but survived.

Waldorf escaped early. He was the first Astor in the five generations since John Jacob I who led a successful life of his own, independent of the Astor gold. He got on at school and the university, as he was to do all his life, by trying harder than anyone else. At Eton he was Captain of the Boats; at Oxford he was a polo Blue. The strain was greater than he knew; as a young man he was told that he had a "heart" and forbidden the steeplechasing he loved.

When Nancy met him in the carefree autumn of 1905 she saw a quiet young man, dark and handsome, with an engaging smile. That Waldorf should fall in love was only to be expected; it was the depth and seriousness of that love, the forerunner of a mutual, lifelong devotion, that hardly could have been foreseen.

Waldorf knew it at once. He marvelled that so much vitality, such wit and gaiety, could be wrapped up in one small package. Best of all, Nancy was not in the least overawed by his fortune. "What I like about rich people," she said happily, "is their money." His heart lifted when she said things like that. With Nancy, he need never again experience the paralyzing stiffness, the isolation, that had so afflicted his childhood. The strain of puritanism, the extraordinary sense of duty that was to be so heavy a charge on his own life, in hers appeared as a vitalizing force.

Nancy was hardly unaware of Waldorf's fortune. It was too tremendous; like one of the wonders of nature, it could not be overlooked. "Think of it," Nancy exclaimed to Phyllis. "I should be the second richest woman in the world!" But this time wealth and virtue and intelligence marched together. This time, too, it was her own life, her own choice. She made it very seriously. For Nancy it had not been love at first sight with bands playing and the sun shining every day. But she knew that she and Waldorf were suited to each other and that he would be the sort of father she wanted for her Bobbie. When she looked at Waldorf, she felt an unaccustomed and longed-for peace. He was so different from Chillie. There would be no thin-skinned, volatile Langhorne goings-on from Waldorf, no shouts of laughter or roars of rage. The sweetness of his smile was not deceptive. He was highly intelligent; she could not have respected him if he had not been. Once before she had been unutterably bored by the trappings of wealth without love, and she was not about to risk that a second time.

Marriage in those days was a profession, and marriage to Waldorf held every promise. Love came slowly, but very surely. On March 8, 1906, Chillie received a cable. "Announce engagement, Nancy."

Far away in Virginia, and only too well aware of her former love, Chillie was momentarily confused as to the identity of the lucky fellow. Nancy straightened him out in a letter written the same day. "Dearest, dearest Father, It's Waldorf. . . . Waldorf's like a lunatic. . . . I am v. much in love. More than I've ever been before in my life."

Obstacles multiplied in their path. Confronted with true love, William Waldorf, Sr., took to his bed with gout; not unnaturally, he would have preferred an English aristocrat to an American divorcée as the bride of the future head of the English house of Astor. There were fears that the London crowd would not tolerate the marriage of a divorced woman; demonstrations outside the church were considered highly probable. No clergyman would perform the ceremony. Their friends the Lennoxes advised a country wedding and offered Broughton Castle, but even the Broughton curate refused to marry them. Nancy kept Chillie informed of these developments. "I will cable my plans," she wrote him, "as soon as they decide about who will marry me!" She begged him to come over for the wedding, but Chillie, with a typical Langhorne sense of style, decided that he too could have a touch of the gout. He remained on the other side of the ocean, thereby maintaining a position as impregnable as Mr. Astor's. But in spirit he was with his daughter, and she knew it. She and Waldorf slipped over to Paris for a few days with their friends the Duke and Duchess of Roxburg, and while there Nancy bought herself a $5,000 trousseau. "I hope and pray you won't be cross," she wrote to Chillie, "but I thought it much best that I should have a nice trousseau—as it would make life easier! And probably some day I shall not mind having spent $5,000 of my patrimony."

The wedding finally took place in London, in darkest secrecy, on April 19, 1906, at All Souls, Langham Place. Neither father was present. William Waldorf consented to have the bride brought to see him for a few moments after the ceremony. "He seemed very much affected . . . kissed me twice and remarked that my 'gown' was becoming. . . . He's curious and not really human, but I think a great man." William Waldorf was human enough not to withhold his blessing for long. He gave the young couple his great place Cliveden as a wedding present, retiring himself to Hever Castle. He really preferred the smaller place. Cliveden had resisted his medieval fantasies; at Hever the original style was more to his taste. There he created a sort of Edwardian

Disneyland, where he lived in a state as near content as he was ever likely to achieve.

At this time a cartoon came out in *Punch* showing Nancy on top of a coach and four, arriving at her new home. On the seat beside her was a colored mammy, complete with turban, who is exclaiming at her first view of that splendid façade, "Lawd, Miss Nannie, yo' done out ma-ihed yo'self!" Actually Nancy was far too sensible to bring a mammy with her to Cliveden. She loved Mirador, the big house of Southern song and story, but Cliveden was one of the great houses of England, and she was well aware of the difference. She had no idea of trying to dilute one with the atmosphere of the other. It was to be an entirely new life that she and Waldorf now faced together.

3

Waldorf and Nancy

When Nancy awoke on her first morning as mistress of Cliveden, she looked on a view hardly matched in England. The house stands on an eminence above the Thames, partly natural, partly raised on the terraces made by George Villiers, Duke of Buckingham, builder of the first Cliveden. Below the first terrace William Waldorf had placed a stone balustrade from the Villa Borghese. A great expanse of lawn, laid out in a classic parterre of yews, leads away from the house to Cliveden Reach, loveliest bend of the Thames. In George Villiers's day the view was lofty but stark. When Nancy saw it, open country was still visible beyond the river, but the river itself and the lawns were cradled by the Cliveden woods. There was a perfect balance between the soft, romantic fancies of wood and river and the ordered progression of the yews.

On the east lawn, flower beds prick out a sword and the date 1688, commemorating an ancient scandal, the duel in which Buckingham killed the cuckolded Lord Shrewsbury while Lady Shrewsbury looked on. After Buckingham came Lord Orkney, Marlborough's Field Marshal, and then the stout Prince Regent, playing cricket on the lawn. Canning meditated here, beneath the oak that still bears his name.

On that first morning Nancy came downstairs quietly, ready to submit to influences she had never felt before. Mr. Neve's pupil could not really believe that she had "outmarried" herself, but whereas life at Mirador had been a sort of private cultural afterglow, the forces Nancy felt at Cliveden were alive, capable of shaping a world. She knew that she and Waldorf were part of a large design, and now for the first time, with history spread out before her eyes, she saw its scope. It was an intoxicating thought: now, if she wished, the world might be their stage.

Every sensitive cell of the house's organization quivered at her approach. A new energy ran through the kitchen and the housekeeper's room, through the gardens, the stables, even the woods. The contrast with William Waldorf's remote control was galvanizing. Chillie's daughter made contact at once; she saw everything, spoke to every one of the regiments of people who kept the great place going. There were twenty-three in the household staff alone; counting the farm, gardens, stables, and miles of woods, a hundred people worked on the Cliveden estate. Cliveden in fact was like a small self-contained village where the staff enjoyed a social life all its own, from the Cliveden cricket eleven to the staff Christmas ball.

The house is approached through a magnificent sweep of lawn. Its central portion is 150 feet long and three stories high, with nine bays, or handsomely recessed windows, across the front of each story. In spite of its size the house is not unwieldy; almost delicate, it appears to float on its elevation above the Thames. The terrace on this side survives from Buckingham's day and is 400 feet long. Curved corridors connect the central portion with flanking wings. Nancy remembered that she was at first "a little horrified at the size of it," but she soon set to work to humanize the many rooms, where William Waldorf's taste had produced a "splendid gloom." Waldorf looked on these activities with delight. Of one thing he could be dead certain:

whatever else the future held, Cliveden was never going to be stuffy again.

The young Astors had a brief wedding trip to Paris, only slightly ruffled by the appearance, in every post, of letters from an old flame of Waldorf's. Crown Princess Marie of Rumania had visited Cliveden, and Waldorf had visited the royal palace in Bucharest. The two young people had become intimate friends. Nancy discouraged advances from Marie at this time, insisting that Waldorf bring this rather excessive correspondence to an end, but it does not seem that any ill feelings resulted. Marie was to remain a close family friend.

Very soon after their return from Paris the really important part of the wedding trip took place. Nancy's impulse was to hurry to Mirador and Chillie. Even in her first letter to Chillie about her engagement she had announced her plan: "We are coming home in July, so please paint the dining room and plant the garden. Please sir." In other letters she reminded him again: "Paint the dining room!!!" and "Please don't let Lizzie sleep in my room!" "Waldorf perfectly understands," she had written to Chillie on her wedding day, "how much I depend on coming home."

She took Waldorf to Mirador in July, then on to spend the rest of the summer with Chillie at Isleborough, the Gibsons' place in Maine. The Gibsons would not be using it themselves that summer and had agreed to lease it to Nancy and Waldorf. Nancy assured Chillie that she was coming home to be with him. "So if you don't want to go [to Isleborough] I will go wherever you like, only I am afraid Virginia would be too hot for Waldorf." However, the week at Mirador was her main concern. Apparently Chillie did paint the dining room and did keep Lizzie out of Nannie's room, for Waldorf's introduction to Virginia was all that she could have wished. There were tremendous and rather miscellaneous parties in Greenwood and Lynchburg in honor of the bride and groom. Isleborough too went off well. Here Nannie had all the people she loved best in the world around her: Phyllis and her family, Chillie and Waldorf, with a cook, a kitchen maid, a parlor maid, her own maid, and Waldorf's servant for butler, to help them lead the simple life.

Waldorf bore up well under the avalanche of Langhornes.

Luckily he found Chillie fascinating rather than appalling; even so, there is nothing to show that he was not relieved to get back to Cliveden in the autumn.

Nancy had been proud of him at Isleborough. Waldorf, unlike his wife, was an obliging and easy guest. But Isleborough was not "real life," and adjustment to marriage had yet to come. At Cliveden, Waldorf devoted himself to his horses and to the new farm he had purchased adjoining the estate. Nancy was busy redoing the house and replacing the servants who had left with William Waldorf for Hever. The heavy mahogany, the antimacassars, and the plant stands in the hall were rapidly vanishing, to be replaced by books, chintz curtains and covers, and flowers. Above all, flowers. No one in England, Nancy found, knew how to arrange flowers. It was the era of sweet peas and gypsophila in stiff silver vases, surrounded by a cluster of framed photographs. Nancy remembered how her mother's colored maid at Mirador used to go out into the garden and pick flowers, then put them all mixed up into a big bowl, and how beautiful they had looked with no photographs or ornaments to spoil the effect. This was the beginning of Cliveden's reputation for flower arrangements, which years later that great connoisseur Harold Nicolson was to describe with enthusiasm.

The rooms became livable, no longer appearing overlarge. But some of the old splendor remained. The Orkney tapestries, a set of three, were perfect where they were, breaking the long line of the entrance hall. They showed Marlborough and his mounted retinue, including Lord Orkney, second owner of Cliveden. The fireplace end of the hall, with its continually tended blaze and large sofas, was actually inviting. Family life, however, centered in Nancy's small sitting room. Here eighteenth-century woodwork, painted yellow, reminded her of Virginia, and a bust of an old colored man, sculpted by Phyllis, stood upon the mantel. The dining room remained as William Waldorf and Madame de Pompadour had left it, rather out of key with the rest of the house, but so superbly elegant that no one wished to touch it. The Louis XV paneling had been lifted bodily from the Pompadour's hunting box and reassembled at Cliveden. Luckily Nancy did not require a special setting or, rather, she created her own out of any props at all so long as they were not fake or too drab and dreary.

Along with the Victorian furniture went some old Victorian friends, standbys of William Waldorf's era, who no longer felt at home under the livelier regime. To the delight of the staff, Nancy began to entertain; she was not after the social lions, but inevitably the lions came. First the Astors invited the people who had been nice to them, for Waldorf too, serious but not stuffy, had been popular with Edwardian hostesses. Queen Alexandra had been a close friend. Soon the highest society was beating a path to Nancy's door. In such circles the young Mrs. Astor shone as easily as she had in Greenwood, Virginia.

Cliveden, of course, was made for entertaining. The size of the staff was a challenge, but Mirador too had required organization; it was only necessary to enlarge the scale. Servants everywhere adored Nancy; whether black and casual, as at home, or correct and English, they did their best for her. Somehow she conveyed to the head gardener and the men under him that she not only liked well-kept lawns but shared their pride in them. William Waldorf had adorned the approach to the house with Italian statuary. Such lawns must be kept immaculate; the miles of wood rides, on the other hand, should be bosky, but designedly so, without a leaf out of place. The gardeners were up to both. Every morning while still in bed Nancy received the housekeeper with a detailed report of what fresh vegetables were available in the gardens that day. "If we can't have first-class friends, we can have first-class food!" Of course they had both. There was always a list, too, of all who might be ill or in need of care on the place. After the housekeeper came Nancy's secretary, and if half her correspondence consisted of warmly impulsive and nearly illegible postscripts, the necessary dates and arrangements were in order.

From early in Nancy's career, the development of Cliveden house parties followed a single line. Once safely arrived, Nancy's guests found their mornings and, if they liked, the greater part of the afternoons to be their own. Spontaneity was the order of the day. What could be more delightful than to write an editorial, if one were Geoffrey Dawson, editor of the *Times*, or to work on a play, if one were Bernard Shaw, and then to emerge for golf or boating, or perhaps not to come down until teatime, when the conversation of others as brilliant as oneself was always available! Nancy was well aware that this was the way to attract brilliant men to Cliveden, and this was the sort of man she was after. Capturing and entertaining the social lions was altogether too easy and not ultimately "worthwhile."

When the first sense of social triumph wore off, Nancy did indeed begin to find society dull. When Edward VII bored her by insisting on bridge until 1:00 A.M., she made a comment that has passed into legend: "I am afraid I can't tell a King from a Knave." Her aversion in this case was not to royalty but to cards. All her life Nancy was to feel that playing cards for money was wrong. She was once persuaded to join a poker game and was much incensed when told that she had lost a hundred pounds. She refused to pay, and Waldorf had to retrieve the family honor by sending a check.

Many of the original planters had emigrated to Virginia from England in the uncertain Stuart times. Some of the great landowners of the Tidewater were of Cavalier origin, but the majority had a Protestant background. Nancy's strong puritan strain, a heritage of her Virginian background, came out in her view of cards and in another, more serious, prejudice—anti-Catholicism. It was rarely spelled out because there were few indigenous Catholics, but for Nancy the fire lit by Cranmer's stake had never quite gone out. To her, Catholicism meant Bloody Mary Stuart; it was simply a synonym for despotism. Protestantism meant the Glorious Revolution, and the liberty and democracy that had come to England when Protestant Englishmen were permitted to read the Bible for themselves, freed from the hungry tyranny of priests.

Nancy may be censored for carrying this ancient hostility to an extreme that had not been appropriate since the time of the Spanish Armada. On the other hand, it remained a prejudice and nothing more; it had no effect on the friendships she began to form in these early days at Cliveden.

At home at Mirador she had been considered the "literary" member of the family, a not very difficult distinction to acquire among the "beautiful Langhorne sisters." Her reputation had been gained by listening to the efforts of the poetically inclined young men who had written odes to Irene. But now that real literary men appeared at Cliveden, Nancy found them cleverer and more appealing than her purely social guests. Hilaire Belloc was her closest literary friend in this period before the First

World War, and the fact that he was a devout Catholic had no adverse effect upon their intimacy. In fact, it drew them together, for Nancy never cared what brand of religion, or indeed of anti-religion, her friends professed so long as the religious sense played a vital role in their lives. Once, deeply concerned over an illness in the Astor family, Belloc wrote: "I will have all my little children pray for yours and that to our Blessed Lady who never fails us. . . ." He could write of his faith in this way and count on her respect, a proof, I think, that Nancy, for all her prejudices, was no bigot.

Far from wishing to convert or condemn others, she was at this time searching for a more satisfying religious expression in her own life. She wanted a religion that might give her a total, all-absorbing way of life, something bigger, more serious, and at the same time simpler than the life of society. She did not find it in the Established Church, which seemed to her bound to old patterns. It no longer fitted her own life and certainly offered her nothing new. She missed the freedom and the sense of fighting convention that had been hers at Market Harborough. During the first years at Cliveden she was often ill, without apparent cause beyond a rather unspecified frustration. Waldorf, on the other hand, was content with life and physically stronger during these early married years than he had been before.

Marie of Rumania had not been a serious threat, but Nancy did have rivals. The objects of Waldorf's passion had four legs rather than two. He was a born horseman and was to enjoy a lifelong love affair with the noble beast. As a young man he had played polo on equal terms with the great Devereux Milburn; mounted on a smart hunter, he had been Master of the Oxford Drag and a hard man to beat when hounds were running. Retired for reasons of health, he began a serious career as a breeder of racehorses. Out of his old steeplechase mare, Conjure, he produced Winkiepop, the winner, in 1910, of more than £12,000. It was a lucky break, but the kind that comes most often to the skilled breeder. He had done it on a relative shoestring, before he had important money at his disposal. The Astor stud was to go from glory to glory and remain an important part of Waldorf's life. Yet the final triumph eluded him; he was never to lead in a Derby winner. Five times an Astor horse ran second.

The fifth time even Nancy was silent. At last Waldorf spoke. "It might have been worse," he said, "something might have happened to the children."

In these early years Nancy sympathized with his love of racing but did not share it. Horses for her were something to ride, not to watch. She was not by nature a spectator; to engage her interest even sport must involve her active participation. But she dutifully entertained Waldorf's racing friends, who bored her, and he, for his part, tried to hold his racing zeal in check. For Waldorf's sake she did her best to adapt, but her best was not always successful. One day she took her Bible to the track, to give herself something to read while Waldorf watched the horses. It became quite clear that Nancy was not about to be a country gentleman's wife.

Waldorf continued to wonder at the marvel he had married. It was enough for him that she returned his spiritual love; undeniably she did not wholly return his passion. In 1906 physical passivity in a wife was rather expected, and certainly not taken as outright rejection. Nancy's experiences with Bob Shaw had not been happy. Nancy loved men, but she loved them as people. Deep down, between herself and any man would come the image of Chillie: Chillie hollering "Shut the door," before one had scarcely entered the house; Chillie, the model of the dominating male. The elder Nannie Langhorne, as Nancy often remarked, had never wanted children, but she had had eleven. The only way to succeed with him was to out-Chillie Chillie, a feat Nancy attempted all her life.

This was no model for marriage, particularly Nancy's marriage, for Waldorf would not fight back. And yet she loved him. He was so good, so nearly always right, and he had that quality which she most admired: He was big, above all petty considerations. Day by day, even when she stormed, even when she was spoiling for a fight, she found herself depending on him more and more.

Waldorf weathered the storms. There is no doubt that it was he, not Nancy, who was the hero of this marriage. When Bill, their first son, was born in 1907, Waldorf wrote to Chillie: "Everyone seems to think I ought to be awfully proud, as though I had done something clever or able. The only thing I am really proud of is being Nancy's husband. She was joking up to the last in spite of all pains . . . I wish you had been here, sir. You would have been proud of your daughter."

The thing that saved him and preserved his independence was his ability to laugh a little, as well as to marvel, at his spectacular in-laws. Cliveden seemed perpetually full of Langhornes, often in a state of crisis. In 1909 Nancy's youngest sibling, Nora, was on a somewhat penitential visit to the Astors. She had recently attempted to run away with one Baldwin Myers, whom everyone but she considered extremely undesirable. Nora had remained a charming child. Gay, pleasure-loving, guileless, she had never been able to decide which of many men her true love might be. In the phrase current in that day, she was "undeveloped." At Mirador, Chillie, tired of finding Nora's suitors perpetually underfoot, had once declared at the luncheon table, in the presence of one of Nora's top favorites: "Damn it, Nora, I'm going to line up all these fellas in a row, and you can take your pick and be done with it!" Nora had fled the room in tears, and the suitors, suitable and unsuitable, remained.

Now at last it appeared that Nora was returning a suitable passion. "He is one of the nicest men I know," Nancy wrote her father, "clean minded, high minded, and clever and charming." This paragon was Paul Phipps. He was all that Nancy said that he was. In addition he had a promising professional future as an architect; he had been to school and college with Waldorf; his mother had been a Miss Butler-Duncan of New York. In short, he had everything that the most exigent parent could want, except money. Apparently, in 1909 insanity in the family, drug addiction, and a dozen mistresses would have been less damaging to one's marital prospects.

Waldorf took a detached view of the ensuing uproar. "Nora is in love!" he wrote to his sister-in-law Irene. "A big secret—so big that nearly everyone is in it. . . . This time it is *the real* article. Everything previous proves to have been spurious and of no account. . . . We are all waiting breathlessly to hear what C.D.L. will do and say."

All did indeed depend on Chillie, and Chillie dragged his feet. He and Nancy both had reservations as to the sort of wife their extravagant Nora would make for a poor man. Nancy wrote that "knowing Nora's love of amusement and thriftlessness" made her nervous, but nevertheless she begged Chillie to send his blessing and, if possible, a substantial check. Chillie did not attempt to conceal Nora's weaknesses from her prospective in-laws. No one in either family could have doubted the superiority of Paul; yet it was Mrs. Phipps who came humbly to Cliveden apologizing for her son's daring to propose "on so little to offer Nora." Nancy hoped that Chillie would not only approve but make Nora an allowance, enough at least to pay for her clothes and her own maid. Without the latter, apparently, Nora would have been not simply poor but destitute. "Oh Pa," Nancy wrote, "do come over and settle this. It's too great a responsibility for me to take, and Nora can't do anything until you decide." To Nancy, as to all her world, it still appeared entirely proper that the fate of Chillie's daughters should depend upon his final word.

In the year 1909, changes with even broader implications than Nora's engagement to an impecunious architect were taking place. Most upsetting of all was the Lloyd George budget. Lloyd George, the brilliant nonconformist lawyer from Wales, was something new in British politics. From a working-class origin he had risen to high cabinet rank. In later life he could never find words for just how hard that climb had been. As Chancellor of the Exchequer, he presented a budget to the country in 1909 that was geared to the needs of his own people; that is, it embodied a wide range of social benefits, anticipating, in kind if not in degree, the measures of the welfare state. Left to himself, Waldorf Astor might or might not have actively supported the Lloyd George budget. He was leading a full and happy life as family man, sportsman, and progressive farmer. But he was not left alone. Six months after their marriage and almost immediately after their return to Cliveden from America, Nancy wrote to Mr. Neve: "Waldorf is going to begin working on his father's paper [William Waldorf owned the *Pall Mall Gazette*] . . . and I hope eventually go in for Parliament. He is too good a man not to help in public things. . . ." Once the initial impetus had been given, Waldorf's eyes opened wide, wider indeed than Nancy's own, to the trend of the times, and the trend of the times had little use for a country gentleman, much less for an unreconstructed Astor. Under the influence of Lloyd George, Waldorf became a man dedicated to social reform.

The far-reaching acquisitive drive of the first Astor had been immoral, perhaps, but socially useful. At least it had been useful to the white settlers in their race across the continent, for the ruthless trader in furs had been there first to open trade routes to the West. As Nancy told Grace Vanderbilt, John Jacob had been skinning skunks long before Cornelius had run a ferry. But from its energetic beginnings, the Astor fortune had frozen into an unimaginative, tenacious grasp of private wealth.

Once turned to the field of social reform, a powerful conscience and a severe logic drove Waldorf to embrace it as his own. It was a way of leaving the unhappy image represented by his father far behind, even of redressing wrongs and relieving burdens that went beyond William Waldorf, far back into the Astor psyche. While Nancy was forwarding Nora's romance and awaiting the birth of their second child, Nancy Phyllis Louise (Wissie), Waldorf was preparing to stand for Parliament as the Conservative candidate for Plymouth. Contrary to the party line, he intended to support the Lloyd George budget.

The provincial city of Plymouth and the Devon country were a revelation to Nancy. She felt at once that she knew them as she had never felt she knew London. It greatly strengthened her sense of the tie between her native and her adopted land. Canvassing with Waldorf was like going back to the old days with Mr. Neve and his horse and buggy. Now, as with Mr. Neve, she was discovering in herself and using the power of instant sympathy with all sorts of people. In the campaign she went from door to door saying, "I am Mrs. Astor. My husband is standing for Parliament. Will you vote for him?" A conversation usually started from there. The extremely successful result surprised everyone but Nancy, who had had no doubt that she could do it. (In England of the period it was almost unheard of for a lady to leap class barriers except in a traditional village setting. It happened that one night on a transatlantic crossing Nancy had stayed on deck instead of going down to dinner. Thinking that the deck was empty, some of the crew had come up from below to get a breath of air. Nancy and the sailors fell to talking. "They told me their troubles and I told them mine." When discovered by the other passengers, this scene created a sensation; Nancy became aware that what she had done naturally was considered extraordinary.)

Winning was not easy for a Conservative candidate in the working-class constituency of Plymouth. On top of this, Waldorf fell ill with the first of the recurring bouts of tuberculosis that were to plague him intermittently for the rest of his life. The campaigners had to retire to an open-air sanatorium in Scotland, an ordeal exquisitely painful to Nancy, to whom isolation and inactivity were the hardest possible things to bear. Besides, there was the climate; they slept on a balcony so cold that she had to wrap up her nose to prevent it from freezing. She did not begrudge a moment of it. "He is so good, so reasonable," she wrote to Chillie. Later on, when she would yield to Chilliesque gusts of temper, Waldorf could take them in stride. He was sure of her devotion.

They returned to Plymouth for three days for the election and, not unexpectedly, lost. Nevertheless, they had a wonderful reception. It almost seemed that the Plymouthers could see beyond the present election to the lifelong union of this young couple and their city. "This beating makes me all the more determined," cried Nancy; "I am going to win Plymouth before I die." There were answering shouts of "You can do it, Nancy!" The crowd took the horses out of their carriage and pulled them back to the house. Nancy had proved herself in this campaign. She felt that at last she knew what she had been born to do; her real life had begun.

4

Social Revolt and the Round Table

IN 1903, only a half dozen years before Waldorf first ran for Parliament, one Elizabeth Crews, aged seventy-seven, living alone amid filth, was listed in the coroner's report as dead of "self-neglect." She had succumbed to blood poisoning from untended bed sores. Was this event ordained by immutable economic law, or was it a criminal abuse of human life, subject to attack by the Lloyd George budget?

The voters of Plymouth had not been sure of the answer. Some were particularly unhappy about that part of the scheme which called for a 20 per cent levy on unearned income. It is hard to realize now the degree to which the Astors were considered, and in fact actually were, social revolutionaries. The budget, particularly its tax provisions, was so anti-establishment, so anti-Adam Smith, that Waldorf's political masters shook in their boots as they sensed the threat to the easy dominion they had so long enjoyed.

Waldorf's defeat as a Conservative candidate in a working-class constituency in his first campaign had not been unexpected, but once the Astors had established their own line, future victory was assured, if not quite the sort of victory the Conservative office had had in mind. After all, Plymouth was a port town, and Nancy had convinced the electorate that the Astors were for God, the British Navy, and the British working man, in that order. Party hierarchy or no party hierarchy, that was going to be a hard combination to beat. Waldorf was elected on his second try, in December of 1910.

For the Astors the city was never to be merely a political base, where one perhaps rented a *pied à terre* for the campaign or even came up from London by the day to make necessary appearances. From the first they meant to be Plymouthers. During the campaign they took a place outside town on the Devon moors, so that the children could have country air. Cliveden remained their home, and they had a London house at 4 St. James's Square, but after the 1910 campaign they bought in Plymouth too, at 3 Elliot Terrace.

It was one in a handsome row of houses facing the Hoe, the splendid esplanade that overlooks Plymouth harbor. The Hoe descends in broad terraces of turf, crossed with macadam paths, to the sea. More than most English places it is geared to people and to the outdoors, to couples strolling under an open sky or sitting on benches sheltered from the wind. Plymouth is both a modern port and one of the ancient outposts of the sceptered isle: Drake played at bowls on the top of the Hoe while the Spanish Armada beat up the coast; and some three hundred and fifty years after Drake the Astors were to hold their city together under the rain of German bombs.

The Plymouth Corporation is distinguished as the oldest town government in England, and a very independent, Protestant sort of place it is. The guns of the Citadel, placed there in the time of the Stuarts, face toward possible rebels in the town, rather than out to sea. The old town, called the Barbican, clusters around the small harbor of Sutton Pool. It was here, from a flight of ancient stone steps, that the Pilgrims stepped aboard the Mayflower, not to set foot on land again until they reached Plymouth Rock in Massachusetts Bay.

The new M.P., who had not so long before migrated in the opposite direction, felt his way delicately into the life of the town. Private charity, as ever with the Astors, combined handily with public measures. First came the Wissie Wee Cot Home for Invalid Children, named by Nancy in what was perhaps an excess of maternal feeling. Other Astor charities were the Francis Astor Creche, a settlement called Virginia House, and the Astor Institute. When one of the old houses in the Barbican became threatened with extinction or a good future site for public housing came on the market, Waldorf would quietly buy it, to hold for a time when the town itself should become conscious of such civic responsibilities. Nancy, talking as usual to any inhabitant who would listen, soon had the feel of the independent Devon people. "Plymouth," she said, "is my Virginia in England," and from Nancy there could be no higher praise.

Plymouth's ancient ties with the new world and its strong Protestantism were among the things that appealed to Nancy. It seemed to these two expatriated Americans the dearest goal in life to draw their two countries together, but in 1910, there seemed to be no inclination at all for such *rapprochement* on either side of the Atlantic. Socially, yes, for the period was noted for its international marriages. That of Consuelo Vanderbilt and the Duke of Marlborough was an unhappy case in point, and earlier there was the celebrated alliance between Jennie Jerome and Lord Randolph Churchill. Friendships and family ties crossed the Atlantic, particularly among the leading families. There was a lively correspondence between Astors and Roosevelts; three times in the past generations Astor money had intermarried with Roosevelt blood. Waldorf was second cousin to Franklin Roosevelt's half-brother and had known Franklin since boyhood—a tenuous relationship, but one that was binding in Hudson River circles and was to have political influence later on. But in 1910 political association between the two countries was at a minimum. America still jealously guarded her independence; England still looked askance at her bumptious daughter across the sea. Politically speaking, the Atlantic seemed wider than ever, when there suddenly appeared on the Astor horizon a group of young men who were deliberately setting out to span the dividing ocean.

Nineteen hundred and ten saw the regrouping in England of "Milner's Kindergarten," that highly regarded group of young men who had been on Lord Milner's staff in South Africa after the Boer War. Milner had gone out as High Commissioner, a latter-day proconsul, but his ideas for a new liberal empire went far beyond the old pattern. Milner had a vision of self-governing people under the British flag. It remained for one of his staff to coin the word "Commonwealth."

Milner's young men were chosen for brains and character rather than for experience. "Who is responsible," demanded a South African newspaper, "for giving youngsters our public undertakings as toys to play with?" The first task of these rather remarkable "youngsters" had been economic reconstruction after the chaos and destruction of the war. In her conflict with the Boers, England had defeated and annexed the two Dutch republics that adjoined her South African colonies. The second phase of the Kindergarten's work involved reconciling and uniting under one government such diverse peoples as the erstwhile enemies, British colonial and defeated Boer.

Britain had lost one empire through her unwillingness to extend her free institutions across the sea to America. The question to which Milner's young men adressed themselves was this: Would British political genius be equal to a fresh start, to create first a new nation in South Africa on the model of the American Union and then, perhaps the wildest dream of all, to create a new sort of empire, a federally united commonwealth of self-governing dominions? In due time the Union of South Africa was achieved, through the joint efforts of British and Boer leaders.

To have belonged to the Kindergarten in those days was a great thing; its members were to carry a sense of identity, a certain political panache, that went back with them to London when their work in South Africa was over.

Obviously their return was no ordinary event. To the Astors, with their binational loyalty and desire to bring together the old world and the new, the idea of a greater English-speaking commonwealth had great appeal. The timing was perfect, for at the very moment that Waldorf was entering politics, the

Kindergarten was regrouping in London. The first act of Milner's young men was to launch their famous *Round Table Review of Commonwealth Affairs*. This was a quarterly, designed expressly to keep open lines of communication around the Empire, a function that might later be performed by official representatives if federation became a reality. Waldorf, although never a member of the editorial board, was soon a bona-fide member of the group, which was now referred to collectively as the Round Table.

Nancy was entranced. Even more than Waldorf, she felt a religious element in the Round Table idea. The ideal animating federation was the dream of brotherhood, of closer union between nations based on cooperation rather than on coercion. "Their coming," exclaimed Nancy, "changed all our lives." It was true. For both Astors the Round Table opened new vistas, new channels of action. For the first time Nancy found excitement in foreign affairs.

Nancy was drawn to one of the group in particular. Young Philip Kerr was her temperamental counterpart; his personal history of restless religious seeking appealed to her. She delighted in his quick flow of ideas. He could put into words things that she had always felt but had never quite known how to say. He was no stolid Englishman or shrewd Yankee but a Celt and an outsider, like herself. Waldorf too fell under the spell. Later on Nancy would say, "Everyone thinks I am in love with Philip, but it's not me. It's Waldorf who can't do without him." If this were not strictly true in the beginning, it became so in the course of an extraordinary relationship.

While in South Africa, Philip had acquired a belief in federal union that virtually amounted to a religion. It was this quasi-religious belief that Philip brought home with him to England and that immediately struck an answering spark in Nancy. (She was less attracted to his formal religion, Roman Catholicism, a deviation from the Anglican norm that had come to the Kerr family with the conversion of Philip's grandmother.) Philip had been one of the first of the group to return to England, in the fall of 1908. Shortly thereafter he and Nancy met. Bob Brand, Philip's immediate chief in South Africa, had been a friend of Waldorf's at New College. In fact Philip's first introduction to Nancy had been while he was still in Johannesburg, sharing a bungalow with Brand. Someone had sent Bob an old copy of the *Tatler* containing Nancy's picture. "Mrs. Langhorne Shaw," the caption said, "who is to marry Mr. Waldorf Astor." "Well," said Bob, "Waldorf anyway has done pretty well for himself." For him the picture brought a delicious nostalgia, a sense of London, of beautiful women, and of all the world that he had left behind him. Philip did not yet know London; but he was struck by the frank, arresting gaze. There was no one in South Africa who looked like that!

Nancy and Philip first met in 1909 at Hatfield, the great country house belonging to the Cecil family. From the time of Elizabeth I the Cecils have been in and out of power in the government of England. After this first meeting Nancy and Philip saw each other constantly. The little band that comprised the Round Table was now enjoying a degree of leisure, meeting, not as of old in the simplicity of the African moots, but amid the luxury of London and the splendid country houses. They went to Hatfield, to F. S. Oliver's place in the Chiltern beechwoods, and to Cliveden. Cliveden, for these young men, was Nancy. If Nancy was affected by the Round Table, the Round Table was overwhelmed by Nancy. She was all they had perhaps dreamed of and despaired of finding. Unlike their sisters and cousins and the daughters of their family friends, she had great beauty and brilliant wit, qualities that they had vaguely associated with the "fast set." But here she was in their midst, extremely frank and friendly, and morally absolutely straight!

Brand and Kerr were regulars at Cliveden, and so was Lionel Curtis, former town clerk of Johannesburg, and Geoffrey Dawson, once Lord Milner's private secretary. Nancy loved nothing better than to hear the sound of their voices, settling the affairs of the world, and then later to join them for talk and still more talk. "Cliveden talks," for this group, became a lifelong habit. The Round Table ideal of international cooperation was adopted by Nancy and applied in her own style to the political house parties that were to make her later fame as a hostess. In those long days before the First World War, no one foresaw the grim 1930s, when Cliveden would slip under a shadow of opprobrium and abuse. Nevertheless, they were all there, the little nucleus, the hard core, the "Cliveden Set" in embryo.

5

The Secret Way

THERE was a great deal, in 1910, to occupy the best minds of the Round Table. After the Lloyd George budget came the Home Rule for Ireland bill. Asquith, the Liberal Prime Minister, was dependent for his majority in Parliament, and hence for office, on the votes of the Irish Nationalist Members in the House. The Conservative opposition were unalterably opposed, and as they controlled the House of Lords, the abolition of the Lords' veto became the imperative issue of the day. Waldorf's first years in the House were thus a time of bitter division, affecting, in a way that had not happened since Cromwell's time, the constitutional balance of the realm and, what was even more dreadful, the intimate structure of British top-drawer society. Cousin was not speaking to cousin. At the Asquith-Cholmondeley wedding it was said that the ushers were instructed to use as a guide for placing the guests not the familiar question, bride or groom? but, Liberal or Conservative? When Lord Curzon gave a ball he explained kindly to Margot

Asquith that she had not been invited because *she* would have been so uncomfortable.

The Astors' friendship during this period of division crossed party lines. There was no break, for instance, in their long-standing intimacy with the Asquiths. Nancy had known Mr. Asquith since at least 1905, before he became Prime Minister or she Mrs. Astor. In fact, just before the Atlantic crossing on which she met Waldorf, she had written the future Prime Minister repeating a joking request apparently made earlier, that he find her a husband. Mr. Asquith had replied gallantly, even breaking into verse:

> You must not reproach me, my dear Mrs. Shaw;
> It's not like a redskin selecting a squaw;
> For there's no tougher problem in logic or law
> Than to find a fit mate for the lady called Shaw.

Only a month after receiving this letter she met Waldorf and the problem was solved.

But by 1912 political differences had begun to put a severe strain on the Astor-Asquith family friendship, which was reflected in some extraordinary letters from Margot Asquith to Nancy. Nancy's reputation for outspokenness pales indeed before some of the effusions from Margot. In a letter of this year Mrs. Asquith in effect told Mrs. Astor that she would never make a political hostess: "You are too young and crude." In a previous letter to Margot, Nancy had referred to "bitterness about Home Rule," which brought advice from Margot to stick to subjects that she knew and "don't talk about . . . Home Rule." A reference by Nancy to "the P.M." brought down upon her head the response, "My poor darling, what have you ever got out of my P.M. beyond a little chaff? . . . Do you suppose when I used to talk to Ld. Salisbury or when I talk to Arthur [Balfour—both former Conservative Prime Ministers] I merely trip them up with a metaphorical toe or a pillow fight after meals?" This was hitting home indeed. The true reason behind Margot's outburst followed in the next sentence but one: "If you are not fond enough of us to risk us meeting your political gods . . . then dearest we must part." Obviously the

Asquiths had not been included in a political party at Cliveden!

To this letter Nancy made the only possible response: she did not answer. Margot really cared for Nancy and soon regretted her outburst. Two weeks later she wrote again: "Darling Nancy, I hope I wrote nothing in my long scrawl that hurt you." For some time after this the course of friendship ran smoothly, but in 1914 a similar complaint erupted in a letter from Margot accusing Nancy of "boycotting" the Asquiths. The accusation was based on nothing more than Nancy's failure to include the older Asquiths in an invitation to their seventeen-year-old daughter. This letter went from bad to worse, and ended on a maudlin note: "If I died lots of you would say you had loved me and been one of my dearest friends."

Mr. Sykes wonders at Nancy's patience under such flagrant provocation. Actually, she was well able to keep silent when she chose, as this correspondence shows. When she spoke impulsively it was because she *let* herself speak that way, not because she had no control over what she said. In Margot's case she took her revenge privately, in one of her classic impersonations. All she needed to do was pop in a pair of false teeth, assume a certain tone of voice, and there was Margot Asquith to the life. The result was irresistibly comic. As was characteristic of Nancy's best acts, it might be produced quite unexpectedly, with no particular relation to what had gone before.

Nancy had beseeched Margot, "Let's not talk politics," for she knew that their views on Home Rule would not coincide. The Astors followed the Round Table line. Characteristically, the Round Table young men saw the Irish problem as an opportunity to apply the federal principle at home. They came out for something that they called devolution, or Home-Rule-All-Around. According to this plan, there would be four local parliaments, one each for England, Ireland, Scotland, and Wales, with an imperial parliament over all. Philip disappointed the more doctrinaire of his colleagues by finding this solution rather impractical. Nevertheless, it won support in high circles; included among the more influential converts to the federal solution was J. L. Garvin, editor of Lord Northcliffe's weekly paper, *The Observer*. Waldorf, with his interest in his father's *Pall Mall Gazette*, was particularly impressed by this recruit.

Garvin rated high indeed on the political scene. He had the

confidence of Arthur James Balfour, the powerful leader of the Conservative or Unionist party; he knew what the Unionists were about to do before they knew it themselves. His public exposure was immense. Max Beerbohm caricatured him, in itself the ultimate accolade. Max showed him as a willowy, popeyed figure pontificating to assembled admirers: "Mr. Garvin giving ideas to the Tory Party." *Punch* apostrophized him: "A Lay of Federal Home Rule":

For a season he ruled as dictator
Till all of a sudden the role
Of national pacificator
Appealed to his sensitive soul.
So, having empowered a commission
Of eight to consider the means,
The realm he resolved to partition
In four smithereens.

Alas for the tragical sequel:
Alas for the frailty of man!
The zeal of his friends proved unequal
To working the Federal Plan.

Alas indeed! When the Conservative opposition, led by Balfour, failed to endorse Home-Rule-All-Around, Garvin found himself very nearly out of a job. His active mind had already made the transatlantic leap; he was convinced that the United States could be included in trade agreements wth Great Britain and the nations of the Empire. The proprietor of his paper did not see it that way. Northcliffe told his editor that if he wished to keep his place on the *Observer* he must find a purchaser for the paper. Garvin readily agreed. He was, of course, in touch with the Round Table group and their friends through their common cause in the battle for Federal Home Rule.

At this time, in the spring of 1911, Waldorf had been strenuously supporting Lloyd George's new Insurance bill, the most comprehensive system of publicly administered welfare yet devised in England. Waldorf, an M.P. of less than six months' standing, again flew in the face of the party leaders, as he had done in the case of the Lloyd George budget. The Insurance bill was one of the things that he and Nancy most ardently desired to "get done." On this occasion he was subject to party discipline and was called to Lansdowne House to receive what Nancy called "his dressing down." Such measures were meant to impress, and no doubt they did. Lord Lansdowne was reinforced by Lord Curzon, the very personification of Toryism. A current couplet described him well:

> My name is George Nathaniel Curzon,
> I am a most superior person.

But after receiving this bolt from Olympus, the young Astor left the combined presences and voted exactly as he had intended to do in the first place.

For Waldorf this was the psychological moment. What is not obtained through party support often comes one's way through the power of the press. Garvin was looking for a new proprietor, and Waldorf "greatly wished" to purchase the *Observer*. In Garvin, an Irishman of working-class origin and brilliant gifts, the Astors found the same imaginative outreach to a larger world that they had found in the Round Table. He also offered something else particularly congenial to Nancy, the smell of newsprint and the smoke of political battle.

To acquire the *Observer* it was now necessary to raise the money, for Waldorf was not at that time in a position to make such a large investment on his own. William Waldorf, now living in Italy, was approached; detailed negotiations went through John Coode Adams in the Astor Estate Office in London. Each of the two principals, Garvin and the elder Astor, was a prima donna in his own right. Waldorf and Nancy had to sit back as patiently as they could while the two older men sparred over their heart's desire. William Waldorf went so far as to inquire into the editor's religion. Luckily Garvin had shed the Roman Catholicism of his childhood for what he had once described to a friend as "the church of Wordsworth." This could be, and was, suitably reworded for William as the "Protestant Church." After this, one or two specifically financial details were ironed out, and the deal was closed. The real partnership, that of Waldorf Astor and Garvin, was to ripen gradually and operate effectively in the political battles of the thirty years to come.

By the terms of the agreement, the Astors retained ultimate

control of policy, but no one, much less young Waldorf, expected to ride the fiery editor on a tight rein. Garvin remained Garvin. On Friday afternoons he came to Cliveden, where he and Waldorf threshed out the weekly line. For Waldorf it was a liberal education, for Garvin a happy experience. Their views, in fact, marched well together, in regard to both federal developments in the Empire and, most important, Anglo-American relations.

There was, however, a gap, not of policy but rather of style, between the *Observer* and the Round Table. Waldorf was the connecting link, and there was naturally a certain amount of rivalry between the two. The note of weekly journalism now impinged on the leisurely atmosphere of the Round Table; the popular style of Garvin contrasted with the Olympian Lord Milner. One essential difference between these two influential figures in the Astors' political life was their attitude toward party. Garvin was closely associated with the Conservatives; Milner, who had been toppled from high position in South Africa by the Liberal victory in 1906, despised the party system and had as little to do with it as possible. He preferred to remain a powerful figure behind the scenes. Garvin referred to the Round Table as "that desolating influence." He wished to detach Philip Kerr, the only one of the lot, he said, who was worth saving. Lady Edward Cecil, on the other hand, told Lord Milner that she found Waldorf Astor "one of the very dearest good fellows I know, and not at all stupid, as he has every right to be if he chooses." She added: "It is unlucky they have Garvin to lead them. He is quite worthless as a guide." It was a matter, almost, of having two gurus, or at least two sage counselors, Garvin and Milner. Perhaps only Waldorf, disarmingly genuine and disarmingly rich, could have kept both happy at the same time. Noted for a judicious ability to hold a steady course between extremes, he went quietly about his business in both camps.

It was a tremendously demanding life Waldorf had chosen for himself, but a satisfying one. On his own, quite apart from the Astor money and influence, he was earning the trust of his colleagues in the liberal wings of both parties. In his first year in the House, meetings of the Committee on Tuberculosis, of which Waldorf was chairman, were held at Cliveden, where some of the important health clauses of the Insurance bill were drafted. The Astors' friendship with Lloyd George dated from this period, as did Waldorf's activities in the field of health. In 1918 he served as Parliamentary Secretary for the Ministries of Food and of Health, all solid work in the course of a substantial career.

Not all visitors to Cliveden at this time possessed the basic seriousness of the Round Table or even of the Astors' Irish editor. There was one young man in particular who attracted Nancy with his lively mind and imaginative conversation but whose attitudes and approach to politics put her off. Nancy admired brilliance and got on swimmingly with prima donnas (Lloyd George and Bernard Shaw certainly fall into this category), but between Winston Churchill and herself there early developed an ambivalence that was to last their lifetimes. She could not discount him, although she tried, but she definitely disapproved of him. As a rising star in the Liberal Party, Churchill was invited to Cliveden one day in 1912, so that Lionel Curtis, a most dedicated Round Tabler, could convert him to Home-Rule-All-Around. Curtis wrote her:

> Last time we met Winston Churchill at Cliveden I came out in the evening on the terrace to look for Bob [Brand] and saw him walking with Winston on the lawn. On joining them I found them engaged in a lively discussion of devolution. Bob was arguing the impossibility of effecting social reform in England in the present congested condition of the executive and Parliament and was arguing that a devolution of certain executive and legislative powers on provincial administrations and legislatives was an essential preliminary. Winston was combatting the idea and indeed ridiculing it until I lost patience . . . and burst out "But what Brand is advocating and you are ridiculing is not his policy but yours–the official policy of your liberal government to which you have again and again declared that Home Rule was only the first step." He laughed, shrugged his shoulders and said something cynical which I forget, and then with curious facility drifted into seeing what could be said for such a policy and what use could be made of it for platform purposes at an election. You know how in private conversation he tries on speeches like a man trying on ties in his bedroom to see how he would look in them.

To the Astors, Churchillian politics lacked seriousness, and, at the worst, verged on opportunism. Nancy and Winston often met socially and always argued ferociously. The most famous of their exchanges occurred during a weekend at Blenheim Palace during this period.

Nancy: "Winston, if I were married to you, I'd put poison in your coffee."

Churchill: "Nancy, if you were my wife, I'd drink it."

Lionel Curtis, to the contrary, always had a respectful hearing at Cliveden, although not always from the younger generation. Curtis, aptly nicknamed "the Prophet" by his intimates, was capable of holding the floor through an entire dinner, until murmurs of "Why doesn't he shut up?" would reach their mother from the children's end of the table. Nancy would then admonish *them* to shut up, all this going on without interrupting the stately flow of the Prophet's periods, all about the commonwealth of nations.

From such men as Churchill and Curtis Nancy was learning fast. Curtis above all was opening a world view and helping her to develop her instinctive desire for the Anglo-American connection in British foreign relations. But at this time she was an apprentice and a spectator, not an actor on the world's stage. The passionate urge to play an active role in life, first nurtured by Miss Jennie and then inspired by Mr. Neve, was not yet satisfied.

Nancy was still suffering from occasional bouts of illness, followed by rest cures that were probably harder to bear than the original disorder. Her problem was sleeplessness, brought on by a sort of restless frustration, which none of her many activities seemed able to assuage. Three Astor children were born in this period: Bill (William Waldorf), 1907; Wissie (Nancy Phyllis Louise), 1909; and David (Francis David Langhorne), 1912. It was Nancy herself, not Waldorf, who wanted a big family. When Waldorf had said that he thought two children would be enough, she had protested. Nothing could equal the joys of the Mirador family life, but only two! That would never do. You see, she told him, she knew what they would be missing. But for herself even a large family was not enough to absorb her energies.

The role of mother in an upper-class British nursery was a highly restricted one. A nurse saw to the daily well-being of the Astor children. Nancy hardly knew what further thing she wanted. She only felt, in an undefined way, that life was passing her by. Her personal ambition had early been given a religious cast by Mr. Neve, but religion alone was not enough to satisfy her inner drive. She and young Philip Kerr were both searching at this time for something that eluded them in the midst of their full and busy lives—Philip for a religious sanction of his secular career; Nancy for a secular expression of her aspirations.

In the fall of 1911 Philip came very near to a breakdown. Religious doubt had plagued him ever since his time at Oxford, and this was now complicated by an unhappy love affair. In his distress he turned to Nancy for counsel. He had fallen at least half in love with the daughter of a family of dyed-in-the-wool Anglicans, "rich," as Mr. Sykes puts it, "with monastic spoils." The religious difficulties were obvious. Beset by doubt as he was, Philip was unwilling to renounce his own faith and unable to ask the lady to renounce hers. They had come to one of those sad and noncommittal arrangements where the affair was to remain suspended for six months, to be resumed then, "unless," as he told Nancy, " she should find the really right person in that time." It was really the prelude to breaking up. Nancy's warm sympathy almost drove out the hurt. "I am perfectly contented today," he wrote her after their talk; "I shall never forget what you did for me." By easing the end of this love affair she had cleared the way for their own remarkable friendship, a passionate-platonic affair that was to last the rest of Philip's life.

Immediately after this Philip had left for India, partly on Round Table business, and partly to see if he could find something in the religion of Gandhi to meet his personal need. He admired Gandhi, but the Indian form of sainthood offered no model for his own active life. He returned in the summer of 1912 with his religious doubts still unresolved.

Nancy had missed Philip more than she would admit to herself. David, born in March of 1912, was her most vigorous child, the one most like herself and Chillie, and he seems to have taken more than his share of her energy. She resented her weakness. It was so unlike what she thought of as "Langhorne." (Chillie had never had a sick day in his life, at least none not adequately accounted for by his current intake of bourbon whiskey.) Now a rest and change of scene were ordered. It was just at this moment that Philip returned from India, also, it appeared to his friends, on the verge of breakdown. There was a full moot at Cliveden to hear his report on India, a masterly analysis of the possible application of the principle of federalism to the Indian states under the British raj. He again attempted to take up his duties as editor of the *Round Table Review*, but it was obvious that he was not up to intensive work. His brother Round Tablers, kindly surrogates for fate, arranged that Philip and Bob Brand should join the Astors on a projected holiday in St. Moritz.

In the cold, stinging air on the white slopes, youth and health reasserted themselves. Depression vanished. When Bob Brand joined them and signed the hotel register Nancy was astonished. "I didn't know you were an honorable," she said; "you don't act like one." Bob was delighted. He was always amused by her, but not so uncritically as Philip and Waldorf were. To put it precisely, he was not in love with her. After a time the little group left the slopes and motored down the valley, through Nîmes, Arles, Avignon, and other lovely places. The two young men wanted Nancy to play golf with them, but she refused, for Waldorf did not play. On their way home they stopped in Paris and she bought Philip "something very nice" at Cartier's. Because she could not have given a present to Philip alone she gave Bob an extremely handsome set of gold waistcoat buttons. When the next day he went to her sitting room to say goodbye, he found her writing a letter, but she sprang up and went to him as he stood by the mantelpiece. "Are you in love with me?" she asked. Bob said, "Yes, of course." What she really meant was: "Is Philip in love with me?" They both knew that the answer was for Philip too.

But once back in London, Philip and Nancy went their separate ways; Philip, still unable to work, idled at home, and Nancy, condemned to even more stringent "rest," went to Dr. Dengler's Sanatorium at Baden-Baden. Nancy's thoughts turned to Virginia and to her "Dearest Miss Jennie." "Here I am," she wrote from Dengler's. "This means no London, and it may mean Scotland." Scotland—the very name struck horror to Nancy's heart. She hated their place there, Glencoe, but Waldorf loved it. She promised herself Virginia in the autumn. "Virginia will cure me," she wrote Miss Jennie from Glencoe in August. "I sleep better . . . and am trying 'new thoughts'! . . . The writer of the *Round Table* is here, Philip Kerr, and he does us all good. He is not only brilliantly clever but so spiritual and high minded that one feels it more than all of his other qualities." The cure had been resumed, and at hated Glencoe!

New Thought, a rather dubious movement then current in America, proved inadequate after all. In February, 1914, Nancy's recurring illness was vaguely diagnosed as "internal abcesses," and she submitted to a painful and apparently not very successful operation. A few years before she herself had designed and Waldorf had built a "cottage retreat," a rather large, rambling, and pleasantly undistinguished house on the Channel shore at Sandwich. It was to this house, Rest Harrow, that she went to recuperate from the operation, lying on a balcony and attempting to soak up as much sun as Sandwich in early spring might produce.

As she lay there within sight of the water the world around her seemed beautiful and peaceful, in painful contrast with her own misery. Even more threatening than present pain was the doctor's insistence that a quieter and more restful routine be planned for her future. To Nancy it was like seeing the prison bars descend between her and life. Her rebellion was total, passionate. "This," she wrote in her memoir, "is not what God wants. It is not what He meant to happen. It can't be that God made sickness. It turns people into useless self-centered people who become a burden to themselves and to everyone else. . . ." Then, as she said, a wonderful thing happened. "Whenever a soul is ready for enlightenment, and awaits it humbly, I believe that the answer is somewhere to hand—the teacher comes." The teacher was Mary Baker Eddy. Nancy first heard of Mrs. Eddy through her sister Phyllis, who told her there were people in America who were convinced that illness could be cured by prayer. These people were called Christian Scientists. Nancy sent at once for a practitioner. "We talked for a long time, I told her how much I wanted to be well, but I said if it was going to separate me in any way from my religion or shake my faith, I would not touch it." The first chapter in Mrs. Eddy's *Science and Health*, on prayer, laid all her anxieties to rest. "From that moment," she said, "fear went out of my life."

But the struggle with doctors was not yet over. Reinforced by Waldorf, they insisted on a second operation. This time things went quite differently. When the doctor came to change her dressing he told her that she was the bravest woman he had ever come across, but she assured him truthfully that she had felt no pain, "except when he prodded" her. To Nancy, Christian Science was the supreme cure for illness. It was not only that. It was also the way of health, the path to true personal fulfillment. She need no longer fear her own inadequacy; like the powers of darkness, like sin and suffering, it was just material error, doomed to vanish before the light of spiritual truth. Her illness had indeed vanished, never to return.

Nancy wanted to tell her friends of the wonderful thing that had happened to her. She wrote to Hilaire Belloc, who replied in a farcical vein, claiming that he wished to convert her to Judaism, a rather sour joke, as Belloc was an unblushing anti-Semite. Philip, of course, was the friend she thought of first; she lost no time in sending him a copy of *Science and Health*. It reached him at a most opportune moment. Staying with the Astors at Rest Harrow in April, only a month after Nancy's own conversion, he was stricken with acute appendicitis. Full recovery, Nancy assured him, could come only through Mrs. Eddy. In this crisis Philip put himself completely in her charge; for the first days after his operation she was with him constantly. After she left he wrote her with a freshness and love that shine through the written page: "Dear Nancy, I'm going on flourishing. Only it makes the day much longer not having you to talk to and see. I'm only just beginning to realize how much you've helped me—that morning before the operation and every hour since. My faith will grow all right, yours is so infectious. . . . I don't miss you—only as I should miss a great pleasure—no aching or real loneliness—that's the wonder of it. We shall never be alone again. Love to everybody from Philip."

After Nancy left Sandwich his mother came down, and his almost beatific convalescence was interrupted and made difficult. There were not only the doctor and the nurses, who practiced the unhappy—not to say fiendish—method of that day of leaving a tube in the wound to "prevent it from healing too quickly"; there was also his mother, with her rigid Catholicism, her every censorious instinct aroused by this new and strange departure of Christian Science healing, to her a perversion, in the religious life of her son.

Nancy's old disposition to equate Rome with a narrow despotism was strengthened at this time, as was her growing reliance on Philip as a guide and counselor. She had given the original impetus, but from very early on in their conversion it was Philip who led the way. Feelings that might have led to a tortured repression of physical love and eventual separation found sublimation in the spiritual love taught by Mrs. Eddy. They were to have their heaven on earth after all. Nancy gave Philip a book in which she inscribed the lines:

> You and I have found the secret way,
> None shall hinder us or say us nay.
> All the world may stare and never know
> You and I are twined together so.

It sealed a relationship that was uniquely their own.

Philip's conversion astonished his friends. One of them, discussing the matter with Alice Roosevelt Longworth, wondered how such a good Catholic could possibly have embraced the religion of Mrs. Eddy. "Perfectly simple," replied Mrs. Longworth; "just a case of swapping Blessed Virgins in midstream."

On the secular side of life, Philip found in the works of Mrs. Eddy a spiritual manual perfectly suited to his temporal goals. In a subsequent reasoned statement of his faith he drew attention to this central point. "The 'ending of war' and the 'unity of men and nations' of which Mrs. Eddy so frequently speaks as one of the objectives of Christian Science will only be fully realized through the establishment of a world constitution and a world Parliament or Congress, paralleling on the political sphere the Manual, which gives complete freedom in their own sphere to branch churches while uniting both individuals and churches in a single world church under a world constitution. . . ." Thus were Philip's worldly doctrines sanctified, as it were, by Mrs. Eddy. For Philip faith was now integrated with personal life. It was the "secret way" shared with Nancy. It was the answer to those "troubles of the soul and heart" which, as he wrote to Brand, "nearly destroyed my body once." They were never to trouble him again.

For both Nancy and Philip, psychosomatic illness became a thing of the past, and Nancy always believed healing to be the most important aspect of her new faith. But for Nancy as well as Philip, Christian Science had its political aspect. Her desire to change the world through personal action was vastly fortified by the new teaching; without it she might never have achieved her later spectacular career.

No matter how striking the public results of a religious conversion may be, the most important changes are interior, in the personal life of the convert. In these matters Philip became Nancy's spiritual adviser, and whether this influence was wholly a happy one is open to question. In a letter of March, 1915, during their novitiate, as it were, in the new faith, he wrote her on the subject of helping others. "Sympathy," he wrote, "in the literal sense, is a snare. It means 'feeling with' another. That doesn't help one snap. What does help is understanding what the root of the trouble is and pointing out how it can be cured." Philip did not realize it then, but this advice ran directly contrary to Nancy's best gifts, and certainly to her best interests. Never slow to tell others what to do, she was thus encouraged to ignore her gift of natural sympathy and to indulge instead a tendency that was later to cause her much grief in her relations with family and friends and even in her own religious life. The loneliness and alienation of her last years were the inevitable result of a lifetime of pointing out to others how to run their affairs.

Philip wrote in depth to Nancy and to Bob Brand, but otherwise was generally reticent about his faith. Asked about it by an overbold friend, he replied laconically: "It works." Nancy was less restrained; although she refrained from making a nuisance of herself, she was never averse to converting others to the new faith. She would no doubt have approached the Pope himself on the subject if opportunity had offered. Nevertheless, Waldorf, her nearest object, did not swear allegiance to Mrs. Eddy for another nine years, and then not until driven to it by an ailing back.

This faith, like others, had its dangers, not only to Nancy, but to Waldorf and Philip as well. By denying the "reality" of evil, it led to an overconfidence in the essential goodness of man. Nancy's interpretations of the doctrine were personal and, to say the least, erratic, but she did earnestly try all her life long to live up to the precepts of her adopted church. It was to be her shield and buckler in many a future battle. It was a rather heavy armor that she donned at this time, but she managed, on the whole, to carry it lightly.

6

War—and Peace?

"ON the political sphere," as Philip expressed it, the Round Table continued to work on the Irish problem. This bitter and ancient battle was no longer confined to Ireland or even to the drawing rooms of London; it was leading Englishmen to the very brink of armed rebellion against their own government. In this crisis the young men were moderate, and the old, reversing roles, were calling for blood. The government wanted Home Rule; Milner and Garvin were among the most violent against it. Waldorf attempted to hold down his editor, but Garvin, aided and abetted by the other firebrand across the water, William Waldorf, was ready to stop at nothing in the battle with the government. He wanted the peers to refuse to pass the Army Annual Act, which alone enabled the British government to support an army. Waldorf was appalled. "The more I think about it," he wrote Garvin, "the more strongly do I feel that action would be both an outrage and unwise. . . . As a statesman I am against it, and as a politician I dread it."

More temperate and more typical of Cliveden's methods was the dinner given by the Astors so that Dawson and Lionel Curtis might continue their efforts to convert Winston Churchill to Home-Rule-All-Around. Curtis was successful; Churchill did speak in the Commons advocating a federal solution for Ireland, and Asquith gave his support to the scheme. Unfortunately, many of the Die Hards, including Milner himself, refused to accept a compromise.

When Englishmen have reached the point of desperation they call upon their king. That is his *raison d'être;* it explains the necessity of his remaining ceremonially pure. Everything else had been tried and failed. Even Churchill's support had not prevailed. In June the King and Queen proposed themselves for tea at Cliveden. Nancy, like any Virginian, never doubted the serviceability of her native manners under any circumstances whatever. The week before she had entertained five hundred members of the Salvation Army. The royal tea party went off as quietly as the other occasion had been noisy, and both were typical of Cliveden. Of the King and Queen she wrote Mr. Neve, "I am far too democratic to get excited over it, though, I confess, I was highly flattered."

Ordinarily no respecter of persons, she did in fact harbor a most unlikely respect for the royal family. They satisfied some unburied feudal instinct from her Virginian past. On this occasion, as she wrote Mr. Neve, there was no party, just a long, quiet talk. What they talked about was not mentioned and perhaps is not important. The mere presence of Their Majesties was a tacit endorsement of compromise between the extremes of the Unionist opposition and the government policy of Home Rule. The following month a conference was called at Buckingham Palace. The politicians played the King card, as they called it, in a desperate but futile attempt to effect a compromise between the warring parties.

While all eyes were on the troubled land across one channel, calm appeared to reign across the other. The autumn before Nancy had stood with an old friend, Lord Wemyss, on the Scottish coast. He had pointed across the North Sea and said, "Virginney [his name for her], the war is not far off, and soon the enemy will sail across that sea." Had Waldorf had the same premonition when he had resisted Garvin on the Army Act?

At least he had seen further than his nose, further than the old frustrating wrangles which again were grinding to failure at Buckingham Palace. The very hour that the conference was breaking up, a member picked up a newspaper and read "Germany's Ultimatum to Serbia." With these words the age of optimism expired.

Late on the night of Tuesday, August 4, 1914, the blow fell: England was at war. Sir Edward Grey saw the lights going out. "We shall not see them lit again," he said, "in our lifetime." No one believed him. When the King, with the Queen and the Prince of Wales, showed himself on the palace balcony, the cheering was terrific. Nancy wrote to Miss Jennie Ellett, "The war came so suddenly . . . it simply knocked everybody off their feet. . . . But those Germans must be licked once and for all."

The wounded had come to Plymouth, men returned from the first three days of desperate fighting at Mons. They told Nancy firsthand of the *Schrecklichkeit*—of the Belgian women without hands. These tales were recounted on "the first day they arrived, before they had seen or heard a newspaper," so that they could not have been inspired by propaganda. They made her feel like sending all her family and going to fight herself. Her whole nature rose, as happened to many in those early days of the war, in a passionate urge to serve and to sacrifice. She and Waldorf offered Cliveden as a hospital, and Nancy hoped that the government might let her put up recreation rooms for the troops in camp. (The recreation to be offered was strictly nonalcoholic.)

As often happens, these offers of service were not immediately accepted. In the meantime Waldorf put up YMCA huts in Plymouth, and finally the hospital plan, turned down by the War Office, was taken over by the Canadian government. It was a fortunate choice, for the Canadians, next to the Yanks themselves, were closest to the Astors' own people. Not since the Sheltering Arms Home in Virginia had Nancy's talents been put to better use.

Waldorf, not well enough for front-line duty, had asked for the toughest home-front service that could be found, to be added to his already full schedule as an active M.P. In 1912 he had been made Chairman of the House Committee on Tuberculosis, and he was now treasurer of the new Medical Research

Committee. A fellow member described him as turning up at one of their meetings "looking very nice in his major's uniform." He had been inspecting camps on Salisbury Plain, where the new army was slithering about in from six to eighteen inches of mud, Waldorf slithering with them. He had the job of checking waste in army management, an ungrateful task at any time but especially hard for a tall, strapping fellow of military age who gave no outward sign of the bad heart that kept him from the front lines.

Philip, more than the other Round Tablers, felt the war cutting solid ground from under his feet. What of the *Round Table* now and of all their work for peace? His colleagues talked him into staying on as editor; he could serve best, they said, in the old manner, "working on the far-sighted line." In September, fully recovered from his April appendectomy, he went down to Southampton to see his young brother, David, off to France. They had a gay evening in Southampton; the next morning David sailed. Three weeks later he lay dead near La Bassée, one of the first of the many thousands of British youth whose blood was to drain into the fields of France.

On the purely human, emotional side, Philip found it harder than ever to keep "working on the far-sighted line." In June, he had seriously considered taking a commission and going to France. It was not the *Round Table* or his recent surgery that immobilized him; before he could take the final step he had to reconcile going to war with the tenets of his new faith. Following old habit, he sought religious counsel, but again found only confusion. Rather to his relief, perhaps, his new Mother Church offered no firm guideline. It was left up to the individual when and if to elect to fight evil by physical means. "The general conclusion," he reported to Nancy, "is that if one has enough understanding of the truth one won't go: if one hasn't one will. Do you understand that?"

In the event, he did not go, but he was not then, and never became, a convinced pacifist. He believed that a time might come when only the sword could combat evil, but that, on the other hand, a shallow and trigger-happy patriotism simply stood in the way of "truth"; peace between nations, as between individuals, must be given every opportunity to prevail. In essence this was the creed to which Philip's whole future was devoted.

"Pacifism," he said, "is not enough, nor patriotism either." His last published words, many years and two wars later, were simply a restatement of his belief in individual responsibility, and of the choices that must rest squarely on every citizen.

Nancy's position was much easier. She never considered that her work in the Canadian hospital conflicted in any way with the tenets of her religion. Her dynamic faith in the love of God in which neither sin nor disease found a place could supplement as well as supersede the work of the doctors. It was her good fortune that the head surgeon, Colonel Newborne, knew how to use her special gifts. Nancy and Colonel Newborne worked devotedly. Colonel Newborne, she said, "is the only living man for whom I ever made mint juleps."

Cliveden's potential as a hospital site was appreciated and used to advantage by the new occupants. The squash tennis courts, open to the sky, made an excellent operating theatre; wards and offices were grouped around it. In the spring of 1916 Nancy wrote to Miss Jennie Ellett that they had nine hundred wounded, and "it was more like a house party than a hospital." If so, it was Nancy who made it that way. She told them, "Now, you boys have got to die or get well. We can't have you hanging around here sick." It was there, she later said, that she learned her lesson of complete service, from the men. Colonel Newborne took to using her as a sort of emergency shock treatment. There were the two sailors so badly wounded in the Battle of Jutland that they had given up and turned their faces to the wall.

"Where are you from?" she asked.

"Yorkshire," said one of them.

"No wonder you don't want to live, if you come from Yorkshire."

He raised himself on an elbow. "Repeat that," he demanded. He told her that Yorkshire was the finest place in the world, and if she didn't know that she didn't know anything. To hell with the Battle of Jutland, he was going back to Yorkshire. And Nancy assures us in her memoir that he did go back.

This scene may strike one as brutal if one did not know Nancy or had not been present to feel the strong current of support flowing from her to the wounded men. These men just had to get well. A former patient wrote her later from Canada:

"They are making a lot of me here. They think I'm a hero. Gee, Mrs. Astor, they don't know how you had to kick me around to make me live!"

Dr. William Osler, the famous surgeon, was the hospital's medical consultant. If he was not at Cliveden promptly every Monday morning Nancy would ring him up and tell him that her children were weeping for him. In fact she was thinking not of Michael, born in 1916, or of John Jacob (Jakie), born in 1918, but of the boys at the hospital whom only Dr. Osler could help.

Nancy's religion, combined with her ceaseless activity, protected her from the old proclivity to physical breakdown, but not entirely from depression and emotional storms. Like a millionaire harassed by fears of bankruptcy, she could sometimes shamelessly and half-seriously depict herself as friendless. Half-seriously, because even in these moods she could joke. A favorite character was the fellow who declared, "I have only one friend, and I hate him." Nevertheless, she could quite seriously tell Susan Buchan (wife of John Buchan and later Lady Tweedsmuir): "I've got no friends, no friends at all, smart or otherwise. I would welcome the butcher's boy from Maidenhead to tea." Mrs. Buchan was so entranced by this statement that the "butcher's boy from Maidenhead" passed permanently into the Buchan family vocabulary.

With the men in the hospital nothing like this was ever allowed to appear. When she could bear no more she would tell them, "When this war is over I'm going to have nothing more to do with this man-made world. I am going into an old ladies' home and I shall just sit and knit." When she became an M.P. one of the men wrote her, saying, "Is this the old ladies' home you said you were going to retire to?"

Will Rogers, after visiting the hospital, summed up his feelings: "If I ever hear social or political foes say aught against her . . . I just rake up the vision of that woman walking among her boys with tears in her eyes, yet telling jokes of each one. So let no woman, mother of a son, ever say evil against her."

Her devoted service in the hospital is symbolized by the statue representing Canada which stands with outstretched arms at one end of the little military cemetery at Cliveden. It is not a portrait, but the Australian sculptor who created it used Nancy's head as his inspiration. "There is not much outward resemblance," he wrote her; "it is your eyes alone which . . . remain." It is perhaps her finest memorial, best of all because so totally anonymous. At the core of this most public of personalities there lay, for those who could see, something essentially private.

The year 1915 had been ghastly. Dead piled on dead in rotting middens. The British Commander-in-Chief, Marshal Haig, continued to pour in troops, with no material gain on the western front. The casualty lists mounted at home. Nancy's gay and very gallant young friends Julian and Billy Grenfell had been killed early that summer. The Grenfell boys were the sons of her old rival for Revelstoke's affections, Lady Desborough. By coincidence the Desboroughs' Taplow Court was Cliveden's nearest neighbor, but relations between the two houses remained cold for years. Even after 1915, Nancy could not entirely forgive the perhaps fancied wrong she had suffered from Lady Desborough or overlook what to her was a serious lapse in morals. However, the Grenfell boys became intimate friends, representing the lighter "social" side of life at Cliveden. After Julian's death Nancy, using influence, had contrived to have a safe staff job offered to Billy, but Billy would not leave his men. His last letter to Nancy, written in the almost sure knowledge of death in the coming attack, exhorts her: "Take care of yourself, my pretty, do your hair nicely, and do not overload yourself with charitable works in this ungrateful world."

What was there to do but drown grief in work? Nancy joined a march to the government offices at Whitehall on behalf of women, to demand that they be allowed to work in munitions factories. She gave talks to the men going on leave, calling up visions of mothers and sweethearts at home, and contrasting them with dreadful pictures of the misery caused by those twin evils, "drink" and "women." She could say anything she liked and they would take it from her. One boy came to her after one of her "horrible talks" and gave her his money to keep for him until the end of his leave. "Here, Mrs. Astor, you have just ruined my holiday."

The worry at home that oppressed those in a position to know was that England was not being properly led. Philip and Garvin, in their respective journals, were advocating a wide program of compulsory service and a separate ministry of defense. Waldorf was backing these suggestions in the House. The Astors were behind any proposal and any leadership that would get on with the war. The Prime Minister continued to move with his customary deliberation, "doing nothing supremely well." It was called the "wait and see" policy. Nancy, in the full flood of wartime enthusiasm, was in no mood to respond to overtures from the Asquiths. She refused a dinner invitation from Margot in June: "I am going to Plymouth on Monday to see about our YMCA huts there and make a recruiting speech—alongside Mrs. Pankhurst (who I wish was in the Cabinet!)" There followed a comment later omitted from the letter finally dispatched to Mrs. Asquith: "Anyhow you would find us disagreeable company these days. The Wait and See Policy has changed me into a fighting woman."

The care used in the composition of this letter (a copy was sent to Geoffrey Dawson) reflects a change in the Astors' position vis-à-vis the Asquiths. It was no longer a question of a personality clash between the two ladies but of a very serious conflict between current government policy and the far more vigorous prosecution of the war advocated by Waldorf and his Round Table friends. This letter in fact foreshadows the formation of the group of anti-Asquith conspirators known as the Monday Night Cabal.

Asquith was no natural fighter. His brilliant son Raymond had fallen on the Somme, and since then his faculties had seemed benumbed. To Lloyd George, in contrast, the casualty lists were a challenge, galvanizing those springs of electric energy and sympathy that were Lloyd George at his best. He did not despise Asquith as did some of the diehard Tories; he respected the Prime Minister's solid judicial qualities. But respect or no, he had his own way of cutting Asquith down. He remarked to Riddell that "Asquith worries too much about small points. If you were buying a large mansion he would come to you and say, 'Have you thought that there is no accommodation for the cat?' " Such insights, irritating to some, were irresistible to the Round Table, who couldn't have agreed more.

The young men of the Round Table were looking for a leader. Waldorf had worked closely with Lloyd George on the Insurance bill and had early recognized his qualities. Milner himself had decided, rather cynically, that Lloyd George was the man to serve the Round Table's political purposes. He was the master of those popular arts that Milner disdained to employ himself, without scrupling to use them for his own purposes when he discovered them in others. Philip, more generous, wrote that "Superior people censure [Mr. Lloyd George] for rhodomontade and sentimentality, but in so doing they miss the point. He is sincere, and speaks to those who are suspicious not of error but of insincerity; he speaks as an idealist to idealists." Lloyd George was clearly the Round Table's choice to win the war. It remained but to put him in power.

For this purpose a "Ginger Group" was formed, so called because its members were dedicated to "gingering up" the war effort, which, they felt, was sadly lagging under Asquith's leadership. To others, less in favor of its objectives, it became known as the Monday Night Cabal. The principals were Milner, Dawson, Carson (Conservative M.P. for Ulster and later member of the Lloyd George cabinet), Leo Amery (associated with the Round Table but not a full member), Round Tabler Fred Oliver, and Waldorf Astor. Lloyd George himself, Philip Kerr, and others were in occasional attendance.

Nothing that took place at Cliveden before World War II could hold a conspiratorial candle to what happened there during World War I. Starting early in the year 1916, the nucleus met regularly on Monday evenings at seven, talked for an hour, and dined together if convenient. It was a sort of informal staff meeting, laying down plans of action and issuing public communiqués in the guise of *Times* leaders from the hand of Geoffrey Dawson. Their main objective was the creation of a supreme war cabinet, a select steering committee that should be able to bypass the large, minuteless, and very loosely implemented meetings of the Asquith cabinet. These Ginger Group meetings were to lay the groundwork for the palace revolution to come.

In May Waldorf took a hand in the game, urging that Lloyd George resign from the Asquith cabinet. Lloyd George explained, in effect, that the moment had not yet come; he was still moving up in the Asquith government. In fact, in July he became Secretary of State for War, which did not prevent him from dining with the conspirators, often twice a week. Nancy and Waldorf, who had long found the knife and fork mightier than the pen, had him to dinner in December. J. L. Garvin was present and developed the theme: Asquith resembled Lord North, a mere party manager; what was needed in wartime was a real leader. Lloyd George listened attentively, his bright eyes taking it all in. In the candlelight, across the polished mahogany, the Welshman, the two Americans, and the Irishman were frankly looking for allies. The ties to Asquith were slipping and the *coup* drawing nearer.

Asquith and Lloyd George, of course, were not engaged in a mere struggle for power. The issues involved were war and peace, touching the very life of the Empire. Britain appeared to be bleeding to death in the trenches of France and starving to death at home through the submarine blockade. The final straw, the thing that drove Lloyd George, the master politician, to revolt, was not political expediency but a sense of military desperation. Henry Wilson, a Corps Commander and Lloyd George's favorite general, came home on leave and dined with the Ginger Group. Asquith, he told them, "has been worth Corps unnumbered to the Boche."

Lloyd George at last agreed that the time had come for revolt. On December 4, 1916, Dawson's leader, written at Cliveden, carried the bold headline: "Weak Methods and Weak Men." He said: "There are men in the Cabinet today . . . who are a clear danger to the state." Asquith was pressured into agreeing to a small committee that should henceforth have supreme control of the conduct of the war. The final break came over the chairmanship; who should really have control? In one breathless weekend Lloyd George cleared the path, first to his own resignation as Secretary of State for War, and then to the premiership. At a meeting of the Unionist Association it was decided that Bonar Law, the Conservative leader, should resign and take all Conservative members of Asquith's coalition cabinet with him. He did this, not out of love for Lloyd George, but in order to prevent a split in the party between his own traditionalist wing and the new Milner dissidents. It was this act of Law's that assured Lloyd George the premiership.

Many years later Churchill, giving the memorial address for his old leader in the House of Commons, summed up the story: "Presently Lloyd George seized the main power in the state and leadership of the Government." (Hon. Members: "Seized?") "Seized." ("Hear, hear!") "I think it was Carlyle who said of Oliver Cromwell: 'He coveted the place, perhaps the place was his.' "

And so it was. The action had been so swift at the last that for some time it was difficult to tell what had really happened. Clearly the Ginger Group, many of whom were Round Tablers, had laid the groundwork for the *coup* by drawing Lloyd George and the dissident Conservatives together. Dawson's leader in the *Times* created an opening into which Lloyd George moved speedily. These events were to leave a bitter taste behind, but the immediate result was glorious. Winston Churchill, as usual, got to the heart of the matter. It was now against the enemy that Lloyd George, the consummate warrior, was to address his skill.

Milner was immediately given cabinet rank; he was to be the master administrator of the new regime. Other Conservative members of the new cabinet were Carson, Bonar Law, Balfour, and Curzon. Waldorf and Philip were given lesser jobs, on Lloyd George's personal staff, but they too went to the center of affairs. Lloyd George, wholesale shatterer of precedent, meant to operate through his own staff; even the sacred arrangements of Downing Street fell before his attack. For nearly two hundred years Britain had ruled an empire from an inconspicuous building on a narrow *cul de saç*. "Downing Street, little wider than a passage, is a hundred yards in length. At its not easily discoverable entrance from Whitehall it is open to vehicular traffic. . . . One would not have been surprised to see a card in the window [of number 10] bearing the word 'Apartments.' " Lloyd George needed space, but he could not, or would not, destroy the time-hallowed intimacy of number 10. He solved the problem by building a series of offices in the garden in which he installed his own men—whence came its nickname, the Garden Suburb, and, with predictable innuendo, the Garden Cabinet. Its members came and went without formality through a little green door in a side wall, to which each had a key.

Nancy had her own role in the intimate group. She too fell under the spell of Lloyd George; like herself he was swift, unpredictable, full of the Celt's wizard charm. Others, baffled, suspected the worst of Lloyd George; Nancy saw straight into the heart of the things he cared for: the welfare of his own people and, even in the heat of all-out war, human lives. Waldorf, after a period of strain in which it seemed he might not be given a place, had been taken into the inner circle of the Garden Suburb. Nancy had them all for dinner at 4 St. James's Square, the Astors' London home, on Lloyd George's birthday. It was his fifty-fourth, although the cake bore a single candle to celebrate his first anniversary as Premier. Each guest was asked to cut his slice without disturbing this sacred flame, thus assuring good luck for the Chief through the coming year. Amid the flood of conversation, Nancy described herself filling out a passport form. Coming to the space for "any special characteristic," she had put "talks too much." After dinner there was a serious discussion of the division of labor within the new secretariat. It was decided that Waldorf should keep the Chief informed of "current ideas, criticisms and discussions" in the House of Commons.

Philip, of all the staff, was closest to the Premier. As the principal private secretary he was to be at Lloyd George's right hand through all the days of power, all the fluctuations of fortune that beset his chief. Philip's first responsibility with Lloyd George had been the organization of the Imperial Conference of 1917. This brought J. C. Smuts, an old friend from the days of the South African Union, to England as one of the Dominion representatives. Smuts, now Prime Minister of the Union of South Africa, stayed on as a member of the Imperial cabinet, in whose hands lay the real control of the war and of wartime diplomacy. There is no doubt that Philip, too, had a considerable share in the international diplomacy of the Lloyd George years.

It was no part of the original Allied war aims to tear the old Austro-Hungarian Empire to pieces. The federal idea, as applied to central Europe, was in fact quite viable in pre-Versailles diplomacy. In the years preceding the war there had been an active Austrian movement toward a federal parliament for the peoples of central Europe, and in fact the assassination of the liberal Archduke Franz Ferdinand appears to have been inspired by German opposition to such a development. In December of 1917, responding to tentative peace feelers, Lloyd George dispatched Philip and Smuts to discuss a separate peace with Austria based on such a central European federation. Unfortunately, it turned out that the Austrians were not willing to detach themselves from their German allies, and the negotiations came to nothing. Philip was loath to give up a plan so much in line with the Round Table's hope of regional federations. "Mr. Kerr," remarked Lloyd George, "being young and of a naturally hopeful disposition," wished to continue the conversations.

In June Philip had taken his chief to dine with the Round Table at F. S. Oliver's. Lloyd George had been in fine fettle, talking of his new house at Walton Heath, and announcing that "his new Peers had not paid for it." Waldorf winced, for William Waldorf, after appropriately huge campaign contributions, had just been elevated to a viscountcy, an event enormously distressing to his eldest son. William Waldorf felt that a peerage was the just recognition due a man of his wealth, while Waldorf could think only of his own promising career in the Commons, which would be cut short at his father's death. For no peer could be admitted to the lower house. Father and son quarreled bitterly on this issue, to a point where the elder Astor attempted, so far as he could, to disinherit his son. Fortunately, most of the vast inheritance was in trust. As long as his father lived, Waldorf cast about desperately for some means of evading the title. In the meantime he continued to work at full pressure in the Commons.

There were new forces moving in the world of which he was keenly aware. In December Lloyd George, dining at 4 St. James's Square with Milner and others of the inner circle, spelled out his political intentions for after the war. "A good many old distinctions are dim these days, and the country is ready for a bold move forward under state inspiration." Waldorf gave an interview from his almost unheated office at the Ministry of Food, where he was working long hours, often into the night. "Autocracy in industrialism," he told the press, "is passing out, just as autocracy in kingship." He was implementing this rather general thought by getting employers and trades union men together for conferences in his home at 3 Elliot Terrace in Plymouth. The Astors were definitely looking toward a new world after the war.

In April, 1917, America came in on the Allied side, but the Yanks did not actually arrive overseas in any quantity until the following year. An early arrival was the Assistant Secretary of the Navy, who visited Cliveden that summer. All the gardeners had gone to war, so Franklin Roosevelt did his bit for England by cutting the Cliveden grass. Nancy liked this handsome American friend of Waldorf's, with his enthusiasm and his obvious inability to conceive of defeat. Like so many of her friendships it was to continue through the vicissitudes of peace and of two wars.

Shipping losses had been up to 500,000 tons a month, but now there were American sub-chasers stationed at Plymouth, and things were bound to get better. Nancy had two thousand American sailors to look after, for this was how she felt about these boys with the American faces and the accents from home. There were few left in Plymouth who had not lost sons of their own, but the town rallied and the people outdid themselves to make the American boys welcome. One party Nancy was never to forget. The ancient cathedral of Exeter is not far from Plymouth; its Bishop's wife, Lady Florence Cecil, was a friend of the Astors and promised to give a large party for the American sailors. Lady Florence had lost two sons, and the week of the party she had confessed to a friend: "I don't believe I could go on if Jack [her third son] was taken." The next morning, Monday, the wire came saying that Jack had been killed. On Thursday the party came off, and the boys, never guessing their hosts' sorrow, were charmed as usual with the cheerful kindness of the Bishop and his wife. Not all the heroes, Nancy knew, were on the front lines.

Nineteen hundred and eighteen brought a new development. Lloyd George, with his gift for snatching victory from defeat, responded to a new German offensive by the creation of a unified command under the French Marshal Foch. It was his opportunity at last to bypass the British Marshal Haig and to break the bloody stalemate on the western front. The Supreme (inter-Allied) War Council formed at this time became the model for an international secretariat which remained in being after the peace treaty. It was the tool that Lloyd George and Philip were to use in Lloyd George's effort to build a new Europe after the war.

The war now was all but over. For the last time under war conditions, Lloyd George crossed the Channel, returning to

Dover on a black night with high seas running. A car from Sandwich met him and took the Prime Minister and Philip to Rest Harrow, the Astors' house on the sea, always kept open for friends in need of refuge. Here the Welsh Warrior rested, home from the wars.

On November 11, 1918, an armistice was signed.

November 11, 1918, a day to be remembered by the people of the Western world! The years 1914–1918 had been a colossal binge, an orgy of mud and blood. Nineteen-nineteen, the year of the peace treaty, was the morning after.

Nancy thought of Lady Florence in Exeter, and of the others who had lost sons, fathers, husbands. "After two years," she had said, "we did not look at the casualty lists any more. All our friends had gone." She knew that there were mothers among the enemy too, and all the anguish turned her mind to healing. "In the hearts of mothers of all countries the seeds of peace are sown." There were others, apparently tens of thousands of others, in whom the excesses of war inspired vindictiveness rather than grief or guilt. These were given a voice, perhaps out of proportion to their numbers, by the more violent press. Lord Northcliffe was a principal offender. "Squeeze them until the pips squeak!" "Hang the Kaiser!" Phrases such as these finally drove Geoffrey Dawson to resign as editor of the *Times*.

Nancy, of course, reposed her faith in Lloyd George. The Premier himself, as he left for the peace conference with Philip, was hardly aware of the fiasco to come. His assistants felt charged with a new hope for the world. Colonel Hankey, who had been Secretary to the War Cabinet in England, now created a secretariat representing all the Dominions, truly a new Imperial Office, the realization of the Round Table dream. It could be continued permanently, he hoped, after the conference was over. It was but one step more to the international secretariat, which Hankey was invited to organize for the conference as a whole. It was a "prototype," he wrote enthusiastically, "that might well be adapted to any world organization." The machinery, in fact, was in order. To make it effective it remained only to educate the popular will. At Versailles, in that pleasant January of 1919, anything seemed possible to these young men.

As in the Garden Suburb, Kerr and Hankey superseded the regular Foreign Office officials and continued to occupy the center of the stage.

The British headquarters at the Hotel Majestic were very gay, "full," as Smuts remarked rather bitterly, "of typists and other females." To top off the whole air of promise and gaiety, the weather was mild, and the Paris sunshine, without heat, shone over all. After the long strain everyone felt enormous relief, the desire to let go, to let down one's hair. Nancy would have loved it, but instead of being at Versailles, where the action was, she was tied down at home with a young family. She had to abandon Philip, still at a vulnerable age, to all those "typists and other females" of whom Smuts had taken a dim view. Of one in particular, Philip took a much kinder view; he even brought the young lady to Cliveden. Alarmed, Nancy enlisted Miss Heather Harvey, Waldorf's secretary, a personable young lady whom she could trust, to distract him from the other, whom she could not.

Sunshine and typists were not enough to keep the conference from running rapidly downhill. Clemenceau, the incredibly tough, single-minded Frenchman, was determined that sixty million united and industrialized Germans should never again threaten forty million Frenchmen. His opposite numbers among the Allied chiefs, Orlando for Italy, Lloyd George, and President Wilson, had no such passionate commitment with which to counter the French tiger. Orlando, not averse to territorial grabs, was a very junior partner; for Lloyd George the only *sine qua non* was Britain's command of the seas; and Wilson—well, Wilson was the key to Versailles and a rather special case. His country had fought, quite simply, to make the world safe for democracy, and this was precisely what he meant to achieve. He arrived in Paris with his dream of a league of free nations, and admittedly it was a great dream. He brought with him fourteen general points. The detailed charter of the League, which the President graciously agreed to adopt as his own, was the work of Smuts and Lord Robert Cecil. In any case it was not concerned with specific boundaries, which were the building blocks, the actual substantive elements of the treaty.

Bob Brand said of Clemenceau that "He was born with one day's good nature inside him, and he used it up pretty quickly."

He could, however, indulge a formidable wit, asking the world to imagine him seated between two men, one who thought he was Napoleon, and the other who believed he was Jesus Christ. (He might have observed that neither, in a worldly sense, had come to a very good end.) Wilson, he added, had fourteen points, whereas the Almighty had been content with ten! Wilson, who had proved himself not a bad in-fighter in Princeton University politics, was prepared to stake his life on the idea of the League; the details of the balance of power were, it sometimes seemed, beneath his notice, an attitude that left the field wide open for Clemenceau. The President's famous principle of self-determination for the small, newly liberated fragments of the Austro-Hungarian Empire was manipulated by France. Versailles created a *cordon sanitaire* of small nations, individually weak, around Germany's eastern border, thereby laying a train of dynamite ready for the inevitable day when sixty million Germans should recover their strength. Lloyd George and Philip would have preferred to see a federation standing on this troubled borderland between Russia and Germany.

In March Philip and Hankey both pointed out to the Premier that individual claims, while tolerable taken singly, were nevertheless adding up to an intolerable whole. Lloyd George responded by organizing one of the most remarkable weekends in the history of diplomacy. On Saturday the twenty-second, he retired with Philip, Hankey, and Henry Wilson to Fontainebleau for an informal conference that resulted in the famous Fontainebleau Memorandum. The preamble, drafted by Philip, ran as follows:

> It is comparatively easy to patch up a peace which will last for thirty years [but] I cannot conceive any greater cause of future wars than that the German people, who have certainly proved themselves one of the most vigorous and powerful races in the world, should be surrounded by a number of small states, many of them consisting of people who have never previously set up a stable government for themselves, but each of them containing large masses of Germans clamoring for reunion with their native land. . . . If we are wise we shall offer to Germany a peace which . . . will be preferable for all sensible men to the alternative of Bolshevism. . . . we will open to her the raw materials and markets of the world on equal terms with ourselves.

This summed up the views of Philip and Lloyd George at the time, views, in fact, that they were never to change. It remained the solid base on which Philip and the Astors rested their political thinking between the wars. It was not, however, adopted by the conference as a whole, nor did it do much to ameliorate the harsh terms of the treaty.

Discontent with the treaty was general in the American and British delegations; it rose to a feeling of passionate rejection among the younger men. A few of them banded together one night at dinner in the Hotel Majestic; out of this meeting came the Royal Institute of International Affairs, also known as Chatham House, after the London office that was soon opened on St. James's Square. Born out of it members' discontent with the Versailles Treaty, the RIIA became a sort of permanent commission of inquiry on foreign affairs. Although it operated very much like a government commission, it was an entirely private undertaking, manned by a small professional staff. It became a model for similar institutions in other countries, such as the Foreign Policy Association in the United States. Since its beginning in 1919, Chatham House has held public meetings, conducted independent studies, and issued regular bulletins in a more or less successful effort to enlighten the public mind. Waldorf served as chairman during the critical thirties, when the question, peace or war? was again facing his countrymen.

Would it have been possible, in 1919, to have achieved a real peace after total war? Certainly not so long as Clemenceau sat unchecked in the peacemaking chair. In its final form, embodying all the seeds of a second war, the treaty was delivered to the Germans. On the afternoon of June 22 the telegram from the government of the German Republic was delivered to the Council of Five: "Yielding to overwhelming force, but without on that account abandoning its view in regard to the unheard-of injustice of the conditions of peace," they were ready to sign.

The day that had seemed so remote, so impossible, dawned at last: Saturday, June 28, *la journée de Versailles*. In the *Galerie des Glaces*, Clemenceau sat under a gilded scroll which proclaimed "*Le Roi gouverné par lui-même*." When the various dignitaries had signed, the guns crashed out all over Paris. "We kept our seats," wrote Harold Nicolson, "as the Germans were led out, their eyes fixed upon some distant point. . . . The

Allied chiefs followed, Clemenceau last, with his rolling, satirical gait. A friend stopped the old man, seizing his gloved hand. '*Oui,*' said Clemenceau, '*c'est une belle journée.*' There were tears in his bleary eyes." Nicolson turned to a Frenchwoman near him. "Are you sure of that?" he asked her. "*Pas du tout,*" she answered.

At the Majestic there was dancing, and very bad champagne. Smuts, who had signed in anguish of soul, refused to celebrate with the great, assuaging his conscience by going to celebrate with less contaminated folk belowstairs. Harold Nicolson wrote *finis:* "And so to bed, sick of life."

To Philip, the servant of Lloyd George, it seemed that the battle for peace had just begun.

7

The Member for Humanity

"A world fit for heroes to live in"—that was Lloyd George's promise to his supporters for after the war. In 1919 Nancy and Waldorf had been working as a political team for ten years, and for the first time it did look as though the path for social reform was clear.

But politics for the Astors was about to fall victim to William Waldorf's craving for honors. At dinner one night in April with the Astors, Lloyd George, and a few other political intimates, Bonar Law had worried about the loss of a by-election at Hull. Lloyd George would have none of such pusillanimity. "The people are with me," he told the company; "they are bent on social reform." Nancy agreed with him wholeheartedly. If only, if only he had not made William Waldorf a peer! She pounced on the unhappy Bonar Law and gave him a good shaking. "You're a mean creature," she cried, for he was responsible for the fatal coronet. Bonar Law submitted meekly, according to Riddell, who was also present.

Everyone knew that Mrs. Astor was wildly unpredictable. The adult Nancy could erupt as spontaneously and with as little regard for convention as the little Nannie Langhorne who had set an audience to cheering at the Chicago International Exhibition of 1893. Lloyd George recognized the showman's gift in young Mrs. Astor. He had a Welshman's respect for money, but William Waldorf's gifts had served their turn, and it occurred to him that Nancy might have something of her own to offer his party—and his country.

She certainly offered a great deal when it came to brightening the statesman's leisure hours. Lloyd George was social in his tastes. In late August, he and Mrs. Lloyd George gathered around them as gay a company as could be found and took the party with them to the south of France—his first real holiday since the war. The group included his press chief, Lord Riddell; Sir Eric Geddes, First Lord of the Admiralty; Riddell's friend Ernest Evans; Sir Hamar Greenwood, the Canadian Chief Secretary for Ireland, and Lady Greenwood; and Nancy and Waldorf. One night, sitting around the fire, Lloyd George had put a question to each one in turn: What quality would you most like to possess? Lloyd George himself chose the power of a great preacher, which of course was already his. Waldorf surprised Nancy by choosing that of a great musician. Later the talk turned to absent colleagues, particularly those whose relations with the Prime Minister had not always been untroubled—Churchill, for instance, and his schemes for sending troops to support the White Russians against the Bolsheviks. Churchill had tried to pull off such a move by the Allies while Lloyd George was absent from the peace conference. But Philip had warned his chief of the maneuver, and the Premier had hastily wired Philip to nip it in the bud. This Philip had done so effectively that he was now rumored to be the chief Bolshevik agent in Europe.

Nancy, never a blind admirer of Churchill, took up the Russian theme: "Why not send him to carry on the Russian campaign? He could call for volunteers and raise the money needed." Riddell suggested that Churchill might become tsar. This thought delighted Lloyd George, and Nancy proceeded to puff out her chest and her lips, portraying Churchill in his new role.

Curzon was their next victim. All too aware of the Norman blood and excessive pride of his Foreign Secretary, Lord Curzon, Lloyd George waxed philosophical upon the chances of fate. William the Conqueror was the illegitimate son of a girl whom his father had met while crossing a bridge. "What a remarkable thing!" exclaimed the Premier. "Had it not been that William's father and mother crossed the bridge at that particular time, there would have been no William the Conquerer, no Norman Conquest, and no George Nathaniel Curzon." It was an appealing thought to the present company.

The party did not get into top form until the arrival of Mr. Balfour, Philip, and Sir Auckland Geddes (Lloyd George's Ambassador to Washington) a few days later. The seventy-two-year-old Balfour, surely the most distinguished elder statesman in Europe, performed a Scottish reel, capped by Nancy and her new partner, Ernest Evans, who did an apache dance. Nancy continued clowning until she was displaced by another guest doing a buck and wing. Auckland Geddes then delivered his version of a Scottish sermon, purportedly describing the agonies of the damned in the depths of the bottomless pit. "As an excuse to the Almighty they will say, 'O Lord, we didna ken!' And the Lord will answer out of his infinite murrrcy, 'Well, ye ken noo!' " (The story may or may not have been new in 1919, but its survival power has been immense.) Nancy and Evans closed the entertainment with her version of a village clergyman and his wife opening a bazaar. Mr. Balfour was very appreciative but evidently astonished. He had never, he said, spent such an eccentric evening in his life—an omission that could have been corrected on almost any visit to Cliveden.

The political mood was as optimistic as the social one was light-hearted. Lloyd George boasted that "the younger Conservatives are with me." There was a sense of old shackles falling away. "I shall be able to get on without greedy people who see the knife at their throats and know I am not in sympathy with them." It was left to Bonar Law to introduce the note of warning: "The Conservatives do not intend," he told Lloyd George, "to scrap their party organization."

A very important part of the postwar social revolution was

Colonel Chiswell Dabney Langhorne, painted by E. Upsen in 1901. *(Photograph by Edwin S. Roseberry)*

Nancy Witcher Langhorne, painted by E. Upsen in 1901. *(Photograph by Edwin S. Roseberry)*

Nancy Langhorne Shaw, 1902.
(Valentine Museum, Richmond, Va.)

Irene Langhorne Gibson,
by her husband,
Charles Dana Gibson.

Nancy and Bobbie Shaw.

The Reverend Frederick Neve, photographed on a visit to Cliveden in 1925.

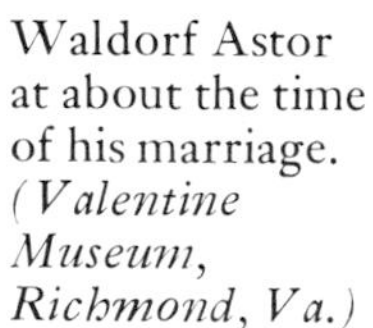

Waldorf Astor at about the time of his marriage. *(Valentine Museum, Richmond, Va.)*

Nancy in 1907, by John Singer Sargent.

Cliveden.

Bill, David, Nancy, and Wissie Astor, *ca.* 1912. *(Valentine Museum, Richmond, Va.)*

Philip, Lord Lothian. *(Wide World)*

Lady Astor's introduction to the House of Commons, escorted by Arthur Balfour and David Lloyd George, painted by Charles Sims, R.A.

Nancy Astor, *ca.* 1925. *(Valentine Museum, Richmond, Va.)*

Lord and Lady Astor celebrate their silver wedding anniversary, May 3, 1931. From left to right: Bobbie Shaw, Wissie, Michael, Bill, Nancy, Waldorf, Jakie, and David. (*Keystone*)

the granting of the franchise to women over thirty. It was generally felt that they had earned it. Many had worked throughout the war in the munitions factories, and most women had assumed a more independent role in the absence of their men. Some people, not all of them men, deplored the measure, expecting chaos; others, like Nancy, believed that it would herald a new and better day in politics. Actually, except in Nancy's own situation, no great change was immediately effected by the women's vote.

Nancy's moment came with the death of William Waldorf in October, 1919. The old gentleman, who had become addicted to the pleasures of the table, dined rather too well on a leg of mutton and a bottle of Beaune and was that evening found dead behind the locked doors of his lavatory. His death, at age seventy-one, had come without warning and much sooner than had been expected. If Waldorf had only had a little more time in the Commons he might have legitimately expected to be moved up to a cabinet post. He had already been seriously considered for chairman of the Local Government Board, the sort of post that could have kept him in the government and in politics independently of a seat in the Commons. In fact, during the last two years of the war, Nancy had taken over many of his minor political chores in Plymouth to save him for departmental work.

But now that the blow had fallen, what to do? The by-election in Plymouth was to take place in a matter of weeks after William Waldorf's death, and rumors were already rife in the press that Nancy would stand for the seat in her husband's place. Should she, or shouldn't she? Like so many of the crucial decisions in life, this one had to be taken quickly. Under pressure Waldorf showed his true quality. While trying desperately to divest himself of the peerage, he nevertheless put aside his own disappointment and encouraged Nancy to stand. Nancy admitted that the idea of being a candidate "knocked me out for a week. Still," she said in her acceptance speech, "he [Waldorf] thinks I can do it." And, after all, she had only to consult her instincts to *know* that she could do it. "I am a Virginian," Nancy exclaimed, "so naturally I am a politician." The election would be the easiest part of it. When her self-confidence was questioned she replied, "Why, don't I know the men, women, and children of Plymouth and can't I tell whether they are pleased with me or not?"

Waldorf had been a coalition Unionist, a supporter of Lloyd George, and Nancy of course stood under the same auspices. Lloyd George endorsed her candidacy in an open letter: "Now that women have been enfranchised I think it important that there should be a certain number of women in Parliament. . . . There are a good many questions in regard to housing, child welfare, food, drink and prices in which it would be an immense advantage . . . to have a woman's view presented by a woman, and"—here Lloyd George reached the crux of the matter—"your sympathies were genuinely with the people long before you had any notion of becoming a candidate yourself, and even before women's suffrage became an accomplished fact." Altogether it was a splendid letter. Perhaps not surprising as it had been drafted by Philip.

Among friends the opportunity to put on a show was irresistible. Dining with Lloyd George, she amused the company by describing what she would wear in the House if elected: "Something quiet. A coat and skirt. In the evening no evening dress. Only a V with a piece of chiffon. Of course I should wear a few pearls." The "Missouri Waltz" was played on the piano, and Nancy showed the company how she might dance up the floor of the House and make her bow to the Speaker. At this time Nancy and Waldorf were both known to be ardent prohibitionists, and Lloyd George gave her good-natured advice on the subject of her favorite cause: "You will have to be careful what you say about drink. At elections you cannot always have the best. You must modify your transports sometimes," advice which Nancy heeded in spite of Philip's urging that she stand uncompromisingly for total prohibition. In matters of practical politics she was always willing to take advice from those who knew more than she did. In this case Waldorf had already blazed a path. Both Astors were for control of the sale of liquor, as a measure more politically possible than total prohibition. The label of "pussyfoot" or prohibition candidate would have been fatal to her chances in the election, and she responded briskly to any such appellation from her opponents. "I have neither been asked to stand as a 'pussyfoot' candidate, nor have I any intention of doing so. It seems to me I detect the claws of some other sort of envious cat in the misleading suggestion." It was necessary to be courageous, but not, perhaps, foolhardy.

When it came to campaigning, Nancy took lessons from nobody. She drove about Plymouth in an open carriage behind a pair of spanking chestnuts. Everyone knew her, and her carriage could be spotted a mile off, with its red, white, and blue rosettes and streamers, Lloyd George's coalition colors. Posters broke out all over town proclaiming "Vote for Lady Astor and Your Babies Will Weigh More." The odd thing about this slogan was that it was perfectly true. Until after World War I and the appearance of Lloyd George, the well-fed and well-to-do had simply taken it for granted that the majority were undernourished and that nothing could be done about it. Nancy was for pure milk, better working conditions, shorter hours for women and children—in fact, for all the things that did make slum children larger and healthier. "I want for your children what I want for my children," she told them. "I do not believe in sexes and classes."

Plymouth was not entirely ready for such revolutionary ideas. Labor supporters set out to heckle her. "Plymouth doesn't want blankets and coal," one shouted. They were suspicious of palliative measures, considering them as subtle devices of the rich to hold down the poor. The ever-useful campaign subject of Astor money was brought up against her. "I probably have far more than I ought to have," she admitted, "but if some of my Socialist opponents had what I have they would not be here asking for your votes" (*cheers and catcalls*). It was her opponents' fond belief that a woman alone on a platform without a man to prompt her would soon betray her ignorance. "Lord Astor can't help her when she is at a meeting." Nancy assured them that they needn't expect long, reasoned speeches from her. "It is not my style."

Nancy was returned with 14,495 votes to 2,292 and 4,139 for the other two candidates, respectively. A Unionist candidate, running against her on the issue of sex, withdrew before the contest. Waldorf, although up to the last moment he had been trying to relieve himself of his title, now rose to the occasion. "I have been asked," he said, "to introduce to you my successor, your future representative [*loud cheers and laughter*]. I have been asked, presumably because I know more about her than anyone else. . . ." The team of Waldorf and Nancy had become Nancy and Waldorf. Whichever way, they were to pass the ball back and forth to each other for the next quarter century of successful political life.

Unhappily Chillie had died in 1919, before the launching of his third daughter's spectacular career. Although he was no supporter of women's rights, success in any form pleased him. What his comments might have been on Nancy's new career make fascinating speculation.

The victory was a triumph for Nancy, but she took it as a triumph for women. "If I should fail," she said, "the consequences would be lamentable, not to me, but to the women of England." For as long as she could remember she had been a feminist. It had started even before Miss Jennie Ellett's school. "I cannot remember a time," she wrote to a friend, "when I did not think that women were as good, if not gooder, than men." She really believed that she had been born thinking it. And now it was quite clear to Nancy that the Lord intended her to prove it. When Members declared that they represented the men and women of England, Nancy said that she represented the women and children. Some evils, like drink, the effects of which she had experienced in her personal life, she hoped to control. If courage were needed then, Nancy believed, courage would be given her, as she had seen it given to Mr. Neve, and as Mrs. Eddy promised it would be given to her disciples.

Her introduction to the House was indeed a test of courage. "They call it the best club in Europe," Nancy said, "but it didn't seem like the best club to me. I can't think of anything worse than being among six hundred men none of whom really wanted you there." Nancy had as her sponsors the two most distinguished Members of the House, Lloyd George and Arthur James Balfour. A new Member is traditionally escorted to the Speaker's table, where he signs his name in a register. To walk even this short distance in utter silence was too much for Nancy; she talked to her mildly embarrassed sponsors all the way up the floor of the House and almost, according to Lloyd George, forgot to sign the register through having a chat with Bonar Law. She knew many of the Members in private life, but for quite some time she was excluded from the easy give and take outside the chamber. One gallant Member, Mr. Winston

Churchill, admitted that they thought if they could freeze her out they would be rid of the female sex for good. He graphically described his feelings on coming upon the new Member: "As though some woman had entered my bath, and I had nothing to protect myself with except my sponge!" "Don't worry, Winston," Nancy is reputed to have replied, "you would be in no danger."

The real test of a new M.P. comes with his—or her—first speech. The old Members turn out in force, they give the new boy a courteous hearing, which is not always the case later in his career. Nevertheless, he is on trial, as to both the matter and the manner of his speech. Waldorf and Nancy determined that she should attack head on; they chose "Temperance and State Purchase of the Liquor Traffic" as the subject of her first speech. It would have been bad enough for a male, but the mind quails at the thought of a female on such tricky ground. But the very fact that she was a woman steeled Nancy for the fray. She thought of herself as something new. Women were citizens now. They had been taken out of the "class of criminals, lunatics, paupers and peers," for these benighted souls were still outside the Parliamentary pale. Nancy saw clearly that in the new postwar society politics was coming into the home. "Up to now," Nancy pointed out quietly enough, "although the home has been implicit in everything our country has done, it hasn't been very much considered in detail." That was the way she meant to consider it: water supply, refuse disposal, pure milk, good schools, early closing of the pubs, guardianship of infants, inheritance laws, social insurance, unemployment compensation. . . . The lady Member's mind was not on "blankets and coal" but on a new society where the details of the home were considered the proper concern of politics.

Where better to start than with the liquor trade? During the war severe restrictions had been placed on the sale of liquor, which it was now proposed to lift. Waldorf and Nancy were for state purchase—that is, government control of the sale of liquor—and this was, of course, anathema to "the trade."

In Nancy's view one didn't rehearse even a maiden speech; she simply marshaled the facts (or, rather, Waldorf marshaled them) and then she let them have it. Interruptions were welcome, encouraging the zest of battle. The great moment came on

February 24, 1920, the memorable day on which a woman first arose to speak in the venerable mother of parliaments. Nancy thought of Miss Jennie and Mr. Neve, who would have approved the matter of her speech, but when it came to the manner she thought of Chillie.

> I am perfectly aware that it needs courage to address the House on that vexed question, Drink. However, I dare do it. . . . The Hon. Member [Sir J. D. Rees, who had proposed the repeal of restrictions] has said that he and his friends were willing during the war to put up with drink control for the purpose of winning the war. It is not true. Ever since the Liquor Control Board started the Hon. Member and his friends have been kicking against it.

Sir J. D. Rees indicated dissent. Viscountess Astor:

> Oh, yes! What did the Hon. Member do in the Great War, he and his friends? No, sir, the Hon. Member and his friends were always kicking against the Liquor Control Board. (Hon. Members: "No!") Oh, yes; . . . I am not saying that there were not some perfectly patriotic brewers . . . but I think that if the Hon. Member and his friends are the real friends of the working man they will urge the brewers to disgorge some of their war profits. . . .
>
> I do ask Hon. Members not to misread the spirit of the times. Do not go round saying that you want England a country fit for heroes to live in, do not talk about it unless you mean to do it. . . . I want you to think of the effect of these restrictions in terms of women and babies. Think of the thousands of children whose fathers had to put up with even more than these vexatious restrictions—who laid down their lives for you. Think of their fatherless children. Supposing they were your children or my children, would you want them to grow up with the Trade flourishing? I do not believe the House would. I do not want you to look on your lady Member as a fanatic or a lunatic. I am simply trying to speak for hundreds of women and children throughout the country who cannot speak for themselves.

The restrictions were not lifted. One imagines that Sir J. D. Rees and his friends retired to the bar for a needed restorative.

"Lady Astor," remarked a supporter, "is always on the side

of the angels even though the angels have no votes, and some people think that they are rather extreme in their views." Nancy had nothing against the angels, but her strength was firmly based on *Homo sapiens*: "What I find is if you care enough about people they will listen to the truth"; and "it is comforting to feel that if you are fighting for what is right and really wanted by right-thinking men and women, in our free system of government sooner or later it comes about." But even this faith had its limits: "Of course," she added, "I refer to social legislation, not, alas, to world peace."

This was Philip's task. After the war Lloyd George struggled valiantly to set up a conference system for the whole of Europe, victors and vanquished included. With this end in view, meetings of the Supreme Allied Council were continued into the days of peace, a nucleus for the larger council, which was to include Germany and Russia. Hankey believed so deeply in the system that he turned down an invitation to become first president of the League of Nations in order to remain secretary to the conferences. Unlike meetings of the League, the conferences constituted a real international executive; they were meetings of heads of state with full power to determine policy. Philip believed, as he told Riddell, that both Russia and Germany "must be brought back into the industrial life of the world." He flung himself heart and soul into this plan to draw Europe together by creating a European council.

It was a noble effort, but success was questionable; certainly it could not be achieved without relaxation of the unconscionable pressures upon Germany, and this France was unwilling to do. In 1922 the eyes of the world were turned to Genoa, where Russia and Germany were to meet for the first time on equal terms with the Allies. The result was a disaster. Russia and Germany broke out of the group and signed the separate Treaty of Rapallo. It was the end of the conference system and nearly the end of Lloyd George. Not only was he faced with the crucial failure abroad; at home the old battle over Ireland had never been resolved. Lloyd George's Home Rule bill of 1921 aroused the ire of Bonar Law, most dangerous of men. The final incident occurred September, 1922, at Chanak, where, the cabinet believed, a Turkish force was moving on the Dardanelles. With Churchill's support, Lloyd George called for armed resistance.

Bonar Law stepped forward: "We cannot police the world alone," he said. Law resigned, and took with him all the Premier's Conservative supporters. It was the end of the Lloyd George era, the end, indeed, of British dynamism. The long years of retreat, what Philip called the Baldwin-MacDonald torpor, now began.

Quite some time before the fall of the regime, Philip had become a chief target of Lloyd George's enemies. Rather like Henry Kissinger in our own day, he had never held elective office, yet obviously he wielded great influence in the affairs of state. Churchill complained to Lord Riddell that Philip and Lloyd George "are formulating schemes which affect the lives of millions and the destinies of the world, and all this is done behind the scenes . . . I told [Philip] so the other night. I said to him 'you have no real responsibility. If things go wrong others have to take the consequences. All you have to do is walk out of Downing Street.' "

From almost the beginning of his years with Lloyd George, Philip had served as chief of the Premier's personal staff and as his principal adviser on foreign affairs. Philip felt that he was becoming a political liability and that the time had come to leave Lloyd George's service. Lloyd George thought otherwise and did not let him go until May of 1921. During these years Philip acted increasingly as the Astors' adviser on foreign affairs; this became his permanent role at Cliveden. As Nancy later exclaimed: "I have never known Philip to be right in domestic affairs, and never wrong in foreign."

In the spring of 1922 Philip went to America—principally to meditate at the Mother Church in Boston, and also to give a series of lectures on the prevention of war at Williams College. He spoke to the ladies and gentlemen of Williamstown with some passion:

> Did the gods of old ever exact a toll of human sacrifice like that which was paid between 1914 and 1918? Are the idols which we worship now going to exact this toll again? Their names are not Moloch, or Baal, Dagon or Ashtaroth today. Nor are they Germany, or Italy, or England, or America. . . . They are *Deutschland über alles*, the *Sacro egoismo Italiano*, Rule Britannia, America First.

The answer, as Philip saw it, was some very loose form of constitution for a commonwealth of all nations, or for all those nations ready and willing to enter into such a bond.

All the assorted tyrannies which now plague us even in "free countries"—the military draft, with its power over individual life and death; government controls on commerce, currency, and even over the individual's right to move freely from country to country—all these have their source in national sovereignty, and in the rivalry and fear between one nation and another. In a world of international anarchy, no man is free. In Philip's more formal language at Williamstown: "We shall only be able to establish a true constitutional balance in our own countries when constitutional government within is balanced by constitutional government without."

All this, he knew, involved far more than a mere change in mechanism. It meant a profound change in moral outlook. A profound change in moral outlook was what the Astors hoped for, and believed in. They too set out for America in the spring of 1922. The immediate occasion was an invitation to Nancy to speak as a woman in politics to the fledgling League of Women Voters in New York. She had not been expected to talk about peace at all, but once she was on her feet it was impossible for her to keep off the subject next to her heart. Where Philip had interested a few serious and idealistic people in the Williamstown audience, Nancy hit the front pages as soon as she stepped off the boat, wearing a black caracul coat with a wide chinchilla collar and, as the reporters avidly noted, five rings. For two hours she fielded questions, told stories, and mingled admonition, attack, and compliments. "If New York is not gifted with an altogether spiritual viewpoint, it is certainly groping for it." She had been told to be careful of American sensitivity concerning the League, but she told the English-Speaking Union, "It's hopeless to go forward when you are looking backward. . . . I believe that the safest and surest way to get out of war is to join some sort of League of Nations." Later, speaking to the Associated Press, she put in an even more daring word, on behalf of conferences. "It is the memory of the anguish of the mothers and fathers who watched for four years [of war] which gives me the courage to speak plainly here tonight. . . . Anyhow, I do believe that America likes people to say what they mean and care about. . . . It is all very well to speak of European entanglements, but the world is already tangled, and we have to think of a plan to disentangle ourselves."

America did like it. After this speech Nancy was besieged with requests for more of the same. Waldorf was in fact the manager of this tour. He described himself as "agent, secretary, manager, booster, adviser of a prima donna, cabinet minister, and circus all in one." So far as such a thing was possible, he drafted her speeches in advance; the difficulty was that Nancy could not be held down to one system of notes, or even to one train of thought. Typically, her best performance was entirely extemporaneous. Waldorf described an occasion in Washington when she attended a meeting, addressed by Secretary of State Charles Evans Hughes and the British Ambassador, Sir Auckland Geddes, and had been called on unexpectedly. "Nancy had two minutes of silent prayer and then went down from her box . . . to the front of the platform. When she sat down the audience gave a huge ovation, and called her back to bow. She was witty, gently sarcastic, spiritual, intelligent and eloquent in her speech." On this tour they stumped the country—indeed, the continent, for Ottawa and Toronto were included—and everywhere Nancy had a tremendous success.

As might have been expected, her hometown receptions reached unprecedented heights. In Richmond their train pulled in ahead of schedule, but not ahead of the reception committee, family, and assorted dignitaries assembled on the platform. All this at 7:10 A.M., with at least the male member of the team unwashed, unshaven, and unfed. Nancy, pointing to the grimy, sooty engine-driver, shouted, "I feel like you look." From that moment everyone proceeded to enjoy the occasion, and an occasion it was. An alley of school children two hundred yards long had formed in the main station. As Nancy entered, a uniformed band struck up "Dixie" and then "Carry Me Back." She walked down the center while the children cheered and threw flowers at her feet. Waldorf, who a moment before had been thinking of himself as a hardened and abused impresario, almost wept. "It was," he recorded in his diary, "a most moving and touching sight, and the sentiment so genuine. People cheering, sobbing, etc."

Danville, visited in company with Irene, brought its own

problems, for neither sister could remember anything or recall any person from the city of their birth. The problem was to some extent solved as the sisters closeted themselves with a young Danville reporter, who had met the train at nearby South Boston. On this last-minute leg of the journey he briefed them thoroughly, no light task, as Nancy estimated that she had sixty cousins in Danville. She may have had sixty a year ago, said Waldorf, but like rabbits since then they have bred much and often. What was more, Danville cousins sat in rows on the porch of their hotel, "rocking, spitting,* and gossiping." Official oratory ran from the warm and folksy, "We are here to greet our baby," to the grandiloquent references to Nancy as "a dove of war and an eagle of peace," and much, much more. Waldorf was not neglected, particularly by one reporter who took him confidentially aside. "Lord Astor, I've seen you called on several times to speak and I want to tell you I think you ought to think seriously about going into public life also."

A welcome corrective was supplied by the conversation of two old countrymen standing near an attentive and apparently anonymous Waldorf.

" 'S that Laidy Astor?" asked one.

"Reckon so—or perhaps it's her sister."

"Why's she called laidy?"

"She married some furriner."

"Is that her husband standing by her?" (looking at an unshaved old boy).

"Reckon 'tis."

"Pity he's so old."

"I don't think she's that pretty."

"No, nor more do I."

And they had moved on.

With this notable exception, Nancy swept the country. She addressed her appeals particularly to women, as she had always done in England, to apply personal morality to the politics of nations. "Can we change [the world]?" she asked them. "Are

* It will surely be brought to the writer's attention that some but not all of the Danville cousins indulged in this habit. I can only say, let him who is without cousins cast the first stone. In this connection it may also be mentioned that Chillie, on a visit to Cliveden, is reputed to have disappeared one day with the Duchess of Devonshire. He had taken her up the clock tower the better to instruct her in this fine art, or at least so they say.

we really different from men? I hope so. . . . There are things bigger than politics, even bigger than countries, though neither party or country likes to think that anything is bigger than itself. If only we, the newcomers of political life, can keep that greater vision. . . ." It was a vision to which she herself held fast through the years. While Philip was building his theoretical federal city in Williamstown, Nancy was asking the women of America, in effect, to believe in it. Waldorf, with his liberal views and modest manners, confounded every American idea of what a British lord should be. Meanwhile he had his own work to do. Not only was he the invaluable "manager," but he and Philip also improved the opportunity and followed Nancy's speeches by promoting foreign policy groups in the United States to parallel the Round Table groups in the Commonwealth. Nancy was their publicist. It was part of their great partnership in a lifelong effort to establish peace by drawing together people of good will.

Nancy had meant to have a long holiday in Virginia, "to renew my youth." Chillie had given Mirador to Phyllis a few years before his death, himself retiring to a small cottage across the road, from which he was well able to observe, and to disapprove of, any changes made by the new owner. But Mirador was still home to Nancy, and it was there that she and Waldorf repaired. As it was, they spent only eleven days in Virginia, and Nancy's youth, as she said, was not renewed! Even here they were pursued by reporters, to the vague discomfort of Virginia cousins. One day at Mirador, Waldorf ran interference for his wife with a reporter from the *Ladies' Home Journal*. "To what," she asked, "do you attribute Lady Astor's success?" "I think," said Waldorf patiently, "it's because she is never afraid to tell the truth. Yes, I think that is it." On her home ground at Mirador Nancy herself might have said it was because she had been brought up to be a fighter. "I hope I am a fighter," she said, "especially when it's a fight for peace."

After six weeks they sailed for home on the *Aquitania*. Waldorf's diary contained this last entry:

"Final visits of friends.

"Final words with reporters.

"Final press photos.

"Ship sailed at 12 noon.

"After lunch I slept till dinner.

"After dinner I slept till breakfast next day."

It was on this trip, I think, that Nancy first attained the quality of magic, the myth-making power, that was to be hers for so long. She was more than an American woman married to an Englishman, more even than the first woman M.P. As one admirer put it, she was the Member for Humanity, the symbol of all that was new and bright and hopeful in the new world of peace. Of course, it was no handicap to have at one's side a handsome and charming husband whose name happened to be Astor. Nevertheless, the success was her own. She told them in Canada, "If you really love people you can say anything you like to them." "The nations of the world," she had said, "have yet to realize that they are really one family, and instead of preparing to fight one another they should prepare to help one another. . . ." Philip could have said no more. The effect was total, and the total was Nancy.

Philip stayed on in America to spend Christmas with Christian Science friends in Boston; Nancy and Waldorf returned home to face the election that followed the fall of Lloyd George. The homecoming was gloriously festive. Nancy wore a "plain cream frock and large apple green hat with ostrich feathers." The Lord Mayor referred to her as "a living link between England and America." The Rev. T. Wilkinson Riddle went even further: "The Free Churchmen of Plymouth rejoiced to see Lady Astor back, and they would desire him to express complete sympathy with her efforts to purify social life, to protect unmarried mothers and unwanted children, to restrict the prodigious traffic in drink, to promote international friendship, and to establish the Kingdom of God on earth." Perhaps unable to cap these compliments one by one, Nancy replied: "I would not like to tell you all I said in America about Plymouth; it might turn your heads."

Clearly she had not lost her grip, but so strong a supporter of Lloyd George was bound to face tough opposition. Besides the Labour candidate there was a dissident Conservative, a certain Dr. Bayly, whose candidacy split the Conservative ticket. The Conservative Association rather rashly came to her aid by suggesting that a vote for Dr. Bayly was a vote for the "double standard" of sexual conduct—that is, permissiveness for the male and strict enforcement for the female. The charge was not soundly based, and if anything it had an adverse effect. Besides competition from Bayly, an unfortunate effort the previous year to put through strict antidrink legislation had told against her. This time Nancy only squeezed through, with a bare majority.

There was also the sensitive subject of divorce. Horatio Bottomley, a newspaper publisher once bracketed by Smuts with Beelzezub, performed true to character, attacking her viciously in his rag, *John Bull.* He accused her of having taken advantage of an easy American law while opposing liberalization in Britain. Actually, as we know, Nancy's own divorce had been obtained on grounds of adultery, which was also, at that time, sufficient grounds in England, so that there was no substance in Bottomley's accusation. It was, however, wonderful ammunition for the perennial hecklers. One man seized the opportunity at a meeting to call out loudly, "What about divorce?" "Poor man," Nancy replied, "are you in trouble too?" Still, the charge rankled and was difficult to refute.

The public reaction to their views on drink caused Nancy and Waldorf to moderate, but not to abandon, their drive in Parliament toward restrictive legislation applied to "the Trade." "Lady Astor's bill," raising from sixteen to eighteen the legal age limit for purchase of alcoholic beverages at a bar, was drafted by Waldorf in 1923 and supported by an opening speech by Nancy in its second reading in the House. It has sometimes been charged that Nancy rarely thought before she spoke. It is quite true that the sort of research and analysis that go into the drafting of a "Private Member's bill," or indeed into any parliamentary bill, would have been quite beyond her training. Miscellaneous reading, no matter how wide ranging, avid, or assiduous, simply does not produce such highly professional skills. Nancy, however, did not speak out of childish inconsequence; she had a perfectly sound grasp of what she and Waldorf were trying to achieve, and certainly at this stage of her career she knew, with few exceptions, what could and could not be said. If she had not drafted the bill herself, she supported it ably in the House.

Nancy drew a good deal of adverse attention in the course of "Lady Astor's bill." The second reading had, by parliamentary custom, to be followed by a third reading, and here Sir Frederick Banbury entered the lists. Sir Frederick was a Conservative among Conservatives, one of those to whom the appearance of a woman in the House had literally seemed to remove every claim to dignity and seriousness from that ancient body. Nancy, an American and a divorcée, was bad enough. She had been shortly joined by Mrs. Margaret Wintringham, a Liberal widow, in 1921. Sir Frederick's suffering was still further compounded by the advent of Mrs. Hilton Philipson, formerly Miss Mabel Russell, star of *The Dollar Princess* and other hits of the musical-comedy stage. And now this intolerable Nancy Astor was about to foist a sort of prohibition upon the unsuspecting male population, at least upon that part of it between the ages of sixteen and eighteen. Sir Frederick waxed verbose if not lachrymose, expatiating upon those good old days when, as a school boy, he had been nourished on beer. His object was to "talk the Bill out" —that is, to carry the debate beyond the time set for a compulsory closing. There was no reason, however, why the bill could not be brought up another day. To a Virginian such a mild form of filibuster must have seemed almost ludicrous, and Nancy took it in good part, only remarking as she left the chamber, "Oh, you old villain. I'll get you next time!" In fact Sir Frederick's act brought him little credit; it was considered unsporting and hardly gentlemanly. The bill later carried by 257 votes to 10. It was piloted through the House of Lords by Waldorf, who remarked that "a relative of mine by marriage" had directed its passage in "another place," which was their Lordships' way of referring to the Commons. Both Astors could feel satisfaction in a job well done.

8

Two Feet Ahead of a Combustion

DURING the period following the American tour Nancy's fame had reached perhaps its greatest height, although the trend of politics was no longer so congenial to the Astors as it had been in the Lloyd George era. Baldwin and MacDonald, the Conservative and Labour premiers, were to alternate in power with little to choose between them. Although rather conservative in matters of divorce and drink, Nancy followed Philip's consistently liberal line in foreign policy. In the 1923 election she had advocated trade with Russia, and she was in fact one of the few Conservatives who voted with the Labour members to recognize Russia in 1924. More than once she expressed the hope that Germany and Russia would soon be admitted to the League of Nations.

Local unemployment had made Nancy's 1923 campaign a stiff one. When the election results were announced she told reporters: "I have not done as well as Lord Astor did. That is awful, but sex prejudice again, you see. He is delighted—look at his smile."

As always, she had run as a Conservative, but the Astors' sympathies seem to have been quite as much with Labour as with their own party. They both had high hopes of the Labour government when Ramsay MacDonald became its first Prime Minister in the 1924 election. Working- and lower-middle-class men had obtained leadership in government before this, but until the 1924 election they had always adopted the mores of the ruling class. The wholesale appearance of working-class accents and cloth caps was something new in official circles. Nancy invited the Labour leaders to dinner to meet the King and Queen and succeeded, as always, in making everyone feel at home.

In more official circles there was a general feeling of treading on social eggs. Ramsay MacDonald was widely praised when it was discovered that the new honors list contained only childless peers, thus preserving the purity of the peerage! Nancy and Waldorf were impatient with such pussyfooting. They preferred more forthright characters, such as Jimmy Thomas, a Labour cabinet member. Sir Alexander Cadogan has described Thomas's performance at an international conference: Thomas replied to the speech of a French delegate with two simple monosyllables: "Oh, 'ell." "*Qu'est-ce qu'il dit, M. Thomas?*" asked the Frenchman. The interpreter replied that Mr. Thomas had listened with great attention and interest and would report faithfully to his colleagues, an explanation that did not wholly satisfy the Frenchman. Thomas was nothing if not genuine, and his style was far more to the Astors' taste than the MacDonald brand of "tact."

After Nancy had been safely returned in the 1924 election she and Waldorf pursued a favorite private reform: they built a public housing estate at their own expense. In 1923 the opposition had made great play with the source of the Astors' income: "We all know J. J. Astor owned half the slums in New York." Nancy had shouted back, "I'll give you 500 pounds if you can prove it," but the ground had seemed a little shaky. Waldorf sincerely wished to abolish slums but did not wish to appear to be buying votes. Even to Mr. Neve, Nancy did not mention their connection with the new housing development in Plymouth, although she wrote to him in February that "the housing question has been getting bad for eighty years and of course it just can't be settled all at once, but I think that the nation, as a whole, is doing its very best."

Obviously the going was sometimes rough. The brewing and liquor interests were especially vocal; Nancy confessed that they almost drove her out of politics in the close election of 1923. As though being a teetotaler wasn't hard enough, there was also this business of being a woman in a man's club. "I really made the male members shiver," she said, "and it also made me shake, though mercifully they never knew it." One Member used to pass her in the House with averted eyes, as though she were Lady Godiva. As for the doughty knight of the sponge, Winston Churchill, he was "fearless and courageous in fighting to keep [the women] out." Nancy was delighted that he lost and the women won. She was still all out, as she made clear, for the women and children of England.

To the American-born Astors public education was always a lively concern. In 1924 Nancy had already advocated raising the school-leaving age, a battle that she and Waldorf were to fight over the years ahead, but her really passionate interest was not aroused until her meeting with Margaret McMillan in 1926. In 1914, eight years before a similar project was attempted in the United States, this indomitable Scotswoman had opened a nursery school for slum children in London's dockside area of Deptford. In Margaret McMillan's school Nancy saw the living realization of her campaign slogan: "Vote for Lady Astor and your children will weigh more." The children at Deptford were in fact half an inch taller and five pounds heavier, on the average, than other slum children their age. Margaret McMillan had seen in a dream that Nancy Astor would help her. A few months after their meeting she wrote: "You haven't forgotten me? I was the poor thing you sent flowers to in the summer."

Nancy replied: "Dearest Poor Thing, There are certain people that you can't forget even though you have never known them."

Miss McMillan's dream had been a prophetic one indeed. With the Astors' help nursery schools sprang up all over England. With this growth came a further need for teacher training. Nancy herself raised £20,000, and Waldorf–it was part of what she loved in him–gave not only time and money but even his own convenience to the cause. They rented Cliveden for "one whole winter," as Nancy said, to raise money for the Rachel McMillan College, named after Margaret McMillan's sister. It opened in 1929.

It was not a one-sided or a bread-and-butter friendship, for Margaret McMillan thought as much of her benefactor as Nancy thought of her. In the close 1929 election Miss McMillan, a foundation member of the Labour Party, came down to Plymouth to speak for the Conservative candidate. It was a gesture not of self-interest but of love. Two years later on her deathbed, Margaret McMillan's last words were for Nancy. "Tell her," she said, "I have no fear. I am happy."

The year 1929 saw a high point for women in the Commons; fourteen were returned in the November elections: three Conservatives, nine Labour, one Liberal, and one Independent. Nancy had long believed that women, acting as women outside party lines, might effect more for the cause of reform than they could within their respective parties. She seized the opportunity offered by the new House to invite all these ladies to lunch, with the soon-apparent object of forming a feminine phalanx. The object failed. It was not soundly based, but even if it had been, party organization was not within Nancy's talents. It required calculation and maneuver; Nancy's forte remained the single devastating salvo. "We're not looking for superiority," she told a woman's meeting; "we've always had that. All we want is equality."

The effort failed, but apparently without disturbing the good relations among the female Members. Characteristically, Nancy's two best friends among the women Members were not in her own party. She was devoted to the motherly Mrs. Wintringham (Liberal) and the fiery little Ellen Wilkinson (Labour). Both were often at Cliveden. Oddly enough, Ellen Wilkinson even figured in one of Claud Cockburn's more imaginative lists of what was later presumed to be the Cliveden Set. Miss Wilkinson admired her ("Lady Astor knows a good deal more than most of her critics about political affairs"), but this did not prevent some sharp exchanges on the floor of the House. On one occasion Miss Wilkinson questioned whether Lady Astor was qualified to speak on the problems of working women, as she herself had never worked. "It makes about as much sense," said Nancy, "as though I should say that you are not qualified to speak of children because you have never had any." The exchange in no way affected the warm relations between them. Of another lady Member, the rough and tough Labourite Bessie Braddock, Nancy remarked: "I take off my hat to her—but I wouldn't put hers on."

If they did not work together, the women in the House did show a certain *esprit de corps*. At about this time the Duchess of Atholl, very much Nancy's junior in the Commons, was given a minor post in the government. Nancy was not hurt. "Nobody wants me as a Cabinet Minister," she told a women's luncheon, "and they are perfectly right. I am an agitator, not an administrator."

There were many plain people, of course, who thought that women with children should be at home minding them, and to some extent Nancy agreed. Her political life was only made possible by "a really wonderful woman," Nannie Gibbons. The first time they had had to leave the children for a trip to the States Nancy asked Waldorf how much he paid his butler. Apparently there was a large discrepancy, in the butler's favor, between his salary and Nannie Gibbons's. "From now on," said Nancy, "Nannie gets the same"—a revolutionary shift in values that has not really been accepted to the present day. Not that Nancy undervalued their butler. Once when that long-suffering man attempted to give notice, there came her instant response: "In that case, Lee, tell me where you are going because I'm coming with you." It was no good; he had to stay.

In the Astors' life of these years, weeks of concentrated politics were alternated regularly with weeks at Cliveden and their seaside house at Sandwich, devoted to the children. Nancy could and did put on as good a show for someone under five as ever she had for Mr. Balfour or Mr. Lloyd George. With children she was a runaway success. With anyone especially sensitive, self-conscious, or pompous, which covers most adolescents and many adults, her methods of making fun and of direct and stirring attack could badly misfire. Children loved it. They adored her imitations and her rapid changes of mood. Even the ritual of the Christian Science lesson read to the children every morning could be interrupted by their mother's suddenly declaring, "Yassir, I'se gonna help yew. Me and Mistah Jesus is gonna help yew." This was pure Mammy Lisa out of Nancy's own past, and to the children, a welcome change from Mrs. Eddy. At night, when there were no guests, the children would lie in front of the fire in her little sitting room, regaled by stories of when she was a little girl. All the black characters would spring to life, and her brothers and Chillie himself. Many of her ideas on child rearing came out of her own experience, not, as might have been expected, in revolt, but in emulation. A scolding could be sudden and overwhelming, followed by an abrupt command to the afflicted child to stop crying. Childish tears had not been encouraged in Virginia. At the same time, no condemnation was carried over beyond the immediate occasion, and sometimes a scolding could be avoided altogether.

The Cliveden family often went out on the river. On one historic occasion they were boating in their flat-bottomed electric canoe with Michael, aged about six, at the tiller. Father, mother, and the other children were in the forward seats with their backs to the steersman. Michael, carried away by the unexpected bliss of his situation, proceeded to enhance it by casting out, at appropriate intervals, a series of colored cushions, which then appeared as a flotilla following in the wake of his flagship. He had just added the finishing touch to his fleet by throwing overboard a large sun hat decorated with a ribbon when his blissful absorption was interrupted by a yell, pejorative in nature. It came upon him that he had done something awful, from the consequences of which there could be no escape. But inspiration to this child of Christian Science was not lacking. He told his mother, "I want to sing a hymn." "You want to do what?" Michael began, bravely piping, "O gentle presence, peace and joy and power . . ." He had figured, correctly, that no one would lay hands on him while he was trilling these sacred words. The critical moment dissolved in laughter. After this it would seem base ingratitude, but Michael was to shed Christian Science as soon as he could escape his parent's influence.

To be Chillie's child had not been easy. As Nancy herself admitted, he had demanded far too much of his children, and he would not let them go. Nancy repeated the pattern. Her success with children was apt to stop rather abruptly at the time of their adolescence. At that age she felt it a sacred duty to run their lives, and the influence of her religion, unfortunately, only invigorated her efforts. She was in the habit of telling her children, do what you *ought* first, then you can do what you *want*. As interpreted by Nancy this was no light admonishment, for what they ought seemed to take up so much place that little room was left for the second half of the program. Michael, for one, felt that she used Christian Science as a bludgeon. He cited the example of Bill, who had been the very proud cox of the Eton eight at Henley. Bill's boat had won the first heat and was eliminated in the second. His mother, surely inspired by her own personal devil rather than by Mrs. Eddy, attributed this failure solely to Bill and his probable neglect of the Christian Science lesson on that particular morning.

Neither son could have known that in writing of this same event to Mr. Neve she had shown herself extremely proud of Bill. She did try, she wrote this old friend, to have an understanding heart for each of these so different children. Although they could have been in little danger of forgetting it, she liked to remind them that all their blood and all their money came from America. They had not, she admitted, turned out exactly as one would have planned (the mind rather boggles as to what that might have been), but they were, she was profoundly grateful to say, all good.

In spite of the pressures that undoubtedly existed in Astor family life, the children were not exceptionally rebellious, which is not to say that they did not rebel at all. Michael, the hero of the incident in the canoe, later upset his mother profoundly by setting himself up in bachelor digs in London, rejecting all threats and entreaties to come home. He had consciously set out to explore a rather more hedonistic and artistic life style than that practiced by his parents. David, at the university, had veered sharply to the political left, a form of deviation much better understood at Cliveden than an inclination toward the arts or toward pleasure. Once David and Waldorf's secretary, Heather Harvey, had been sitting together on a sofa when Waldorf came in, beaming. Suddenly a chill descended. "David, don't keep Miss Harvey up too late," and he had left the room abruptly. "What's wrong?" asked Heather. David silently pointed at the whiskey and soda in front of him. But Waldorf had little serious to complain of. Michael saw his father as stern but often secretly pleased when a son asserted his independence. It was Nancy who found it hardest to give way.

During the years when the children were growing up, there was never a lack of Langhornes on the Cliveden scene. Chillie, complete with whiskey and chewing tobacco, was a frequent visitor. Nora and Paul Phipps had a house on the grounds or very near by, as did Alice Winn, daughter of the eldest Langhorne sister, Elizabeth, and her family. Alice was almost always an available companion; Phyllis, now married to Bob Brand, came frequently with her family; and Irene, although more detached, visited from time to time. As in their girlhood, the sisters would disappear upstairs for the lethal "truth parties" in which each told exactly what she thought of the others. Nancy throve on it, it was Mirador all over again, but Phyllis, perhaps the most civilized Langhorne, found herself a little oppressed.

There were times, too, when Nancy and Nora would reach an impasse in their rarely tranquil relations. Paul continued to be an ideal husband, but Nora, as Phyllis put it, would go on conducting flirtations, if not more serious affairs. The result was predictable. Nancy would go on giving Nora digs, Waldorf would go on looking pious, and Paul, Phyllis pointed out, would go on being mush. Nothing Nancy could say or do, and she was certainly outspoken, had any effect on the family patterns. When challenged with writing a "disgraceful" letter to Irene, Nancy looked honestly surprised and exclaimed, "Well, there's no doubt about it, there's a sense lacking in me." Try as she would, it was impossible for her to reach that pure love and Christian charity that Mrs. Eddy's followers were supposed to enjoy. One day, arriving late for lunch, she told the company: "For ten minutes in the car I have been trying to purge my mind of all malice and uncharitableness. Have I succeeded for ten minutes? No. For one minute? No. It's all human nature."

She was a perfect hostess but, her sisters complained, a terrible guest. "The Viscountess in company with the Marquis has just arrived," Phyllis wrote in 1930, shortly after Philip's accession to this title. Phyllis had put Nancy down for a tennis tournament and given her the best partner, "and now she says she is not going to play as it ruins her golf!" The truth was that she wanted to play golf with Philip. She had been in the house for one hour, half of which had been spent eating dinner and the other half swamped in newspapers. "Oh my! Oh my!" Phyllis exclaimed, "She will never be a private visitor again." This was the rub. What would have been expected and forgiven in a man was a little hard to take in a woman, and in one's own sister, perhaps, most of all.

Those who complained most strenuously were those closest to her, or, on the other hand, those who hardly knew her at all. There were legions in between for whom she could do no wrong. When she did not feel impelled to improve one's character her charm disarmed; her generosity and largeness of heart bound one to her for life. There was, for instance, Miss Jennie. When someone as rich as Nancy makes a present it is a touch-and-go thing; the gift must be given with a freely loving heart or it will be resented in the end. Her generosity to Miss Jennie shines through the letters of those years. "I was so glad you really needed that coat at that moment! Dearest Miss Jennie, it's such a joy to feel that you know how much I love you and have always. I love the chance of doing anything that I can." Miss Jennie visited often and was assured that she was "Waldorf's favorite guest."

In the family Buck was a rare and much beloved visitor. He was the only brother left to her after Keene and Harry both died in middle age. His high spirits and gaiety never failed to divert her; squalls were never serious when Buck was with them. After a riding accident at home he had come over to convalesce, and they had gone to St. Moritz in a family group. She had planned to read and gather her thoughts in the evening, but Buck, laid low from the aftereffects of his accident, made them all eat their dinner and laugh in his room. "No one could resist," she wrote exuberantly to Miss Jennie, "a Swiss winter day. . . . I really am resting and thoroughly enjoying [myself]." Buck was talking the whole time as she wrote so Miss Jennie must forgive this letter, but she obviously loved the interruptions. His only fault, she felt, was that he sometimes lacked seriousness, especially in politics. Buck had served a term in the state legislature in Richmond. When he had first arrived, so the story went, he was asked to express an opinion on taxation. "Well," drawled the new legislator, "that's a question I think each man should decide for himself." "What a world!" the feminist Langhorne exclaimed, "when they put

Buck in the Legislature and won't give Aunt Lizzie [the respected relative] the vote!"

Langhorne brothers and sisters always tended to assert seniority, and Buck, as the youngest save Nora, ranked low on the scale. Nancy sometimes treated him as though he were about sixteen years old. It did not worry Buck in the least. Even Nancy found it impossible to quarrel with this light-hearted brother

As the children grew older, Nannie Gibbons could no longer relieve Nancy of responsibility. In 1928, Phyllis wrote her sisters that Nancy was "two feet ahead of a combustion." This was the year of Wissie's coming-out ball and of Bill's coming of age. Both events meant tremendous parties and, for Nancy herself, double work. Her nights, she said, were spent in the ballroom, and her days at her desk or in the House of Commons.

Although outwardly a free spirit, Nancy still had a considerable faculty of respect, which she continued to lavish on the royal family. They were surrogates, as it were, for Chillie, filling her need for a paternal symbol. For her the high point of Wissie's party was the appearance of the Duke and Duchess of York, who were later to become King George and Queen Elizabeth. It was rather a large party, she confessed to Mr. Neve, but she thought it had all been a great success. There was no need to apologize, even obliquely, for Bill's party. It was just the sort she loved, fireworks at Cliveden, and everyone invited—from the sheriff of the county (local bigwig) to the boy who brought the papers.

In these letters to Mr. Neve describing family life she poured out her religious thoughts as well. In one sentence she could describe her day—"the Queen of Spain to luncheon, just a big friendly party. . . . spoke in the House of Commons this afternoon . . . now off to a public dinner, etc."—and in the next speak of the universal love of God: "What a beautiful thing spiritual unity is!" Every morning there was the Christian Science lesson, read to sustain her through the day. What if several newspapers, the breakfast tray, and her youngest climbing over the bed were all competing for her attention? Nevertheless the lesson got read. She could say with truth, "I read and study Our Lord's word daily." It was here, and in her letters to her old counselor, that her own thoughts on peace were matured. She knew that before peace could come to the nations it must come first to the hearts of men. "I love what you say," she wrote to Mr. Neve, "about expecting great things to happen because you know that God is at work."

But Nancy was not apt to leave it up to God, not, at least, without a helping hand from herself. The late twenties were to find her engaged more and more in work for peace. They also brought into her life one of the longest, deepest, and most remarkable of her friendships.

George Bernard Shaw's interest in Nancy was first aroused by hearing her quoted as exclaiming "Rats!" in a House of Commons debate. As this precisely summed up the famous playwright's opinion of most parliamentary speeches, he willingly accepted an invitation to Cliveden. Their friendship, as so often happened with Nancy, was off to an instant start. Both were masters of the art of comic abuse; each found the other a perfect foil. They soon found, however, that they could be tremendously serious about certain important things. Both attempted to set the world straight by making simple, commonsense statements that the world was apt to consider hilariously funny or, alternatively, outrageous and infuriating. Nancy was rather less intransigent in her statements than Shaw, but the effect she produced on people was often quite similar to his.

Shaw and his wife Charlotte first visited Cliveden at Christmas 1927. By Christmas 1928 their friendship had progressed to the point where the Shaws appeared as a fixture, and GBS as the leading light of the festivities. There was the usual tremendous house party. Two enormous fir trees were set up in the great hall, festooned with heirloom decorations and surrounded by flocks of children. To Cliveden children on these occasions, distinguished guests appeared as more or less natural objects, around whom they played with total unconcern. And well they might, for the party would go on for three weeks, with as many as forty-five in the house at one time. No politics, however, for at Christmas Cliveden drew to itself its own. In 1928 Shaw dressed as Santa Claus and handed out presents to the staff, an easy role for the great man to play as he had his own natural Santa Claus beard.

Shaw, who could work as well at Cliveden as anywhere else,

was in no hurry to leave and wrote a good deal of his play *The Apple Cart* during that holiday. After the jollity abated he would sit under a lamp and read scenes aloud as he finished them, while Nancy and Mrs. Shaw knitted. The play, true to Shavian politics, presented a benevolent dictator, King Magnus, as the future answer to the world's problems. At teatime, Nancy, nettled by the master's undemocratic strictures on the House of Commons, demanded to know, "What would we do if we were in Russia now?" If this was a serious question, it did not receive a serious answer. "If we were in Russia," replied Shaw blandly, "you and I would have been married and divorced long ago." Whereupon he helped himself to a third cup of tea and a fourth piece of cake, causing fellow guests to stare. Nancy was delighted. He was her best sparring partner, her adored, her Mephistophelean Santa Claus.

By the following March *The Apple Cart* was ready for a complete reading to a group of distinguished guests at Cliveden. The author brought T. E. Lawrence with him, and so began for Nancy one of the closest and surely the most spectacular of her friendships.

The year 1929 also brought into her the hard test that must come sooner or later to anyone who truly holds an unworldly faith. Wissie, now "out" in London society, had developed into a lovely and popular girl. Staying with her cousins Nancy and Ronald Tree at Kelmarsh Hall in Leicestershire, she had been hunting on a treacherously wet and slippery morning. Although at this date young women were already riding astride, Wissie still rode sidesaddle. This anachronistic device exposed the rider to great danger, for if a horse fell at a fence it was almost impossible for the lady, hooked firmly in place by two special pummels, to fall clear of her mount. Wissie's horse slipped on take off, crashed through the fence, and rolled on her on the other side—the sort of fall every rider fears.

Nancy and Waldorf left London for Leicestershire immediately by car. On the way they convinced themselves that nothing serious could have happened to Wissie. Two local doctors had already been called in, and on arrival the Astors were faced with the harsh truth; there had been structural injury to the spine. They were told that Wissie must have immediate orthopedic attention, a "rearticulation" of the spinal column.

Nancy went white but recovered herself in a moment. She did not want a surgeon to be called. The exterior pressures were intense: doctors, family, friends, all insisting that, for Wissie's sake, a surgeon must be brought in. It was the moment of choice. Should they refuse a surgeon and restrict Wissie to Christian Science healing, perhaps at a great cost to her, who was at that moment the dearest object of their lives? Nancy had cooperated with doctors before. Now, almost under duress, she agreed to compromise and to call on her old surgeon, Sir Crisp English, who had operated successfully on both herself and Philip. Sir Crisp was an abdominal specialist; his rage and frustration when confronted with a serious spinal injury that he was powerless to treat broke Nancy's resistance to an orthopedic surgeon. What Waldorf felt we do not know, but Nancy was able to believe that whatever the surgeon did scarcely mattered. Wissie was put in a plaster cast, and her parents were told, as they firmly believed, that Wissie would recover. She would never be completely normal, the doctors said, or able to bear children in the ordinary way.

Wissie's recovery was complete, if long and painful, and she had no later difficulty in normal childbirth. At the Canadian hospital during the war, Nancy became used to working with doctors while giving the credit of cure to Christian Science. It did not seem false to her to play down the role of the plaster cast in Wissie's recovery. Her attitude may be open to question, but she was perfectly sincere in believing that love and faith, not plaster, wrought Wissie's cure.

In this time of trouble their friends rallied round. Philip participated in the healing, and so did Charlotte Shaw. She "worked" for Wissie's recovery in her own thoughts, in a way that seems to resemble the Christian Science method but to which Nancy took exception. T. E. Lawrence took up arms on Charlotte's behalf, writing to Nancy to insist that she "allow Mrs. Shaw . . . to work for [Wissie] and say the right word." Exactly what that "word" would have been we do not know, but we do know that the Shaws seemed to share Nancy's opinion of the medical profession. (Shaw was once asked by a reporter, "Have we lost faith?" "No," replied GBS, "but we have transferred it from God to the National Medical

Council.") The Shaws were always unorthodox in their beliefs, which in this case apparently did not quite meet Nancy's views. Yet the Shaws' offers of help were sincere and heartwarming. The friendship, initially based on mutual entertainment, acquired a new depth during Wissie's illness.

9

Mr. Kellogg, Comrade Stalin, and Mr. Keynes

ALTHOUGH it is difficult to realize now, there had been for some time a real sense of U.S.–British naval rivalry. In 1922, at the time of the Washington Naval Conference, an unmistakable Southern drawl had come clearly over the international radio hookup, telling the women of America and the British Commonwealth overseas that instead of worrying over the size of each other's navies they would do better to cooperate for peace.

> As yet we may not be exactly in the seats of the mighty, [but] we can be mighty powerful. I feel certain that when women have political rights they will bring pressure on their governments to

take some risks for peace. After all, they are really far smaller than the risks we create by preparing for war. The women must be as brave about peace as the men were about war. Our men dared to die. Can't we dare to trust one another a little more? I think it is one of the things that we ought to dare to do.

During the second half of the 1920's, it looked as though America had heeded these brave words and that some risks were to be taken for peace. These were the years of the Pact of Paris, by which the delegates of fifteen nations, led by F. B. Kellogg of the United States, agreed to eliminate war as a means of settling international disputes. In August of 1926 Waldorf talked to Kellogg, President Coolidge's Secretary of State, about these matters. He wrote to Philip from Mirador: "Kellogg says war between U.S.A. and Britain is unthinkable and that therefore neither side should aim at [naval] superiority. . . . If nations bind themselves together for purposes of war whether defensive or offensive why should not the civilization of two countries like U.S.A. and Britain enable them to agree to have points of dispute or differences settled by arbitration?" By the following February he had carried this thought to its logical conclusion: "If war between us is unthinkable, why not make it unlawful?" Thus did Waldorf anticipate the idea of the Kellogg pact, by nearly a year.

So far as Philip was concerned, the game involved a great prize, that of enlisting America in a system of world peace. When Mrs. Chapman Catt, feminist leader, asked Lady Astor to address a giant women's demonstration for peace to be held at the Albert Hall, Nancy turned to Philip for help. A resolution was to be proposed: "This committee recommends . . . the renunciation of war as an instrument of national policy in favor of the pacific settlement of international disputes." Philip advised caution: "You know the natural instinct of the country-born Yankee to suppose that any proposition that Great Britain approves of must necessarily involve a bad bargain for the U.S. If you support it, therefore, do it in your capacity as a representative woman and not as a British M.P." In politics it was sometimes necessary, as Lloyd George had told her, "to modify one's transports." But when she asked him later what she should say to the Overseas League luncheon, Philip put the crux of the matter exuberantly, in her own style: "There are a great many people now going about in both the United States and Great Britain talking nonsense [about naval parity], . . . but the common sense thing is for Great Britain and the United States to think less about armaments and more about friendship."

In 1927 Nancy longed to go to the naval conference at Geneva with Philip, but the children were holidaying at Jura and she felt that they needed her. In this dilemma she wrote to her sister Phyllis, "David is longing to go to Geneva and says he won't go unless I do, so I feel I ought." Phyllis, quoting this masterpiece to Irene, exclaimed, "Now I ask you, and to *me!*"

In 1930, at the death of a cousin, Philip became the eleventh Marquis of Lothian and heir to three large estates, Newbattle and Monteviot in Scotland, and Blickling in Norfolk. There was also an ancient border stronghold, Ferniehirst Castle, which he ingeniously turned into a youth hostel. The new heir regarded his noble estate with mixed feelings. He wrote to Lloyd George: "Largely as a result of your all-too-admirable work, a well-diluted peerage is now possessed of almost no power, and I discover that I shall have to pay to an exhausted Exchequer almost 40 per cent of the capital value of a mainly agricultural estate. In my capacity as an ordinary citizen I think highly of these arrangements, but as an inheritor of a title and estates thereto they will prove somewhat embarrassing."

To add to his troubles, Blickling Hall, the major part of his inheritance, had been allowed to go to seed. It was a mare's nest of priceless heirlooms, Victorian horrors, and discarded belongings of all sorts. What did one do with a little girl's dress and apron that had belonged, it was said, to Anne Boleyn, or with the peer's red robes in which Stafford had been beheaded by Henry VIII in 1521, all now attracting moths in a long-abandoned closet? Philip sold off the less useful treasures of the Blickling library in order to pay the bills and enlisted his sister, Lady Butler-Thwing, to supervise the task of bringing the beautiful rooms back to life. Bedrooms were brightened with white carpeting and Chinese-patterned chintzes; larger state rooms retained their character while acquiring comforts unknown to Anne Boleyn. Philip's guests gathered for sherry in the long library, which happily was not completely denuded of books, and looked through tall west windows onto the formal gardens below. Tall and handsome, obviously enjoying his guests, the new owner was a perfect host. Blickling had become once again a house to be enjoyed and to be lived in, although it had taken a year to make it so. Many of the political house parties formerly held at Cliveden now took place at Blickling, but Philip never lost the habit of Cliveden and of Astor family intimacy.

The Bernard Shaws continued to visit the Astors as their friendship flourished. GBS admired Nancy and Waldorf; their hard work and Spartan habits were exactly to his taste. No tobacco, no alcohol, cold baths, and exercise were surely not everyone's idea of the life of the idle rich, but they were the choice of the lady of Cliveden. Shaw, of course, had a weakness for intelligent women. In Nancy's case this most didactic of wits cheerfully undertook to civilize the Virginian savage; he tried to reform her into someone rather like Beatrice Webb, the leading spirit in the Socialist Fabian Society, only livelier. That the task was hopeless probably pleased him most of all, for he obviously enjoyed Nancy as she was. The public highlight of their friendship was their trip to Soviet Russia in 1931. Shaw was a Fabian —that is, a highly theoretical and nonrevolutionary socialist. Having made a fortune from his plays, he was that interesting paradox, a wealthy but, as he put it, "implacable Marxist." He delighted in driving about with Lady Astor in *his* chocolate-colored Lanchester limousine. When he was invited to visit Soviet Russia it seemed to him perfectly sensible, and intensely Shavian, to take Lord and Lady Astor to pay homage to Comrade Stalin.

Philip seized the opportunity to join the party; he had in fact been the first to suggest that the Astors make the trip. Surely Shaw, the socialist sage of England, would penetrate where others would be barred. Russia's emergence into the twentieth century had taken place behind closed doors, but if Europe was to come to terms with her, and it was one of Philip's cardinal beliefs that Europe must, then the first requisite was to get to know her. In 1929 he had written in the *Observer*, Russia "has dethroned usury from the altar on which it now stands in Western Civilization, has rendered it almost impossible for anyone to live, or at least to live comfortably, except by the fruit of his own work, and has made the huge engine of economic production and distribution function for the general good and not for private profit." Nancy was a little more skeptical. "I would be a socialist," she said, "if I thought it would work."

At the last moment before their departure, the trip had almost not come off. Bobbie Shaw, Nancy's son by her first marriage, had been a problem for some time and was now in serious trouble. Perhaps he should have been a traveling player, if such a thing had been possible for an upper-class Englishman of his time. Instead he was a Guards officer, a senior subaltern of the famous "Blues," a crack steeplechase rider, and a rather dissipated man about town. He was also homosexual, in a society where homosexuality was often tacitly ignored but was punished as a crime if thrust upon the public notice. Bobbie was found drunk on duty and forced to "hand in his papers"—that is, to resign from the Blues. After this he had become increasingly reckless; finally, and inevitably, he was arrested on a homosexual charge.

Bobbie's past had admittedly been a special one. His half-brother and -sister had accepted him as one of them, but it is not certain that he himself ever felt fully integrated in the Astor family life. At home at Cliveden he displayed what his half-brother Michael described as a "devastating—perhaps too devastating" wit. Family photographs of Bobbie show something sad and remote in the handsome boyish face. He was successful as a steeplechase rider, at the cost of two serious falls, and twice fractured his skull. Socially as well as physically, Bobbie seems to have been on a collision course. At the time of his arrest he could have avoided prosecution—the police offered him a chance to leave the country for a year, perhaps less—but he chose instead to go to jail. This was an act of courage and integrity; it may also have been a part of the savage, half-unconscious war long waged by Bobbie and his mother.

Nancy and Waldorf stood by him. Bobbie had once been the whole world to her, and she to him; at some primal level, this relationship remained the most real thing in both their lives. They would attack each other fiercely but always soon made up. It was a familiar pattern for Nancy, but here the bond was closer and the attacks went home. Bobbie knew her weaknesses as she knew his, and they could always draw blood from each other. In this period of grief the trip to Russia was delayed, but it could not be postponed without causing the publicity that they had so far managed to avoid. Nancy set off courageously, still carrying Bobbie's trouble in her heart.

The Russians, of course, had made elaborate preparations for the reception of the sage. Shaw, for his part, was delighted to frustrate any possible appearance of pomp, even Communist pomp. He egged Nancy on to do her worst, and she was, to say the least, outspoken. A formal interview had been arranged with Stalin. "Of course," Shaw said, or words to this effect, "I may bring Lord and Lady Astor." "And of course," said Nancy, "you will wish us to bring Lord Lothian." Two lesser members of the party, Miss Gertrude Ely and young David Astor, regretted that the additions ended there. Once met, the principals appeared to be in no hurry to part, but for two-and-a-half hours exchanged some rather pointed questions and answers.

Nancy: "When are you going to stop killing people?"

Stalin: "When I think it is necessary to do so."

Stalin then remarked how strange it was that a small island ruled one-third of the world.

Nancy: "Look at the map. It can't be might; it must be right. It's something in their thinking."

It was the same wisdom, in fact, that she was in the habit of imparting to her nieces and nephews, to cabinet ministers, and to anyone else who would listen.

As an expert on nursery schools, which indeed she was, she had been taken to see the Soviet version. She took her host to task; the Soviets did not know how to treat children. Stalin made a gesture with his arm like the slash of a whip. "In England you *beat* children." That may be, said Nancy, but "Why were those prettily dressed little girls at the collective farm not out of doors?" The nurse said that it had rained that morning. Rubbish! A child should not know nor care whether there was rain or shine. And the spotless dresses and the clean faces and hands! The unbroken toys! "A child should be grubby, dirty, except at meals! … . Send a good sensible woman to me in London and I will take care of her and show how children of five should be handled." Stalin took an envelope and asked her to write her address on it. This homely gesture resulted in the subsequent arrival in London of not one but a dozen sensible Russian women to be instructed, entertained, and taken to nursery schools. Perhaps one should not trifle with dictators.

Nancy described Stalin as "a quiet, dark-eyed person, well behaved and very grim." To Shaw his manners appeared perfect, "if only he had been able to conceal the fact that we amused him enormously." Lord Astor attempted to give the interview a more conventional turn by speaking of the friendly feeling for Russia that existed in England. Shaw would have none of this and advised the dictator "to keep your powder dry." Philip spoke to Stalin of the plight of his own Liberal Party in England: its remnant had divided, its right wing joining the Conservatives and its left wing actually now left of the Labour Party. He suggested that Lloyd George, as Liberal leader, be invited to Russia on an official visit. This rather interesting advance was declined. Stalin replied that he would welcome Lloyd George as a private tourist, but that Allied interference in Russia after World War I had made it impossible to receive him officially. Churchill was mentioned, no doubt as the *enfant terrible* of British-Soviet relations, and Nancy exclaimed, "Oh, he's finished!" Stalin repeated this with some relish to Churchill after the latter became Prime Minister. This Russian was interested in power, not in ideology.

After the Astors returned from Russia Bobbie Shaw came out of jail a marked man. Now, as in the case of Wissie's accident, the Shaws took the matter to heart. They suggested another jaunt, to include "the whole Shaw-Astor tribe," this time with the obvious object of helping Bobbie back into the world again. In any event, the Astors did not go, and Shaw and Mrs. GBS took off for Africa alone. It was on this trip that Shaw wrote *The Adventures of the Black Girl in Her Search for God.* "We need the help of one another's bodies," he said, "and the help of one another's minds; but our souls need to be alone with God." The Shavian life style seemed to illustrate the third part of this statement to the exclusion of the first two, yet none could be a warmer or truer friend than Shaw was to the Astors. He offered a trip and his own company, simple forms of bodily help. The "mind" and religious aspects of the problem were far deeper, but to these too Shaw gave full effort. "Mrs. Eddy," he told Nancy, "is no use." He clearly wished to protect Bobbie from too severe an onslaught of the councils of perfection. The end of the black girl's search for God was a garden cultivated by an old philosopher (GBS in one of his disguises). "Therefore come in," he tells the wandering girl, "and help to cultivate this garden to His glory. The rest you had better leave to Him." It was this last admonition that Nancy found it so very difficult to obey.

Looking around him after his return from Africa in 1932, Shaw had good reason to despair of the local condition of the garden. Whatever may have been the case in Russia, the British economy was in serious trouble. The mistakes of the 1920s were emerging to haunt the economy of the 1930s. Already in 1929 it was no longer possible to sweep economic ills under the rug. At Christmas that year Nancy had written to Virginia warning the grownups not to expect any presents that year. "I have adopted a town," she told them, "so I need every penny." It was in one of the "special areas" in South Wales where the coal mines were either closing or cutting back, leaving whole townsful of the unemployed. "You cannot think what the suffering and want is."

There had been no far-reaching reforms since 1925. In that year Winston Churchill had "crossed the floor"—that is, changed parties—for the second time and become a member of the Conservative government. A natural for the War Office or the Admiralty, he was placed at the Exchequer. However, he brought his accustomed energy to the new post. T. E. Lawrence, who had once served under Churchill in the Colonial Office, described him as "strutting about with a large cigar in his mouth saying 'I'll make the blighters save! I'll make 'em save!' "

So long as the great financial institutions known collectively as the City of London had been in existence, and that had been for a very long time, Britain's position vis-à-vis the world money market had been the very foundation of her wealth. There was a sort of mystique about gold. The squire's roast beef, the workingman's pint of beer, the easy gentlemanly credit of the City, where a man's word was as good as his bond—all this, it was held, depended on the value of the pound in gold. Although he was no student of economics, Churchill did make an effort to inform himself on this key factor in the economy. One evening at dinner the subject was argued at some length. John Maynard Keynes, then considered revolutionary, now known as the father of modern economic theory, was present. Keynes strongly opposed a return to the prewar standard. It was not the return to the gold standard in itself that he feared but the return to the prewar parity, which would overvalue the pound in relation to the dollar. But politically the words "prewar parity" had the right overtones; it was something like offering an American Mom's apple pie, a nostalgic recall of past well-being that had an irresistible appeal to the postwar voter. There was also, of course, the impressive urging of City men, who should certainly know whereof they speak. So in his budget speech of April, 1925, Churchill proudly announced the return to the gold standard; all England rejoiced that the pound could once more outface the dollar. Some experts agreed with Churchill, foreseeing inflation in the United States which would improve the relative position of the pound. This did not occur. The results in England were declining exports and an undermined trade balance, at the cost of unemployment, strikes, and unlimited suffering in the "depressed areas."

As Keynes put it in his fetchingly titled book, the economic consequences of Mr. Churchill were indeed disastrous, culminating, as he had foreseen, in the General Strike of 1926. The Conservatives managed to weather that crisis. Sparked by Churchill's unyielding demand for unconditional surrender, the government won a decisive and many thought a ruthless victory over Labour. The Labour Party never forgot the repressive legislation passed at this time. The Trades Disputes Act, passed in 1927, was one of the principal causes of Churchill's defeat in 1945. The suppression of the strike, moreover, was soon found to have left untouched the basic ills from which the economy suffered.

Unfortunately for Labour, it was in 1929, that year of universal economic disaster, that they again came to power.* In America the crash of the stock market sent waves of shock throughout the world banking system. The Labour government wobbled, attempted a minor public-works program, and finally

* The first Labour government had been under Ramsay MacDonald (1924–25).

settled for the old economics. MacDonald now called the Liberals and the Conservatives in for consultation, but only the Liberals came. Philip, who had worked on a joint Liberal-Labour commission on unemployment and was already favorably known to both parties, was the Liberal representative at meetings during this summer. It was a rather thankless job, for, as he had told Stalin, not even Labour appeared ready to act on liberal principles.

The Labour government, in fact, was caught in a vise between the old-style party stalwarts who would rather die than cut wages and unemployment benefits, and the immense weight of authority behind the Bank and the Treasury Bench. When continuing deflation and unemployment caused a political crisis in August, MacDonald and Snowden, his Chancellor of the Exchequer, were easy converts to, or victims of, if one prefers, fiscal orthodoxy. Further economies seemed to them to be the only way out. This was directly contrary to the developing Keynesian theory of public spending, a course which had been anticipated by Lloyd George's recommendation of a program of public works as early as 1924.

The panic of that time can hardly be understood by those who do not remember how many New York brokers leaped from tenth-floor windows. Neville Chamberlain, for one, was to have the fear of insolvency lodged in his very bones. It was one thing, however, for Sir Montagu Norman, President of the Bank of England and high priest of fiscal orthodoxy, to demand cuts in the miserable dole given the unemployed; it was quite another for Labour leaders to impose these cuts on their own people. Pathetically, almost tragically, MacDonald and Snowden were led to believe that the cuts were necessary. MacDonald saved his political skin, but not his reputation, by forming a new National Government, in which the Liberals agreed to serve. Philip took the post of Chancellor of the Duchy of Lancaster (a minor cabinet post) in this government, but not without first registering a protest against the reactionary budget. He had recommended a capital levy as a fairer means of sharing the burden between rich and poor.

Nancy and Waldorf had had high hopes for the MacDonald government. The Astors felt very much involved in an effort to bring the classes together. Nancy believed that the country was gradually working itself "out of the capitalist state into the cooperative Commonwealth of capital and labor." It was to her the great experiment, the vital issue of the day, whether all classes of people could not obtain an ever higher rate of living under the capitalist system. Following Philip and Lloyd George she was a consistent advocate in the House of trade with Russia and her support was, as usual, highly personal: "Will the Hon. and Gallant Member [Winston Churchill] pay more attention to the silent members of the House, who want to trade with Russia, and not pay so much attention to the Die Hards, who do not want to trade with anybody?" Hardly silent herself, she was for liberalizing world trade and opposed the Baldwin-MacDonald swing toward protective tariffs.

In the election of October, 1931, Philip, unduly swayed by the sense of financial crisis then sweeping the country, was persuaded to stay in the MacDonald coalition cabinet in spite of its Conservative tariff policy. "I am no good at politics," he admitted to Lloyd George. Nancy, on the other hand, was. At a meeting of the Conservatives hers was the only voice raised in angry protest against this election, which formally committed Liberal Free Traders to a tacit support of the protective-tariff policy of the Conservatives. At the time of this clever party maneuver, Neville Chamberlain was moved to exclaim: "Truly the Conservative Party is a wonderful embodiment of good sense, patriotism, and honesty"–an example of moral obtuseness to be exceeded only by Chamberlain himself seven years later at Munich. Although Baldwin remained the titular head of the party, there was no doubt that Chamberlain was the coming man. In Lloyd George's pungent phrase, he possessed a "retail mind in a wholesale situation." Where Baldwin had drifted backward, Chamberlain positively led Britain's retreat from the world scene. For a long time before Dunkirk, the British world had been drawing inward, while in Germany and the United States explosive and unorthodox forces, which Chamberlain failed to understand, were in their different ways breaking up the old economic patterns and fashioning a new world.

Ever since her first campaign, Nancy had understood the role of government in the economic life of the nation. Unemployment and its allied ills served to stimulate her interest further; she was increasingly convinced that she herself had a useful role to play. In the twenties Philip had served with Lloyd George on the Liberal Industrial Inquiry, and Waldorf in the early thirties became involved in a similar study with the Next Five Years Group. Both were exposed to the influence of Maynard Keynes, both endorsed the idea of public spending. Their Russian trip had been undertaken largely to find out what they could of economic conditions under Communism, and in 1932 Nancy and Waldorf went to the United States to study relief measures there.

Nancy explained her position to reporters in Boston, repeating her earlier statement. "If I thought it would work I would be a socialist." As it was, she was trying to make the capitalist system work better—indeed, she might have said in those grim years of depression, to make it work at all.

In November they went to stay with their friends Franklin and Eleanor Roosevelt at Hyde Park, and all four attended church on Sunday morning. Fixing his eye upon the two prominent couples in his congregation, the minister intoned his text: Matthew 4:16: "Behold I send you forth as sheep in the midst of wolves: be ye therefore as wise as serpents, and harmless as doves." He was aware, of course, that he was preaching to the President-elect of the United States, for the election results placing Franklin Roosevelt in the White House were already known.

Few days in the Western world can have had greater significance than March 4, 1933, the day of Franklin Roosevelt's inauguration as President of the United States. On that day in Germany they were celebrating the Day of the Awakening Nation. The new Chancellor, Adolf Hitler, addressed his people. In the streets of Berlin there were "monster demonstrations, cheering crowds . . . the open display of brutality and violence, with the police standing by in silence." On that day in Washington it was cold and windy. Ragged men were selling apples in the streets as Franklin D. Roosevelt took the oath of office. From a thousand bands, over a million radios, came the tune: "Happy Days Are Here Again." At Cliveden they listened to the inaugural address on the radio. A few days later Waldorf Astor sat down to write to his friend: "I . . . have heard [Keynes] evolve his remedial schemes for currency. . . . The ideas seem to be fruitful and I thought you might find them suggestive at this moment of crisis when ordinary proposals seem quite barren."

Franklin replied: "I shall be delighted to read the Keynes articles. We *must* bring these problems to a satisfactory solution."

The Keynes dynamite was forwarded under plain cover, in the shape of four typescript articles that were later to appear in the London *Times*. Keynes's biographer, R. H. Harrod, suggests that in the decisive early months of his administration Roosevelt was not a Keynesian, and that it was his "clever backroom boys" who later brought the Keynesian theory to bear on policy. Be that as it may, we now know that a comprehensive statement of Keynesian theory reached him directly in the first weeks of his administration from the exemplary hand of the Lord of the Thames, himself the heir and lineal descendant of the greatest robber baron of them all!

As a matter of fact, Roosevelt's refusal to stabilize the gold value of the dollar was a directly Keynesian act, one clearly indicated by the articles sent him by Astor. In essence the Keynes prescription was for increased employment through government expenditure in public works. The direct result would be an increase in the yield of taxation and a decrease in the burden of the dole. The new and startling insight that Keynes now gave to the economic world was that it was the deficit itself, rather than the public works, that was the potent agency in starting the economic ball rolling. His conclusion was completely contrary to economic orthodoxy: "There is no possibility of balancing the budget except by increasing the national income."

One cannot imagine today the moral outrage caused by these simple propositions. Not only did they fly in the face of every principle of sound finance, they also struck at the very heart of the Protestant ethic. They seemed to suggest that one might eat one's cake and have it too. Traditional wisdom taught that long ago a just God had sent His angel to bar the way to such as Keynes and his clever boys. And yet the logic was irrefutable. One could say, and many did say, that if there were no taxes and no dole, the logic would not work. And yet there *were* taxes, and there *was* a dole, and somehow, as Roosevelt said, the modern industrial world must be made to work.

Ideas of retribution varied. The first obvious one of fiscal disaster, of one's children's children paying for the mad extravagance of their sires, gradually retreated into a future so indefinite as to lose significant menace. But what was more immediate, and not lost upon Keynes's critics and those of the New Deal in the United States, was the attendant increase of bureaucracy and the power of the state. This of course was principally feared by those captains of industry big enough to have been previously free from restraining power counter to their own. Yet the fear of it was not completely without foundation; indeed, the abuse of state power in its absolute form was all too soon to become visible to all in Nazi Germany. Keynes might have pointed out that although a tool (his economic theory) may be misused, it is not therefore inherently evil. He himself believed in the moral and even, one might say, the aesthetic virtues of individual freedom. His economic theory prescribed and documented the sort of liberal capitalism that did in fact come to prevail in the Western democracies, which have not thereby, in the ordinary view, lost their freedoms.

Unlike Sir Montagu Norman, president of the Bank of England, Keynes never considered his own views as holy writ. In this he was a twentieth-century man, yet in other ways one would have to go back to the Renaissance to match the extraordinary diversity of his gifts. He was a professional economist, and of course a very great one; he was of the inner circle of Bloomsbury, most rarefied of intellectual cliques; he was a suave man of the world; a Wall Street operator; a university scholar. By the intensity of his belief and the breadth of his vision he had transformed the dismal science. His mission, briefly, was the same as Roosevelt's: to add economic freedom to the political freedoms already enjoyed by the democracies. Both radically changed the development of their world.

Keynes's economic views were world wide in scope. He had said: "Indeed, there will be no real hope of raising world prices without substantial and simultaneous action to increase loan expenditure in many different countries." If there could be a world economic order, it was but one short step to see it as the portent and precursor of a political order. The latter, in fact, in all probability must depend upon the previous existence of the former. From the early 1930s on, the demonstrated "demonic influence of national sovereignty" began to take second place in Cliveden's councils to the evils of economic sovereignty. The difficulty was that framing the new concepts required a new language. It was imperfectly understood at home, while across the Channel one could take it for granted that words on the lips of Lord Lothian or Professor Toynbee meant either nothing at all or, more often, something quite different when heard by Adolf Hitler.

10

T. E. Lawrence: A Friend on the Wild Side

During this period of political confusion in the early 1930s, Waldorf wanted Nancy to stand down as candidate for Plymouth in favor of their son Bill. Dr. Thomas Jones, secretary of many philanthropic organizations and intimate of the Astors and of Baldwin, was Waldorf's emissary, sent to bring her around to this view. He found her propped up in bed, surrounded by bibles, large and small; she was reading the Christian Science lesson for the day. Jones recorded the scene in his diary:

> I argued for half an hour, secretly admiring her more and more as she swept aside my appeals to prudence, health, the work needing

> to be done outside the House. I felt humble and ashamed in her presence. Flippancy was far away from her speech this morning. I sat at the foot of the bed looking straight into the eyes of the most remarkable woman it has been my fortune to know intimately. I kept thinking of Joan of Arc, precisely as when I saw Sybil Thorndike play the heroine in Shaw's play, I could not get Nancy Astor out of my mind.

Clearly Dr. Jones (always referred to as T. J.) did not stand a chance; nor did Waldorf or Philip. Nor, probably, would Mrs. Eddy herself. (This last is an interesting speculation. An irreverent Astor son once asked a Christian Science practitioner staying at Cliveden what he thought would happen if Mrs. Eddy and his mother should meet. There was a moment of silence, after which the man pointed at the Cliveden clock tower. "Mrs. Eddy," he said, "would have taken off right over that tower.")

Nancy remained firmly established in the House. Bill was the only one of the boys who was seriously interested in Parliament as a career. Although he never became the Member for Plymouth, he was elected the Member for East Fulham in 1935.

In the reconstruction of the government after the election of 1931, Philip accepted the job for which he was supremely fitted, the Undersecretaryship of State for India. The Government of India Act, finally passed in 1933, paved the way for the liberation of the great subcontinent. The constitution then adopted, based on Lionel Curtis's principle of dyarchy (the division of power between central and local governments), was the embodiment of what the Round Table thought federation should be. Its inception went all the way back to the moot on India held at Cliveden in 1912. In this one case, at least, the federal idea had come into its own.

To Philip the outcome was a real triumph of faith in man and in the dual nature of unity and freedom. There had been, however, a spirited opposition. As happened in so many political issues between the wars, Churchill and the Astors were on opposite sides of the fence. Until the fatal errors of judgment made at Cliveden in regard to Germany in 1938–39, we may say that the Astors were invariably right—that is to say, in tune with the times—while Churchill's thinking remained that of an earlier day. In his view of the Empire he was never to outgrow the attitudes of Lieutenant W. S. Churchill, polo-playing and pig-sticking subaltern of the 4th Hussars. To this Churchill, Gandhi was a half-naked little man wrapped in a sheet, who should never have been permitted to set foot in the viceregal palace. India, his India, was still the first jewel in Victoria's crown.

Churchill now engaged in a vigorous last-ditch battle, organizing a minority resolution repudiating the Labour government's compact with Gandhi. Baldwin, the Conservative leader, unwisely made the resolution public. Nancy hit the ceiling. She burst in on Tom Jones, Baldwin's *fidus Achates:* What, she demanded, did he think of his leader now? She made Jones go to see Baldwin at once, which he did within the hour. Jones, who often acted informally as a speech writer for Baldwin, now wrote a speech aligning Baldwin with the government's position rather than with Churchill, thereby saving both India and the Conservative leader, who in this instance had backed the wrong horse. It was a perfect example of the Round Table method of exerting indirect influence on affairs of state. Methods such as these, later to fail with Chamberlain, seem to have worked with Baldwin, undoubtedly the greatest sail-trimmer of all time. Baldwin was later to reap much credit from the Government of India Act.

During the London Conference on India Philip was often with Gandhi. One morning after breakfast he brought Gandhi in to meet her ladyship.

Nancy: "So this is the wild man of God."

Gandhi: "I hope I can live up to that certificate."

Nancy (clapping her hands in his face): "Think of the trouble you have made in the world."

Gandhi: "I have been warned to beware of Lady Astor—perhaps she is a wild woman of God."

After this exchange she informed him sternly that the British had created something in India. He replied by listing what the Indians had created: the village revival, improvements in temperance and in drainage, the emancipation of women. "The British," he admitted, "have taught us how to govern. Now we can do it ourselves." Nancy could feel only sympathy for that. Feeling him to be so much on the right track, she could not resist suggesting that he study the works of Mrs. Eddy. Gandhi gallantly replied that people who tried to convert him to their own faith had helped him a great deal. "Because they all quote the finest things in their religion, they give me the greatest literature." Nancy, because she so clearly meant well, rarely offended people whom she attempted to convert. A Mahatma obviously could take her in stride.

During this period Nancy was seeing a good deal of another wild man. In 1924, she had written to T. E. Lawrence: "I am one of the people who are very wealthy and would like a copy of your book, but I don't promise to read it. However, as that is your wish, you won't mind." The book was the subscribers' edition of *The Seven Pillars of Wisdom*, Lawrence's account of his much-publicized career in the desert war, which he had made virtually inaccessible through the fantastic price he had put upon it. Although he may have remembered this letter, which was typical of Nancy, he doesn't seem to have made the acquaintance of its author until considerably later. In this period Lawrence, fleeing from his own reputation, was undergoing the purgatory of enlisted service in the Tank Corps, and although he was writing frequent spirited and amusing letters to a circle of celebrated friends, a rich woman who did not expect to read his book was not among his correspondents.

Lawrence already had contacts with many of the intimate Cliveden circle. He had first met Lionel Curtis at the Peace Conference, and Philip had used his influence with Lloyd George to get Lawrence's Arab friend, the Emir Feisal, named an official delegate to the conference. Feisal's hope of becoming the ruler of an independent Arab state in Syria was disappointed, much to Lawrence's shame and distress. Lawrence had been the moving spirit behind the Arab revolt that had aligned Feisal with the British against the Turks in the Near Eastern theatre of war, and it now seemed to him that England had betrayed her Arab allies. Like the young men of the RIIA, he had been bitterly disillusioned by the treaty. In the preface to *The Seven Pillars of Wisdom* he wrote: "When we achieved and the new world dawned, the old men came out again and took from us our victory, and remade it in the likeness of the former world they knew."

Lawrence's personality seems to have been unable to survive

the demands of his genius. Guilt was lodged so deeply in his psyche that the strands are difficult to trace. One was the obvious and widely recognized one of the betrayal, as he saw it, of the Arab cause; he had made Feisal promises in the name of his country that he more than half realized at the time were false. But deeper than this was his revulsion at the circumstance of his own illegitimate birth. His father, an Irish baronet, had run away with his children's governess and started a second family in England under the assumed name of Lawrence. Lawrence liked to be called T. E. because, as he told a friend, "It is the only part of my name which belongs to me." His psychopathic revulsion toward sexual relations apparently stemmed from his illegitimate birth. In a revealing letter to Curtis, Lawrence wrote: "We are all guilty alike you know. You wouldn't exist, I wouldn't exist, without this carnality. . . . Isn't it true that the fault of birth rests somewhat on the child? I believe it's we who led our parents on to bear us, and it's our unborn children who make our flesh itch."

With sentiments such as these it is no wonder that Lawrence could not himself bear, much less carry about in the world, the public personality of the heroic "Lawrence of Arabia." In 1922 he fled both his public and his private selves and buried himself in the enlisted ranks of the RAF, calling himself T. E. Shaw. When asked by a superior officer why he had enlisted, Lawrence replied almost inadvertently, "I think it was a sort of mental breakdown, sir."

"Report that man for insubordination," snapped the officer.

In spite of such slips, Lawrence did succeed in what amounted to a self-cure during his years in the enlisted ranks. He never lost complete control and in fact delayed the drastic step of enlistment until he had brought his Arabian adventure to what he regarded as a satisfactory conclusion.

At the Peace Conference he had concerned himself with the changing status of the Empire. In 1921, serving under Churchill at the Colonial Office, Lawrence was instrumental in securing Transjordania and Iraq as Arab states under British direction. This arrangement in some degree satisfied his conscience. He had written Lord Curzon, then Foreign Secretary, in 1919 that "the Arabs should be our first brown dominion, and not our last brown colony," a concept that was congenial to his Round

Table friends. Some of his biographers have accused Lawrence of dreams of imperial power. Churchill, indulging in some romantic dreaming of his own, wrote to Lawrence in 1927 comparing him to the young Napoleon or Clive, "if only the stupid twentieth century had not made peace." Actually, both Churchill and Lawrence were well satisfied with the early twentieth-century solution of the client state, although as a compromise it fell short of Lawrence's original dream of Arab freedom.

By 1929, when Bernard Shaw first introduced him at Cliveden, Lawrence was beginning slowly to emerge from the years of near-breakdown that he had spent in the enlisted ranks, hidden away from the scenes of action in the great world. The virtual recluse, the poor aircraftman, self-stripped of all worldly rank and power, would appear to be at the opposite pole from Nancy Astor, the wealthy peeress and lively, extroverted hostess. Actually they had much in common, a hidden kinship that seems to have been apparent to both of them at the first meeting.

Among the numerous descriptions of Lawrence by his friends there are some that clearly reveal his resemblance to Nancy. Hilda Chaundy, an Oxford friend, wrote: "He seemed to read the minds of the people he was with. . . . He was merry, with a dancing puckish humor, a lightning comprehension that glanced out of his intensely blue eyes." Nancy's eyes, too, were intensely blue, radiating an electric sympathy as well as "lightning comprehension." If one substitutes "a taste for schoolboy pranks" for "puckish humor" this description would fit both Nancy and Lawrence to perfection. His own description of Nancy at their first meeting was written to a friend: "a rare creature, very swift and yet kind." Their friendship was instinctive and had nothing to do with their outward circumstances, although Lawrence was not above reminding her of the fame that he presumably wished to forget. A few months after their meeting he wrote her:

> I do not know when, or with whom, I have ever maintained for so long so hot a correspondence. Clearly we are soul mates. Incidently, an American dealer pays twenty pounds for interesting letters from me: so heaven knows the prices which infatuated collectors will give for yours. Are we worth it? I mean, aren't we rather wasting our sweetnesses on the already sweet?

Nancy, whose life had been closest to those two highly rational men, Waldorf and Philip, must sometimes have longed to find in another something of the irrational, the intuitive, even the neurotic elements in her own nature. Lawrence had always indulged himself in the opiate of speed. In the years before and after her divorce from Bob Shaw, Nancy too had courted speed and danger. No horse had been wild enough for her, no fence too big. It appeared that Lawrence revived in her something of this old passion. It was their common attitude toward the body: That poor forked creature must be subdued and risen above; at times it must be made to hang on the very edge of destruction. Nancy enjoyed scaring Alec Cadogan half to death by driving that infinitely precise little Scotsman at sixty miles an hour over winding country roads. Nancy (laughing wildly, according to Cadogan): "Here come a turn. I shall slow down here." Cadogan, almost speechless: "I should hope so." But this sort of thing was only fun, not the real abandonment to speed, "the hurling oneself beyond the body," bones, blood, flesh all pressed together, as Lawrence practiced it. Now stationed at the Plymouth base, Lawrence indulged this reckless passion on his motor bike *Boanerges*. The second time Nancy saw him she had screamed out "Aircraftman Shaw!" as *Boanerges* had passed her car. The next day she got herself invited to the station on Plymouth Sound.

The most significant thing about Lawrence was his genius, which he had deliberately placed in a straitjacket. By the time he met Nancy he was nearly, but not quite, ready to re-emerge, reconciled or hardened at last to the open use in the world of his tremendous gifts. Shunning any physical contact with women, he was most at ease with them in the few cases where the sexual element could be left out. With men he was apt to be on the stretch, atempting to prove himeself: hence self-conscious and open to the frequently made charge of exhibitionism. With Nancy he was completely relaxed. He even verged, as he did with Charlotte Shaw, on revelations of his personal life, but with Nancy he concealed the sexuality that tormented him in bizarre ways. He let her see only the puritan streak that was most sympathetic to her own: "Over the Christmas season two men and four women have sent me fervent messages of love. Love carnal, not love rarefied, you know: and I am uncomfortable towards six more of the people I meet, therefore. It's a form of lunacy, I believe, to fancy that all comers are one's lovers: but what am I to make of it when they write it in black and white? If only one might never come nearer to people than on the street —Miss Garbo sounds a really sympathetic woman! The poor soul. I feel for her."

Nancy, through her connections, opened channels of influence which he was willing, if he could remain in the background, to manipulate in his own interest, and in the interest of his beloved RAF. Somehow, some day, he had to believe that the constricting chrysalis of his neurosis would be broken, and that he would escape, *into the air*. The same desire for freedom from the material world that had taken him, as Lawrence, to the desert now was satisfied by the idea of flight. The air, he told Charlotte Shaw, is "the purpose of our generation." He planned to write a book about it, to be called "A Confession of Faith." "It would include the meaning of speed, on land and water and air."

In 1929, when Nancy sought out Aircraftman Shaw, she made him ride her pillion on *Boanerges*, as though she too wished to enter that secret world of speed. The first time they rode together she took him to look at something practical, the housing estates that she and Waldorf had built in 1924. On later rides they would plunge for miles through the Devon countryside. For Nancy it was not just a prank but a real release from self that Lawrence and *Boanerges* could give her. Waldorf, as usual, was tolerant, only abjuring Lawrence not to find new ways for his wife to break her neck.

On the lighter side was the vegetarian luncheon to which she took GBS on the base, which proved to be no easy culinary task. Lawrence, of course, was present. Arriving early, he advised their hostess, his CO's wife, "Oh, just make it out of old bits of wood and string." It would be difficult to imagine a more delightful party than the one lunching off "old bits of wood and string" at Wing Commander Smith's. The three "Shaws"—for Nancy, too, had once been called Shaw—could sustain a personal relationship with each of the others and at the same time, in a group, enhance one another.

For Lawrence, friendship with Nancy meant the chance of ease, the haven of 3 Elliot Terrace and of Cliveden, and also access to a larger world, which he wished, on his own terms, to keep open. But this he might have found in other houses; with Nancy he had a unique comradeship. He was not, he said, normally "a good taker," but of Nancy's kindness he happily made free. Their letters to each other are easy and full of fun. When the house of Curtis (called "the Prophet") burned, Lawrence wrote: "I sent condolences and the monster replied: 'Yes, all my clothes were lost but are well covered by insurance!' . . . What would *you* put for price on the P's clothes? . . . 'I was lucky to be sleeping at All Souls, so [only] Pat [his wife] was . . . in the house.' " Nancy, who knew and sometimes suffered under the Prophet's egocentricities, enjoyed this picture; it reminded her of Curtis's reply when Pat had reproached him for *always* putting the commonwealth of the world ahead of her in his thoughts. "But, my dear," he had assured her, "I always think of you second."

With Philip, on the other hand, Lawrence was a little uneasy, and perhaps a little jealous. Continuing the theme of the Curtis fire, he wrote to Pat Curtis: "Blickling, of course! I never thought of it. When your croft was burned, I had imagined your relapsing cosily into little Cliveden's modest splendour. But Blickling is far, far more grand: and the Marquis has so many other houses . . . that you do him a kindness to air one or other. Excellent."

Nancy and Lawrence made good partners in some projects they took seriously. By 1930 she was trying to get him up to London to attend the naval conference. In this instance he refused to be drawn: "Dear Lady Astor, what an undisciplined person you are!" She knew that the RAF had forbidden him to consort with "great men." The official object was to keep Lawrence away from politics, so that the category "great men" had to Nancy's delight included her and excluded GBS. The effect of the stricture appears to have been slight; Lawrence continued to speak in the halls of the great, if only indirectly. "I should like to hear Lord Thomson's [Secretary of State for Air in the Labour government] opinion of my abilities! My opinion of his character hasn't been asked for, but I am quite willing to hand it on through your 'curious but direct' way if you think it would be wholesome. It is not very kindly."

Although he did not care for its minister, Lawrence brooded

lovingly, like a surrogate parent, over both machines and men of the RAF at the Mt. Batten (Plymouth) station. This was the home of the big Iris III flying boats, capable of carrying a crew of twelve. The people of Plymouth were quite used to seeing the large airships on their training flights over the bay. On a bright, windless day the deceptive mirror surface of the sea will betray any but experienced seaplane pilots. On such an afternoon Lawrence, standing on the shore, watched one of the Iris III ships fly nose first into the surface of the bay. As one of the rescue crew he was first upon the scene, but only three of the nine crewmen aboard were saved. Lawrence cursed the slow, unwieldy rescue craft bumbling through the water and identified himself with the lost crewmen, "Six of us crushed together in the crushed cannister of the hull were bubbling out their lives."

It was common knowledge at the station that the ranking officer on the flight, Wing Commander Tucker, was not a flying-boat pilot, and that all ranks were afraid to fly with him. On the day of the crash Flight Lieutenant Ely had been piloting the ship; Ely survived and testified at the inquiry that Tucker had seized the controls, even knocking his hands off the wheel, as they had come in for the fatal landing. The testimony might never have been taken, and certainly never publicized, if Lawrence had not applied pressure through his "curious but direct friend," Nancy Astor. The results were, first, permission for Aircraftman Shaw to work on improved design for future RAF rescue craft; and, second, regulations that placed command of an airship in flight solely in the hands of the pilot, regardless of rank.

Lawrence wrote Nancy a congratulatory letter: "I *think* the battle is won. . . . I need hardly say how grateful I am to you for your help. It is such a pleasure to get things done cleanly and naturally without fuss. Nobody knows that anything has been done, and yet, I fancy, there will not be another case of this sort in our memories."

It was just the way he liked to "get things done." Like the Round Table, he was adept at pulling levers behind the scenes, and, also like the Round Table, he preferred to remain anonymous. Waldorf and Nancy, although less addicted to anonymity, were also willing to pull levers on occasion. It surely should not follow that such operations, because they are not conducted in the full glare of publicity, must have sinister motives. In the case of the Iris flying boats, they clearly did not. Lawrence's wholly innocent but revealing letter ended with "Ring me up, and let me take you up the Tamar for a picnic tea."

Lawrence's Christmases were deliberately austere, spent either in camp or at his cottage retreat at Clouds Hill. There would be, however, chocolates from Charlotte Shaw, and in 1932 Nancy sent two heating lamps, a thoughtful gift for the cottage. Though he, like everyone else, could only half-decipher her letters, their intimacy continued to progress. In 1933 he wrote "Yours MI PIRESS, was the only Christmas greeting I sent."

He paid Nancy the compliment, the great compliment never paid her by GBS, of writing to her seriously about his reactions to a work of art: O'Casey's *Within the Gates*. "This play deals with the life we all have to lead (temporarily) and so we dare not detach ourselves from it and criticise or pass judgment. That's why I do not want to see it again." In O'Casey's character of the young whore, illegitimate and haunted by guilt, Lawrence could see himself.

In speaking to Nancy of his "temporary" life he was telling her that he was still earthbound, but achingly, hurtfully so. He spoke to the note in her of the otherworldly, to the demon that they shared. By signing his letter "your airman" he referred to all that he found tolerable in his present life and looked forward to, the freedom of the air as he had described it to Charlotte Shaw. One day the air might be his special kingdom, cleansed of the gross carnality of the material world.

In their letters Nancy and Lawrence sometimes played the "I" game, underlining every appearance of the first person nominative pronoun. They believed that this multiplicity of "I" was created by attachment to things. They longed to throw off their multiple material selves so that, as Lawrence said, pure mind might triumph and "roll unchecked over the place where the material world had been." This was the sort of thinking that Shaw and Lawrence and Nancy all might share. Lawrence, asking her to underline the "I's" in a letter from him of January, 1932, remarked wryly that she might create a "Japanese sunset effect," so often did the wicked pronoun occur. When it came to competition in the number of times "I" appeared in their letters, he pointed out that he was ahead by three to one. His self-consciousness, far greater than Nancy's, remained to cut him off from the everyday world.

Not the least of Cliveden's charm for Lawrence's ambivalent spirit was Nancy's way of divorcing any sense of self-indulgence from the enjoyment of luxury. She herself never became attached to the material luxuries that Cliveden so abundantly offered. After Waldorf's death, when the great place belonged to her son Bill, the only thing that she appeared to miss was the security of the night watchman on his rounds. Lawrence's celebrated asceticism, self-willed, was more selective. It did not include denying himself huge drafts of the finest reading, and storing his books was a recurring problem. He kept a supply at Cliveden, often retiring there for quiet reading, stretched out usually on his stomach in some large, well-appointed bedroom with airy windows looking out over lawns to the river. Winston Churchill had once remarked that "Lady Astor, like Mr. Bernard Shaw, enjoys the best of all worlds. She reigns at once . . . as a leader of fashionable society, and of advanced feminine democracy. . . . She denounces the vice of gambling in unmeasured terms and is closely associated with an almost unrivalled racing stable, etc., etc." Mr. Churchill continued in this vein for several pages. He might have added another Shaw to his list of those adept at extracting the best of widely varying worlds. In Nancy it was straightforward. If she sometimes sounded a bit more English in Virginia, and considerably more Virginian in England, it was nevertheless true that she was essentially the same person in the ballroom, the House of Commons, or a settlement house in Plymouth. Lawrence, on the other hand, was a conscious chameleon, constantly straining after relationships that, in his own view, eluded him. With Nancy he relaxed his defenses. She was contriving during these years to reconcile this deepest-dyed of neurotics with some portion of his true self. At Cliveden, where conversation flew around the table, Lawrence was often persuaded to let high policy take precedence over flying boats. He was being led by imperceptible degrees into the practice of his supreme gift: the ability to bring policy, men, and events into one brilliant whole.

By early 1934 the challenge was not lacking. Garvin, in Waldorf's *Observer*, was calling consistently for greater effort to build Britain's lagging air power to meet the German threat. Lawrence listened and undoubtedly was thinking of drawing "the tides of men into his hands" once more. He was rapidly becoming a sort of British Lindbergh, without Lindbergh's fascist bias. His ideas on air power were given careful attention, and he was quite free in expressing them. He was already aware of how formidable the "German kites" would be, not like the "French junk." In a letter to Lionel Curtis in March, 1934, he set forth a detailed plan which, if followed, would have put a quite different complexion on the British position vis-à-vis Hitler at Munich. He would build *capacity* to expand production rather than aircraft, which would rapidly become obsolete. He wanted fifteen new airdromes, at a cost of £20,000 apiece. He thought that large surface ships were sitting ducks in the air age (a lesson not fully learned until the loss of *Repulse* and *Prince of Wales* in 1941).

It would have been possible, of course, for Lawrence to think in a clear, far-sighted way without being emotionally able to act, either to promote or to direct the necessary effort. Yet he was clearly considering action. His chance would come, he told B. H. Liddell Hart in June, 1934, if "somebody big" took him under his wing. By "somebody big" he meant Winston Churchill. Nancy was ready to give the final needed push toward active service; after his enlistment ended in February, 1935, she gave him no peace. He responded by declaring that sometimes he thought he would like her better if she were bedridden. A month after his retirement she forced the pace. "Philip Lothian is right, as usual. I believe when the Government reorganises you will be asked to reorganise the defense forces." Perhaps it was no coincidence that the *Observer* called for Churchill's return to the cabinet, to head up Defence, for Churchill, with Lawrence as his technical adviser, would have revolutionized Britain's arms. In May, Nancy wrote to Lawrence: "I will tell you what I have done already about it. If you will come to Cliveden Saturday, the last Saturday in May . . . you will never regret it." Among others, Baldwin, the Prime Minister, would be present.

Lawrence, puttering about his cottage and still recovering from retirement shock, put her off in a letter of May 8, 1935. "No, wild mares would not at present take me away from Clouds Hill. It is an earthly paradise, and I am staying here till I feel qualified for it. Also there is something broken in the works, as I told you: my will, I think. In this mood I would not take on any job at all. So do not commit yourself to advocating me, lest I prove a non-starter."

Lawrence, from long habit, was adept at putting off people who unwisely made demands upon him. If the idea could have been his own, he might have gone to Cliveden that weekend. In fact he might have gone in any case if fate had not been waiting on the Bovington Camp road. Not long before, he had dropped a hint to his friend Sir Herbert Baker that he ardently desired "to do some great national work." The job he probably had in mind, and that would be offered him on the Cliveden weekend, was deputy and eventual successor to Hankey, then Secretary of the Committee of Imperial Defence. On his visit to Baker, Lawrence had exclaimed, "Hankey has too much to do." A straw in the wind, but indicative of the wind's direction.

After the letter to Nancy on May 8, Lawrence's next and last correspondence was with another friend, Henry Williamson, who approached him with the at that time not too fantastic idea that he should go to see Hitler. Henry Williamson was an extraordinary character, a dreamer and an idealist who recognized these same qualities in Lawrence. Williamson, however, was deluded by his dreams, as Lawrence was not: Williamson dreamed of a new age of peace, based on Anglo-German friendship, and Lawrence, he thought, was its destined leader. With this end in view, he wrote suggesting the interview with Hitler. Unknown to Williamson, Lawrence had already been approached by emissaries of the Nazis who wished influential contacts in England. He had decisively rejected their advances. His military reputation may have suggested fascist leanings to the Germans, but Lawrence had made it quite clear that he wanted no part of such activities. Williamson's mission was surely doomed to failure. However, the two men were drawn together, and Lawrence obviously desired the meeting. He had gone next day to dispatch a telegram in reply to Williamson: "Lunch Tuesday wet fine cottage one mile north Bovington Camp."

This meeting never took place. On May 13, on his way back from sending the telegram at Bovington Camp, Lawrence and his motor bike suffered a fatal smash. It was an ordinary accident, not a case of mad speed, of "bones, blood, flesh, all pressed inward together." This Lawrence had tested often enough, gripping with his thighs and forcing the machine to its limits of speed. But even routine speed was too much—Lawrence, in fact, had planned to give up his high-powered machine, never built for country roads and village traffic. It appears that a van traveling in the opposite direction (later mythicized as a mysterious black car) had caused him to move to the left side of the narrow road, just as he was approaching the crest of a hill. As he came over the hill he saw directly in front of him two delivery boys on bicycles; swerving and changing gears, he nevertheless struck one of them (who was not hurt) and was himself hurled into space. Lawrence was taken to Bovington Camp Hospital, where he died from the effects of skull fracture six days later. He was buried on May 21st in Moreton Village churchyard.

The last Saturday of May was still four days off. He might have gone to Cliveden after all, to meet the Prime Minister; the partnership of Nancy and Lawrence might have borne magnificent fruit. He might have revolutionized Britain's posture of defense, thus changing the course of history at Munich; or he would at least have mitigated the indiscriminate bombing and wholesale destruction of World War II. Certainly he would have been at Churchill's right hand. Or, alternatively, he might have been simply crushed once more, sinking into madness or suicide. We will not know: all speculation ends on the road to Clouds Hill from Bovington Camp.

On May 21st the great and non-great assembled at Moreton churchyard. Funerals in Virginia are social occasions; one is cheerful except in the presence of the most intimately bereaved, and even then one does not commiserate or yield to grief. With eyes red from weeping Nancy did her best, moving from one mourner to another. "That was a bloody fine sermon," she told the officiating clergyman, "the first time I've heard you sound really sincere." But when her old friend and enemy Winston Churchill was ready to leave she ran to him and clasped his hands. "Winnie, Winnie," and the two wept together.

With Lawrence something bright, unpredictable, the wild side of her own spirit, had gone out of her life.

11

The "Cliveden Set"

In the early thirties, Nancy's and Waldorf's concern with the problems raised by economic depression had taken them to Russia and to the United States. At Cliveden they continued to entertain, on a larger scale than ever, representatives of all shades of political opinion. Among others, Charlie Chaplin, then on a triumphal world tour, was drawn into the charmed circle. Chaplin, the boy from the London slums, had made good as the great clown of the silent films. On an earlier trip he had refused to be introduced to Bernard Shaw, preferring to wait until he could meet England's greatest playwright on equal terms. Now they matched wits at Cliveden. Chaplin attempted to broach the subject of art and propaganda, but Shaw, on this occasion, refused to be drawn. Cliveden offered Chaplin a platform, and later, with Lloyd George present, the comedian made a serious speech proposing his own solutions for the depression. He touched on slum clearance, world trade, abolition of the gold standard, a reduction of working time, minimum wages—in fact, the whole gamut of the social reforms of the day. Many of the ideas exchanged on this trip were to appear in Chaplin's film *Modern Times.*

The high point of this visit was the opening of *City Lights.* On the first night, that most nervous of occasions, Chaplin was seated between Nancy and Shaw, two formidable wits quite capable of annihilating him. To his great relief, Shaw enjoyed the picture. (And well he might. It is a masterpiece and, further, was to net some $5,000,000, a measure of success to which Shaw was never immune.) Chaplin was so excited that when he was called upon to speak, "Nothing seemed to come out."

Nancy was naturally in sympathy with Chaplin's views on reform, but she was soon disillusioned by his irresponsible be-behavior. Accustomed to Shaw, she was willing to make allowances for the egotism of genius, but in Chaplin this was aggravated by the circumstances of his childhood. Intellectually, if not professionally, he was still a poor boy making up for lost opportunities. He did not hesitate to skip an engagement with the slum children at his old school in favor of a luncheon party in the great world, an act that Nancy would never have committed. When, on the opposite side of the social scale, he ignored a royal command to perform at a benefit graced by the King and Queen, Nancy's disapproval may be imagined. The natural good manners of her poorest countrymen in Virginia would have been superior to Chaplin's.

The premiere of *City Lights* was only one of the many pleasures and excitements of Nancy's life in the early thirties, when Cliveden parties surely reached a peak of perfection. In January, 1933, an especially festive party was given for the newly arrived Italian ambassador, Grandi, and his wife. A thank-you note from Lord Salisbury described the entertainment:

> My Dear Lady,
>
> I came away from Cliveden yesterday full to the brim with gratitude for kindness received and also with information on many grave subjects. I could now . . . write an essay on the relation between Great Britain and America and another on the Italian constitution—also upon how to play (and cheat) at musical chairs.

Nancy as a hostess had an actor's sense of timing; when political talk flagged—musical chairs. She was expert at arranging groups after dinner: "You mustn't talk to him. You wouldn't care for him at all." A Southern accent was irresistible during these maneuvers.

Also in 1933 came the Parliamentary Golf Tournament, in which Nancy lost to the Prince of Wales. T. E. Lawrence congratulated her on her tact: "Admirable," he said, "wholly admirable." It had probably not helped her game that on the morning of the match Wissie rang up to tell her mother of her engagement to Lord Willoughby d'Eresby. "That's the way it is done in these days," Nancy complained. "The young girls today simply ring up and inform their parents!" Actually she had not done very differently herself, at least the second time round. In fact she and Waldorf were delighted by the match, and the "quiet country wedding" in July, 1933, at Taplow church was all that could have been desired by the most Victorian parents.

Golf, in spite of the Prince of Wales, remained her favorite sport, principally because it meant playing with Philip. For a weekend golfer, Philip was truly remarkable. He would pick up a game whenever he could, sometimes in ordinary shoes and a business suit; even so, he was good enough to start one year in the British Open against men who devoted their lives to the game. And that, Nancy admitted, was too good for her. However, she practiced faithfully, taking her golf in much the same way as she did her cold plunges in the Channel waters at Sandwich. Although golf is hardly a hazardous game, Nancy was once injured, hit in the face by a small boy swinging a mashie. She cheerfully ignored her black eye, only remarking in the House of Commons, "As long as it is not taken as a sign of connubial infelicity, I don't mind." "My word, Nancy," exclaimed a colleague, "what must the other bloke be like?"

A. P. Herbert, writing in *Punch*, gave a marvelous picture of a fictitious interview with Nancy and GBS on the golf course:

> Why don't Americans practice their *principles* in England, Lady Astor?, so she said Why don't Englishmen take their *morals to Paris*, which my dear I thought was *rather* rapid and pertinent, however after that she gave the caddies a *brief* homily about their *private* lives and arranged for *all* their children to join the *Band* of Hope, and then *off* she went like an *electric* race horse, with

> Shaw striding beside her like a *Norwegian God*, my dear *too* perpendicular, and making the *most* carbolic remarks about golf, and of course your *frail* little friend trotting *feverishly* behind them from one gorse bush to another, *can* you *see* the picture?

Herbert, besides being a journalist and wit, was a fellow M.P. Whether or not she remembered reading this piece, Nancy later clashed with him in the House. During one of her periodic forays against the nefarious "Trade" she accused Herbert of being the "playboy of the drink world." The Member for Oxford responded: "May I suggest that a regular course of narcotics would be extremely good for the noble lady? She would be less restless." "The Noble Lady," she told him, "will be restless in this House long after the Member for Oxford Universities."

No one, except perhaps GBS himself, could hold her down and make it stick. In the case of the Stroble portrait bust GBS surely did his best. She was sitting for Kisfalud de Stroble, the Hungarian sculptor, who complained to Shaw that the conditions under which he worked were impossible, as his subject was incapable of sitting still. The one thing in the world that Shaw really respected was the discipline and craft of the artist. He wrote Nancy:

> I suggested chloroform, but I now appeal to one of your several better selves. He is a very fine workman and should be treated with genuine respect. And he is too amiable to resort to the poker or the broomstick, which is what you deserve. Unless you enable him to super finish that bust angels won't never love you. Nor will G.B.S.

The bust, which is at present rather impersonally lodged at Westminster in the Speaker's quarters, does not appear to have been greatly cherished. Lawrence, somewhat of an authority on the subject of portrait busts, had congratulated her, but said that the artist should have been Epstein. Why, he did not say. For himself he had preferred Eric Kennington or the more openly romantic Augustus John.

By 1934 new concerns were crowding to the center of the stage. At the Astors', conversation literally raged—about defense, about Germany, about Britain's precarious position in the Far

East. On a typical evening a small group, including Brand and Roosevelt's special emissary, Norman Davis, assembled for dinner at 4 St. James's Square. The Astors wished Davis to exert his influence on the President and if possible to extract an expression of American solidarity with Britain and France in a stand against Germany. There were also personal contacts with the President in Washington. An invitation from Cliveden to Sara Delano Roosevelt was declined by FDR: "I cannot let Mama go over because I am sure she would cancel all the debts."

Philip had a formal interview with Roosevelt in October of 1934 in which he brought up the big guns of his argument for American and British cooperation in the Pacific. He told the President that "the danger lay on the 'front,' Canada, Hawaii, Philippines, Singapore, and that here the United States must be on the front line. . . . The real question was whether the democracies would wake up to the situation in time." It was Philip's favorite theme: that the two great naval powers, Britain and America, should pool their forces and coordinate their diplomacy in order to prevent large-scale aggression anywhere in the world. The President, he told them at home, did not demur, but neither did he express consent. If Roosevelt overestimated Britain's potential strength, it was not the fault of his friends at Cliveden.

At this time Neville Chamberlain, already the coming man on the political scene, was acting as the "head and front of the pro-Japanese party." Smuts, the Commonwealth Prime Minister, who had come to England and was staying with Philip at Blickling, spoke of Chamberlain and his supporters as "being all over the place, like a snake in the grass." Nor was the government any stronger in its position vis-à-vis Italy, which, like Japan, was also flagrantly defying the League.

Up until 1935 Philip still had hopes that the League might keep the peace; these hopes ended with its failure to effectively oppose Italian aggression in Abyssinia. Under pressure of the fall elections, the Conservative team of Baldwin and Chamberlain, then Chancellor of the Exchequer, had encouraged the Foreign Secretary, Sir Samuel Hoare, to commit Britain to support League action. After the election they had Hoare go to Paris and sign the Hoare-Laval Pact, which quite simply reneged on their formal commitments. Baldwin then disavowed his Foreign Sec-

Nancy and Waldorf as they appeared in a family Christmas card, undated but probably *ca.* 1930. The note reads, "Best love to all—I am snowed under with work."

Nancy and GBS on their trip to Russia in 1931, photographed with a group of intellectuals in Leningrad. *(Wide World)*

Nancy campaigning in the general election of 1931. *(Wide World)*

Nancy with President-elect Franklin Delano Roosevelt, 1932. *(Wide World)*

British aviatrix Amy Johnson, Charlie Chaplin, Nancy, and GBS. *(Wide World)*

Lady Astor robed for the Coronation, 1937. *(Valentine Museum, Richmond, Va.)*

T. E. Lawrence on his motorbike with George Brough, its manufacturer. *(From* Lawrence of Arabia, *by Anthony Nutting; Clarkson Potter, 1961)*

Justice Felix Frankfurter talks with Nancy after receiving an honorary degree at Oxford University, June,1939. *(Wide World)*

"The Shiver Sisters Ballet, 1938," by David Low. *(Reproduced by permission of the Proprietors of the* Evening Standard)

Plymouth under the blitz.

Winston and "Clemmie" Churchill tour the blitzed areas of Plymouth with Nancy, 1941. *(Wide World)*

On her twenty-fifth anniversary as a Member of Parliament, Nancy was honored by the other women Members, 1944. *(Wide World)*

Irene and Nancy, 1948. *(Wide World)*

Waldorf, *ca.* 1948. *(Wide World)*

Nancy denouncing Senator Joseph McCarthy in a speech at a Red Cross luncheon in Washington, D.C., 1953. *(Wide World)*

Nancy, still delighting audiences, speaks at the unveiling of a memorial to Christabel Pankhurst, the suffragette leader, in 1959. *(Wide World)*

retary, and Hoare was forced to resign. Rumors were put about that he had been ill, subject to blackouts after a fall on the ice at St. Moritz, and so on, and not himself when the pact had been signed. Waldorf, who had seen Hoare daily at St. Moritz, scoffed at these stories. "Sam," he said "had never looked better."

The Astors, like many others, were fed up. Although Nancy still had the Baldwins for weekends at Cliveden, she had privately taken their measure. Baldwin's assurances of his "mingled respect, affection, and admiration," and signing himself "your obedient S.B.," did him little good. At Cliveden they said that his "capacity for hiding his incapacity" grew greater from one premiership to the next. At the time of the 1935 election Nancy rang up the faithful Tom Jones and regaled him with a perfect replay of Mrs. Baldwin's election speech to the party. Mrs. Baldwin had touched on social welfare, ending up with the extremely imitable peroration: "I appeal to every one of you to make it your business to be responsible for one expectant mother."

Nancy, whose own campaign speeches had advocated collective action by the League to end the Abyssinian affair, now put her disillusionment clearly on the line: "I have fought long and hard for the League of Nations, but I am not going to fight a day longer for a sham." Peace, if there was to be peace, must surely lie elsewhere, most probably, she felt, in stepping up Britain's own defense effort. It was at this time that she had put pressure on her friend Lawrence in an attempt to harness his proven military genius. Given the steadfast opposition of Neville Chamberlain at the Exchequer, any plan at all would have been doomed for lack of funds. In 1934 Mr. Chamberlain had confided to his diary that he had "practically taken charge of the defense requirements of the country," cutting the proposed five-year expenditure from seventy-six to fifty million, including ship-building. It was not a heartening prospect for those who had an improved defense posture in mind.

As had happened in earlier periods of frustration, the Astors and Philip pinned their hopes on cooperation with the United States. In order to draw the United States back into a world system, Philip felt that Britain should keep herself free of what the Americans regarded fearfully as European entanglements. He honestly believed, and until 1937 continued to believe, that Europe would establish her own regional balance more effectively without British intervention. He visualized a community of "good Europeans" within a world league based on Anglo-American seapower. But the United States, he felt strongly, would continue to hold aloof so long as there was any question of involvement in a local European quarrel. Like his friend Smuts, he was deliberately taking the world view. Smuts, he believed, was the one man best fitted to persuade the new world of its coming role in global politics.

One can imagine with what satisfaction Philip learned that the old warrior, unable to bear his isolation any longer, was on his way to England, and with what joy he welcomed him to Blickling. Here the two old friends put together at first hand all those ideas they had been exchanging in long, slow-moving letters across the seas. Waldorf, of course, was alerted to the arrival of this important ally to their cause, and he immediately invited Smuts to make a major address to the Chatham House audience. Chatham House itself was not considered large enough; the Savoy Hotel was chosen as a suitable setting for one of the Royal Institute's greatest evenings. Smuts was the one indisputably great figure to emerge from the overseas Empire in the last war, and, unlike the influence of Lloyd George, his power had survived the peace. When the time came for him to mount the platform at the Savoy Hotel, there was complete, almost awestruck attention. Out of the perplexity of the times might there come a saving word?

Smuts started speaking of the Nazi trouble, which both he and Philip hoped might pass away. After a few words he turned to the East, to that area where, he told them, the great decisions of the future would be made. Here the "ultimate destiny" shared by the Dominions and the United States would be played out. He appealed to his audience to recognize that "there really is a society, and not merely a collection, of nations. . . . The driving force in this human world of ours should be, not morbid fears or other sickly obsessions, but this inner urge towards wholesome integration and cooperation." It was Philip's view, Philip's faith, expressed in eloquent language. But at the end Smuts warned of "new sinister forces . . . imperilling what centuries of European effort have accomplished. . . . I feel," he said, that "the hour for action has come, or is rapidly coming."

On his departure from England Smuts wrote warmly to Philip:

"I am glad to know that you are there to follow up . . . and organize any necessary campaign." Philip had in fact already acted; he followed Smuts's eloquence with a precise strategic analysis in the *Observer.* Once Japan had secured the island chain across the seaway between the Philippines and Hawaii, she would be in striking distance of Singapore and Pearl Harbor. So he had told the President. At home the man to convince was Neville Chamberlain. Unfortunately there was no doing anything with Mr. Chamberlain, who told Philip that "at the proper time" England and the United States must take a common stand, but "that it was better to avoid a rupture [with Japan] just now." This was an early example of the delaying tactic employed to such devastating effect in 1938. Chamberlain remained diametrically opposed to the Smuts-Lothian concept of foreign policy, to the idea, basically, of cooperation of the democracies to hold the dictatorships in check.

Having failed to rouse first Roosevelt and then his own government to positive action in the East, Philip attempted a rearguard action in Germany. His two interviews with the Führer, especially the first one, in January, 1935, were directed mainly toward buying time for the democracies. In essence the argument was that if Hitler would rule out the use of force for, say, a ten-year period, some peaceful adjustment of the Versailles frontiers might be his reward. If force were not employed, such an arrangement, in Philip's eyes, would not have been a cynical *quid pro quo;* it had long been felt at Cliveden that adjustments were right and no more than Germany's due. The attempt at diplomatic persuasion was perhaps logically sound, but psychologically it was all wrong. It did not appeal to Nancy, and when opportunity offered she refused to meet her second dictator. Philip, always sensitive to the reactions of Americans, seems to have had no internal warning system in regard to Hitler. He was perhaps too intent on the great global strategy in which Germany still appeared to him to play only a minor role. He approached the Führer in much the same spirit as he would a study-group meeting at Chatham House, with no more concern for outward effect or propaganda value than he would have felt in St. James's Square. His mind was entirely fixed on the business at hand, on the ideas exchanged, and on the hope, as he told the Führer, of a political settlement.

The man across the table from him was engaged in an utterly different course, yet was somehow able to convey the impression of a successful meeting. To the trained, legalistic mind of the Englishman, Hitler opposed the art of sizing up his man, of lulling his doubts, and of using him for whatever purpose seemed handy at the time. He was a consummate actor, skilled in projecting any impression that would help him in his play for power. In such moments the performance far outran mere craft and conscious deceit. Hitler seems to have taken absolute joy in his own creation, not merely as an intellectually successful ploy, but as a feat of emotional empathy. It is a fact that many men of different views left his presence convinced that in some essential way their minds had met while in actuality they had been divided by unfathomable depths. It almost seemed that the greater the division, the easier it was for Hitler to cast this particular spell.

In the case of Philip and Hitler there were differences of philosophy so profound that true communication was, as the Führer himself might have put it, ruled out. Hitler spoke of the state as the vehicle of German Kultur; Philip thought of the state, preferably federalized, as a mechanism for protecting the freedom of its individual citizens, and for promoting confidence and cooperation, if possible through a loose organization of federal unions, with its fellow states. A quotation from an essay by Fichte illuminates the vast discrepancy between these two views: "The Germans understand by Kultur an intimate union between themselves and the natural forces of the universe, whose action they alone are capable of apprehending, and as a tribal discipline designed to turn those forces to account." Both ideas of the state are directed toward an extension of political union, but the methods involved are irreconcilable. The one involved a long and painstaking intellectual effort to build a new internationalism; the other a glorious union of blood and steel, a return to the atavistic unity of tribal values and tribal conquest. If the immediate goals of these two systems seemed at some points to overlap, it could only be out of context, unrelated to the two utterly different schemes of which they were, respectively, part.

The appearance of the liberal Lord Lothian to talk disarmament in Berlin must have seemed to the Führer a most fortunate incident. It was his first chance to deal with a prominent Englishman, and, to do Hitler justice, he did, in the beginning, attempt to have a "sensible" conversation, touching those points at which, in his view, British and German interests coincided. Lord Lothian, happily, had opened the interview with a reference to possible agreement on armaments based on a prior political agreement. The Führer could fall in with this most eagerly.

Lothian told him that what England wanted was a political agreement that would "stabilize Europe say for ten years. . . . It was necessary in order to protect ourselves to have an agreement which included Russia, so as to prevent an armament race. . . . Stability in Europe depended upon an arms agreement."

Hitler "entirely agreed" in principle. According to Philip's notes, he said: "There cannot be any doubt that Germany is determined not to have war. . . . If he now could speak not as Chancellor, but as a student of history, he would say that the best means of preserving peace would be for England and Germany to make a common declaration that anybody who breaks the peace shall be punished by these two powers."

Lothian now quoted Rhodes's view that the U.S.A., England, and Germany would together preserve the peace of the world. England was at present anxious, because she did not know what to make of the new Germany, was it expansionist or not?

Hitler protested. "War was a great madness."

The fascinating thing about this meeting is that two men could use the same words, and yet obviously, at least in retrospect, talk of two totally different things.

Philip, who had been led to expect the mesmeric glare of those famous blue eyes, was rather surprised at the tameness of the interview. The Führer, he told his sister, "left me completely cold." He came away hardly enthusiastic, but prepared to believe that Hitler would make no military move for the specified period of ten years. He had said openly at the interview, "At the end of ten years one did not know what conditions would be." Privately Philip could hope for much—for British rearmament, for U.S. support, for the encouragement of moderate forces in Germany, which, if treated fairly, might be expected to throw out the gangster types to whom desperation alone, in Philip's view, had driven them. For Hitler's part, if he had substituted "until Germany is ready" for "ten years," his passionately affirmed love of peace would have been quite genuine.

Six weeks later, Hitler's open and unilateral announcement of military conscription and his point-blank refusal to enter into any kind of Eastern treaty shocked Philip into at least the beginning of disbelief. Full realization was not yet, but it did occur to him that a language utterly foreign, expressing an entirely alien *Weltpolitik*, might now be in use across the Channel.

Another shock was in store. On the weekend of March 7–9, 1936, a rather special company had gathered at Blickling: Norman and Mrs. Davis, who were now perhaps the Astors' and Philip's closest American friends; Vincent Massey, later to become Governor General of Canada, and Mrs. Massey; the Astors; Sir Thomas Inskip, about to become minister for the Coordination of Defence, and Lady Inskip; Walter Layton, Chairman of the liberal *News Chronicle*; Professor Arnold Toynbee, the mainstay of Waldorf's Chatham House; and the ubiquitous Tom Jones. The Anthony Edens were expected. Altogether a congenial group not bent on anything more serious for this spring weekend than golf, or perhaps strolling in Philip's gardens.

On Saturday the Edens had not arrived, and late in the afternoon a telephone call came through. Eden was Foreign Secretary in Baldwin's cabinet, and his presence was needed at the Foreign Office. German troops were entering the Rhineland. The company could think and talk of nothing else, and after dinner they all gathered around the radio. At about eleven o'clock Layton received a message from his office: France was demanding withdrawal of the German troops. The dreaded moment, the moment of possible armed confrontation, had arrived.

All agreed that Germany would never withdraw voluntarily once she had set foot on the soil of the Rhineland. The only alternatives were acquiescence or the immediate launching of preventive war. Even if Germany had been checked in 1936, and of course there was the possibility that she might have been, would she not have broken out all over again a few years later? Philip could not find it in his heart to condemn Germany's entrance into "her own back garden," as he put it. Memories of Fontainebleau and Lloyd George's constant warnings that the

Rhineland, like Alsace-Lorraine to the French after 1870, would remain a sacred cause in every German heart now assailed him. How could one justify the use of armed force to deny to Germany what was so manifestly hers? The Führer's methods disturbed him, but Philip did not see in 1936 how far these methods were to go. He wished the British stand to come at a point where Germany was manifestly in the wrong.

Waldorf and Layton, the two newspaper publishers, showed considerably more concern. Waldorf in particular had been backing Garvin, who had issued repeated warnings of Hitler's intentions. Now he challenged Philip: "We made such a fuss about Italy's aggression in Abyssinia? What about Germany's breach on the Rhine?" The general consensus at Blickling that weekend was that there was nothing for it but to try out Germany's good faith. England, after years of disarmament, was hardly prepared for any other course. The Baldwin government responded more or less as expected. A questionnaire was sent to the German foreign ministry, rather naïvely asking them what treaty they *would* be prepared to honor. No answer was received.

The question of the Rhineland now had to be submitted to the intense scrutiny, not only of the Foreign Office, but of the specialists of Chatham House. Here matters of policy long discussed at Round Table moots could be opened to a wider audience. Speakers expressed their own views and unanimity was not required, but we must remember that the Royal Institute of International Affairs was a product of the Peace Conference and of its founding members' desire for justice to Germany. It is not surprising and certainly not in the least sinister that its open discussions should continue to lean toward the policy later known pejoratively as "appeasement."

The basic question was not the justice or propriety of Germany's being in the Rhineland. Most Chatham House members agreed with Philip's later widely quoted statement about her own back garden. The question, rather, was one of future intention. Was this act, perhaps not unfair in itself, merely the thin edge of a much larger wedge? The active members of Chatham House had prepared themselves with the greatest care in their attempt to assess German intentions. First Philip, and subsequently Professor Toynbee, had had personal interviews with the Führer. The atmosphere created for their benefit had been one, if not of sweet reasonableness, at least of a rational, measured diplomacy. One wishes that Nancy had not turned down the opportunity for an interview with Hitler, for she might have shifted the ground to a less rational and more realistic basis.

During the Chatham House meeting Toynbee used a story to illustrate the position as he saw it. Four children had been kidnapped from a poor widow woman. She had screamed until every last one was returned, but she would not have screamed for a fifth that did not belong to her. Was Hitler like that screaming woman? Toynbee thought Britain should make it clear that there were Eastern as well as Western limits to what the Führer might hope to gain with his screams. Philip put it clearly on the line: "Let us tell Europe the kind of settlement we will fight for. . . . The real danger is that we shall . . . say, 'Oh, well, don't let us raise difficulties. We have got round the Rhineland corner. We will wait till we get to the next corner and then turn that.' That next corner is likely to be Austria—and then something else."

In his summing up, Waldorf, in the chair, assumed a judicial position. He found that an unanswerable case could be made for both France and Germany. He too had talked with Hitler and had been struck by the Führer's genuine conviction of the Communist danger. Hitler was probably quite sincere in his belief that the Franco-Soviet pact, concluded just before the occupation of the Rhineland, had justified his act of aggression. It had been, of course, a clear violation of the peace treaty, but the treaty was now nearly seventeen years old. Waldorf quoted Gladstone on the bindingness of guarantees; they could be reasonably affected by the subsequent position of the parties to it. He sincerely hoped that something in the nature of peaceful change would shortly take place to remove all sense of injustice and grievance, not because it paid to do so, but because it was right. Although eminently fair, he did wish to draw a line, and at this point, like Garvin, he felt that the line should be drawn at Austria. "Arms are being smuggled in from Germany," he wrote his friend Norman Davis, "and at no very distant date the Austrian Nazis may be ready for a putsch. . . . If England and France acted together they might by their joint influence help to establish an independent reasonably democratic form of government [in Austria] which would be supported internally by . . . groups which are anti-Nazi and anti-fascist and non-Communist"—in short, by the Social Democrats and those who would cooperate with them. An optimistic view, perhaps, but certainly not pro-Nazi or pro-appeasement, as these terms later came to be understood.

Unlike the visits of Philip and Toynbee, Waldorf's meeting with the Führer had not had a primarily political focus. He had gone at the behest of the Mother Church in Boston to intervene on behalf of the Christian Science churches in Germany, which were then beginning to feel the weight of Nazi oppression. Waldorf was received politely by Hitler and said his piece without meeting any untoward difficulty. In fact, the Führer displayed no particular animus against the Christian Scientists. Waldorf, having finished his prepared statement, turned to general matters. As he later told the Chatham House audience, they touched upon Russia, where Hitler seemed genuinely afraid of the Communist threat. However, there was another question that Waldorf wished to bring up. He told Hitler that it would be difficult for Germany to have normal relations with other countries so long as the mistreatment of the Jews continued. To Waldorf's consternation, the Führer broke into an emotional tirade. It went on and on and finally brought the interview to a close. Waldorf had not been unprepared—it had taken moral courage to broach so loaded a subject—but Hitler's reaction had been beyond any imagining. It was that of an obviously sick mind, in strong contrast to the courtesy and equanimity that had been shown to Philip and Toynbee. If Waldorf had had any disposition to trust the Führer, which is doubtful, it was removed by this interview. As chairman at Chatham House he had maintained a judicial attitude, while privately he was well aware of Hitler's threat to the peace of Europe. "A very dangerous man," he told an American friend. There would seem to be nothing in his remarks to have provoked the "Cliveden Set" stories launched by Claud Cockburn in the leftist press. Nevertheless, these stories now singled out the Astors and placed upon their heads all Britain's sins of omission and commission during the troubled thirties.

Cockburn edited and in fact did all the writing on a small news sheet called *The Week*. He was also the London correspondent for *Pravda*. The Labour Party, for which Cockburn was generally spokesman, had assumed a position difficult to defend: while free with their attacks on Hitler and Mussolini, they were simultaneously objecting to conscription and an increased defense budget at home. Cockburn had first tried to put this line over in a "longish think piece" that, in the author's own words, "made about as loud a bang as a crumpet falling on a carpet." However, this agile journalist was receiving "inside tips," as he described them, from anti-Nazi factions in the Foreign Office, the City, and "the so-called Churchillian wing of the Conservative Party." These stories, he said, "had that particular zip and zing which you get from official sources only when a savage intramural departmental fight is going on." Thus inspired, Cockburn decided to personalize his story. He headed his next piece with the words "The Cliveden Set" and used this phrase several times in the text. "The thing went off like a rocket." From that moment, in June, 1936, the legend of a pro-Nazi conspiracy at Cliveden took root in the public mind. It nurtured a whole irrational system of thought concerning the origins of Britain's foreign policy.

The "Set" was given a brilliant cast of characters, who were, of course, all habitués of Cliveden. Geoffrey Dawson, Philip Lothian, and Nancy herself had the starring roles. It was Cockburn's method to put together truths and half-truths until the sum of the parts came out as a lie. For example, Dawson: as editor of the *Times* his influence was so mystically English as to be virtually incomprehensible to non-Englishmen; yet "half the statesmen in Europe pored anxiously" over his editorials. This man of tremendous power was pictured by Cockburn as putty in the Astors' hands. He had been an Eton scholarship boy, an experience, said Cockburn, that gave him a nice respect for the "importance—in upper English society—of the right people." Philip was characterized as "a super nationally minded Englishman" and "a friend of the Third Reich." Both Philip and Dawson were part of "the queer Anglo-American gathering" at Cliveden.

As the legend picked up momentum the phrases multiplied. It was soon referred to as "Schloss" Cliveden, "Britain's second Foreign Office." In all this it was Nancy's "whims, prejudices, and well- or ill-conceived notions" that played the decisive role, or at least one of "absurdly disproportionate importance." There appeared to be something irresistible in this concoction. Even Nancy's denials played to the box office. "People must have lost their sense of the ridiculous," she exclaimed, "if they swallow this nonsense about my directing Cabinet policy and exercising more power than Queen Elizabeth, Marie Antoinette and Cleopatra all in one."

The general idea Cockburn wished to put over was that if the Astors would only stop exerting their pernicious influence, Britain might be able to check Hitler without any increase in the "defense effort," as armament is always described in every country. Because this theory was so appealing, the public simply brushed aside its patent illogic; the Cliveden Set drama, as staged by Claud Cockburn, continued to be a runaway success. Cockburn later admitted in his autobiography that the phrase "Cliveden Set" soon ceased to represent any particular group of individuals. "It became the symbol of a tendency, . . . a condition, as it were, in the state of Denmark." In short, it gave the public someone to blame and, by inference, an easy way out of the real problem that faced Britain in the late 1930s.

All this, of course, was damaging to the Astors, but, perhaps less obviously, it was damaging to England too. It suggested that the Astors wished to increase the defense budget and ultimately to conscript manpower, not to defeat Hitler, but simply to indulge the natural passion of the rich to grind the faces of the poor. It followed that if one were, unlike the Astors, a poor but honest Englishman who supported the principles of the League, Herr Hitler might simply go away. Such specious reasoning as this blinded many people to the real cause of Britain's weakness, which sprang from a quite different source. While Nancy was voting for increased expenditure and while Philip called for national service for rich and poor alike, Neville Chamberlain at the Exchequer was remarking with sublime complacency: "I have had to do most of the work on the [Army] programme, which has been materially modified as a result. . . . If we were now to follow Winston's advice [or Garvin's, or Nancy's] and sacrifice our commerce to the manufacture of arms, we should inflict a certain injury on our trade from which it would take generations to recover." At the same time that Mr. Chamberlain was penning these reflections the Führer was weeping with emotion at the noble spectacle of rank on rank of his work batallions, flashing their spades aloft and crying in unison: "*Krieg Heil, Krieg Heil, Krieg Heil!*"

As for Mr. Baldwin, he was becoming more and more attached to his pipe, his books, and his slightly sycophantic friend Tom Jones. It did not matter, for Chamberlain, an impatient crown prince, was waiting in the wings. Where Mr. Baldwin erred through laziness, Mr. Chamberlain erred through conviction and was by far the more dangerous of the two. The Baldwin administration came to an appropriate end with its leader's most memorable achievement. If no hero in the foreign field, Stanley Baldwin did now prove his prowess in an affair of the heart. At the end of 1936 he crowned his fifteen years of service as Prime Minister by defending the Empire from an American lady, twice divorced, who, while prevented from making off with the crown, did manage to whisk away the King. Nancy, who had once written a harried sister-in-law that she "was an expert on young women," might have been ready to handle Mrs. Simpson single-handed, but fortunately, according to Tom Jones, Nancy was in Bermuda at the height of the crisis. Philip, perhaps because he was a bachelor and known to be "good with Americans," lunched with Mrs. Simpson several times in an effort to work out a compromise. He combined the priestly function with that of man of the world, and their meetings went rather well. The lady was willing to accept a morganatic marriage, and the King agreed, but Mr. Baldwin, *in loco parentis* to the Empire, rejected the plan so decisively that it never became a serious possibility.

At the end the crisis came to a close with breakneck speed. The King made his "At long last" speech and departed. Nancy, asked to explain these most un-English occurrences over the air to her countrymen in America and to Canada, had little time to prepare. T. J. found her walking about the house, throwing ideas at a pad "like darts at a darts board." Philip and Waldorf were both present, Philip rather unhelpfully suggesting that she ask Americans how *they* would feel about Mrs. Simpson in the White House. In the end Nancy followed a surer guide, her own feeling about the monarchy. The crown, she told America, belongs "in a very special legal sense" to all the Dominions as well as to the mother country. "This crisis . . . has shown yet again that the foundations of the English-speaking race are based upon principles, and not upon persons. . . . Those who will not obey the rules cannot rule." After all, had she not told Stalin himself, when speaking of that flag upon which the sun had not yet quite set, "It can't be might, it must be right"?

12

The Last Best Chance

HAVING saved the country from Mrs. Simpson, Mr. Baldwin proceeded to hand it over to Mr. Chamberlain. At this point of history, Nancy and Waldorf admired the new Prime Minister for his expertise in their own field of social welfare. Personally they found the Chamberlains a bore. Neville was far too stiff and humorless for Nancy's fun and games; at a Cliveden weekend Tom Jones described him as "in the company, but not of it." But he would be useful, they felt, in areas where Mr. Baldwin had dragged his feet.

Waldorf's bipartisan study group (the Next Five Years Group) was grappling with the sort of economic questions raised by Keynes. An important plank in their program was an increase in the school-leaving age. A bill to raise this age to fifteen came before the House in February, 1936, and here, as often happened, Nancy carried her share of a joint project by speaking for it in the House. It was also, of course, an extension of her long fight for the welfare of children. Near the beginning of her career a fellow M.P., who seemed rather ambivalent in his attitude toward the noble lady, had remarked: "She is one of the few I know who unite a charming personality to a frumpish psychology." "I am not ashamed," Nancy declared stoutly. "We who fight for moral and spiritual aims are always laughed at for being frumpish." She could console herself with the knowledge that, in her case, the combination had worked! She could report that in twelve years prior to women's suffrage only five measures of benefit to women and children had been passed, but in the twelve years since, twenty had been enacted. She gave all the credit to the women's vote ("In countries where they didn't have it," she told a reporter, "like Italy, Spain and Russia, the most appalling things go on"), but in retrospect it would appear that the lion's share of this credit should go to Nancy herself.

As late as 1931 she was fighting to reduce the seventy-two-hour work week then in effect for children aged fourteen to sixteen. In the fight to raise the school-leaving age in 1936 some of her old opponents among the Labour Members accused her of trying to prevent working-class children from giving needed support to their parents. They recommended that exceptions be incorporated in the government's education bill. Nancy fought this in a dramatic debate lasting late into the night of February 13, 1936. She reminded them that a century earlier some parents had similarly opposed reducing the work hours of ten- to twelve-year-olds. Nancy told the House: "If we are to consult all the parents we shall never get any advance."

The program advocated by Waldorf was far more extensive. It included nursery schools, extension classes for fifteen- to eighteen-year-olds, and much more. The hall of 4 St. James's Square was plastered with pictures and charts; elegant guests arriving for dinner were unexpectedly faced with the Ten-Year Education Plan. Nancy was more conservative in her recommendations to the House; nevertheless, some of her arguments anticipated the larger program. "Why do not ministers have imagination enough to . . . tell us of this new age in which machinery has taken the place of craftmanship?" The Astors saw clearly that the machine age demanded public education because children could no longer be adequately trained in the home, as they had been in the age of craft.

"We plan for everything else. Let us have a plan for juveniles. I can give the government a plan if they have not one. . . . It would be accepted and welcomed by the country. . . . We call it a ten-year plan, but at the end of ten years you would have completely changed the outlook of a generation of our children." She took a moment more to give a percipient look into the future. "This government, like every democratic government, knows that we must educate not only for industry but for leisure. . . . It is only a question of time before we have a five-day week. I should be positively frightened of having great masses of idle people without taste and without occupation." Her good friend Captain FitzRoy, Speaker of the House, who previously had often had occasion to call her to order, this time did not find it necessary to interrupt. When at last she sat down the next speaker, a certain Mr. Balfour, began very seriously: "I shall not attempt to follow the Noble Lady at this hour of the night."

The moment of success ended in laughter, her own among the rest.

The bill to raise the school-leaving age was passed, but some exceptions were added, so that Nancy's goal was only partially attained.

Nancy, harassed and depressed by what she saw of the world of nations and of politics, thought longingly of Virginia. "It must be lovely at home now," she would write to Mr. Neve, or, "I long to be in Virginia again." She loved Devon, but "it doesn't smell like Virginia in spring, no place on earth does." And when Mr. Neve wrote suggesting an international brotherhood her disillusionment broke through: "Professing Christians don't even love one another! So as a politician I should be a humbug if I began to plan a world based on Christianity." She had once hoped that peace would come to the world in her own time, but that hope had dimmed. Through their isolationism, she felt, her countrymen were shirking their share of the great task. "I wonder," she wrote Mr. Neve in that summer, "how much America's self-centered attitude has to do with her conditions of freezing winters and drought-ridden summers just now." In her mind such physical ills could be, and probably were, linked to a blindness to spiritual truth. Still, she could not be downhearted for long. The very fact that the Christ mind *was* coming to men could be the reason for the troubled times, the wars and rumors of war, even though there appeared to be little evidence of the millennium at present. It comforted her greatly to think of Mr. Neve and to remember that "the effectual fervent prayer of a righteous man availeth much."

The year 1937 was no prelude to the millennium; it was the lull before the storm. Unknown to most of those involved, it was also the year of the last best chance of avoiding war.

"Self-centered" as the United States might be, Nancy came more and more to agree with Philip that, as she told the House: "The only chance of real peace in the world is in the British Commonwealth of free nations and the United States holding the ring, and then . . . other countries will come in."

Since a visit to southeast Europe in 1936, Waldorf's hopes for a settlement had hinged on economic adjustment, and here he found ample support in America. It was a favorite theory of the Next Five Years Group that increased trade, by reducing pressure for territorial change, would also reduce the danger of war. Philip had advanced the same thesis in his Burge Memorial Lecture in 1935: "Mankind can now only live in peace and prosperity if the constant [economic] adjustments which are necessary inside the state are also made in the international sphere." Waldorf saw Cordell Hull's policy of lowering trade barriers not only as a step in the right direction in itself but also as a means of drawing the United States onto the international scene. It was with this object in view that Norman Davis arrived in London in the spring of 1937. Davis had been FDR's original choice for Secretary of State, but on the advice of Felix Frankfurter he had been eliminated as being too close to the world of banking to be acceptable in a New Deal cabinet. The President, however, used him frequently as a personal emissary, particularly in his dealings with London. In March Philip had told Halifax that "Roosevelt is looking for an opportunity to do something for peace on the international front." Halifax at this time was in the cabinet as Lord Privy Seal, and often deputized for Eden at the Foreign Office. The next month Norman Davis was sent to London as a delegate to a conference on sugar then taking place, but also with instructions to sound out the British government in regard to a possible world economic conference which the President himself would attend.

Naturally the Astors rallied round to forward such a project. At luncheon at 4 St. James's Square with Philip, Davis, and Tom Jones, it was agreed that T. J. should arrange a meeting of the American envoy with the Prime Minister, with a view to planning preliminary talks with the President. Mr. Baldwin "thought there might be some advantage" in a talk, but the prospect of his actually leaving the country for any purpose more strenuous than taking the waters at Aix did not seem at all likely. They next tried Mr. Chamberlain. The idea of going to the States seemed to appeal to him—in fact, Mrs. Chamberlain had said, "Neville, I think you should go"—when Davis suggested that some modification of the Ottawa tariffs would be a welcome preliminary. At this a pall fell over the luncheon table. It was a few weeks after this meeting that Chamberlain became Prime Minister. Very shortly afterward (July 8) he wrote to Norman Davis postponing the proposed visit.

Early in May Philip made one last effort to get through to Hitler. Even to the congenital optimist he was, this had become a rather tired hope. On his return he reported that "temper in Germany is changing. . . . If we are confronted by . . . a predatory combination of military imperialist powers . . . then Great Britain should herself organize a definite military alliance."

Nancy, in Virginia with her brother Buck that spring, had been warned by Philip not to rock the boat by speaking publicly on the subject of their dearest hope, an international conference in which America should take part, but in private with the President she could say what she liked

Roosevelt always looked forward to their meetings. In April a friend had written him, "I have a not altogether diplomatic message for you from Nancy Astor." "I am curious to know," wrote back FDR, "what the scurrilous message is from Nancy." When she was in Virginia in June she wrote for an appointment. ("If you are too busy I will understand. Gosh! The heat of my beloved Virginia in June is something I had forgotten! But I am glad to be here with my brother. Love to Madam President.") Roosevelt memoed to his secretary, Marvin McIntyre, "I want to see her before she goes back. Will you fix a time?"

At the time of this meeting Roosevelt was being attacked in the press about as viciously as the Astors were, on their side of the water, by Claud Cockburn. While Cliveden was being called "Schloss Cliveden" and "Britain's second Foreign Office," Roosevelt was labeled "a traitor to his class," "a war monger," and, with inexpressible venom, "that man in the White House." In an interview with the *Washington Star* Nancy spoke out of fellow feeling: "It's a remarkable thing that a man so hated can keep from hate himself. It's a wonderful thing to be able to not hate back." She sent a copy to Marvin McIntyre with a note attached addressed to "Dear Fellow Virginian," a touch that would have been forever lost if the President himself had not deciphered her impossible handwriting, adding a gallant postscript for Mac's benefit: "This gives you a chance to write her a *billet-doux*."

Underneath all these pleasant personal exchanges was the serious business of drawing the two countries together, with the hope that economic adjustment and even "peaceful changes" in Europe might yet take place without plunging the world into war.

Roosevelt, rebuffed by Chamberlain on July 8, wrote again on July 28, leaving the door to a later visit as wide open as was consistent with any sort of national dignity. Not until two months later, with only the briefest and most offhand reference to his incredible delay, did Chamberlain definitely decline the President's invitation. After some extremely faint expressions of good will he gave Roosevelt his usual recommendation: to "wait a little longer." His real evaluation of the American offer may be seen in a private letter written to his American cousin Mrs. Morton Prince a few months later: "It may well be that a point will be reached when we shall be within sight of agreement [with the dictators]. . . . In such an event a friendly and sympathetic President might be able to give just the fresh stimulus we required, and I feel sure that the American people would feel proud if they could be brought in to share in the final establishment of peace." Junior, the Prime Minister seemed to say, might be allowed to help, but he was definitely not expected to take the initiative. This presumably was to be left to older and wiser heads such as Mr. Chamberlain's own. In his talk with Philip, Hitler had expressed doubt "whether U.S.A.

would depart from its policy of absolute detachment." He could hardly have imagined that the Prime Minister of Great Britain was busily engaged in preventing this departure from taking place!

In the meantime Philip had been carrying on a running debate on this very subject with Lord Robert Cecil in the Lords. Cecil was courteous, soft-spoken, and deadly in debate. Such a man contrasted nicely with Philip's open style and was, moreover, a foeman of his own intellectual caliber, something not frequently found in the Upper House. There was a particularly sharp exchange on March 2, 1937, in which Philip was handicapped because he did not feel free to give full weight to the probability of American cooperation in the very near future. Any hint in advance might easily have compromised a project still in its delicate formative stage.

Lothian (near the close of his speech): "It is not inconceivable that the United States would be willing to extend the Monroe Doctrine sufficiently to make possible cooperation between the United States Navy and ours to prevent an explosion either in the Far East or of Europe across the seas."

Cecil: "My noble friend Lord Lothian's proposal is, to my mind, at any rate, an entirely novel one. . . . Indeed it is one of the great charms of his speaking that every time he speaks he has a new principle for dealing with the new situation in which we find ourselves. But this particular novelty seems to me, I must say, more ingenious than plausible. He says that the right thing is to have an Anglo-American Alliance."

Lothian: "No, I never said anything of the kind, and I do not believe in it at all."

Cecil: "I have used the wrong word. It is an Anglo-American understanding by which the two countries shall act together. Will that do?"

Lothian: "If I may say so, that we should not form part of the European Alliance system and that America should not form part of it either."

Cecil: "Now I venture to think that any system which is going to be based on Anglo-American cooperation in any practical sense is really not a thing which is worth considering."

Thus did Lord Cecil dispose of America. It was not the first time he had disposed of a rather large slice of the world's population. After four years as Minister of Blockade in World War I, Cecil, as related by Professor Toynbee, was shown a map of Austria. He not only did not recognize it, but at first refused to credit that this was one of the countries he had been blockading. Finally convinced that he was indeed looking at Austria he had said ruminatively, half to himself, "What a funny shape Austria must be." "The English," quoted Toynbee, "are they human?" An irresistible question, taken by Toynbee from the title of a popular book.

What Lord Cecil had failed to grasp and what Philip himself had not been able to fully reveal was the extent of his hopes from Anglo-American cooperation. A basic tenet of his thinking in regard to the United States was that the maritime neutrality on which Americans set such store was really dependent on British cooperation, just as the effectiveness of Great Britain on the seas depended on American cooperation. This, as he told Smuts, constituted the common ground between them, and this made an alliance of sorts the most natural thing in the world—indeed, almost inevitable. However, there was one hitch, a possible development of British foreign policy which, as Philip saw it, might torpedo the whole prospect of joint Anglo-American action. A firm British commitment to intervene in Eastern Europe, which might oblige her to take part in a local war over a perfectly legitimate readjustment of frontiers, would prevent the overt statement of common aims by the United States and Britain. He did not wish to call such a statement an alliance, especially then, when the whole project hung in the balance, but an alliance for peace it would most certainly have been. In the case of a large general war to prevent German domination of Europe it would become, as it later actually did become, an alliance for war. It was Philip's not unfounded belief that the alliance for peace which Lord Cecil so belittled could have saved the world from its second great war.

The business of drawing the United States into an active international role, if not a specific Anglo-American alliance, hung in the balance during these months. In October Philip had another talk with Hull. In his famous "quarantine" speech of October 5, the President went far indeed, further in fact than political prudence dictated, in condemning the dictators. Hull, at this time, was dragging his feet, not quite imaginative enough to follow the President's lead. FDR's chief and almost sole supporter in the foreign policy field was now the Under Secretary of State, Sumner Welles. Welles, like Roosevelt himself, was the correct but not unadventurous product of an upper-class background and a Groton-Harvard education. Between them they came very near to meeting and even exceeding Philip's fondest hopes. In the "quarantine" speech the President specifically condemned the invasion of territory in violation of treaties and gave the dictators an unmistakable warning against further interference in the internal affairs of other nations. The United States, while avoiding war, intended to cooperate with other peace-loving nations in the search for peace. "Some of President Roosevelt's sentences," Philip wrote in the *Observer*, "have almost the authentic Wilsonian ring."

The President, who described himself as "an impatient soul," was not one to wait on Chamberlain's dilatory tactics. His speech was followed by a proposed peace plan, drafted by Welles, but unfortunately never implemented. On Armistice Day, November 11, that day dedicated to those who had given their lives to abolish war, the plan proposed that the President call a meeting of the diplomatic corps in Washington, representing all the nations of the world. Welles outlined an agenda: "Ways and means should be discussed [to obtain] an ultimate international economy based on reduced armaments, a greater common use of world resources, and the improvement and simplification of economic relationships between all peoples." The President intended to ask for an agreement on four major points: (1) essential principles of international conduct, (2) most effective methods for achieving limitation of armaments, (3) equal economic opportunity for all nations, and (4) humanitarian measures in the event of war. Stressing point three particularly, this can be said to represent the Cliveden program.

Hull panicked. He demanded that the President consult British and French leaders before taking such an initiative. The Roosevelt plan would have brought America into the lists as nothing else would have done, and this was clearly as distasteful to Chamberlain as it would have been to Hitler. Neville Chamberlain had already made up his mind to political concessions to the Rome-Berlin Axis which certainly disregarded both the sanctity of treaties and the territorial integrity of independent nations. In plain language he considered such concessions to be no one's business but his own. On his own line he was not slow to act and now sent Halifax to Berlin.

The Halifax trip drove Cockburn to a veritable frenzy of fabrication. "The conspiracy continues," proclaimed the November 17 issue of *The Week*. Cockburn accused Halifax of going to Berlin to give Hitler "a free hand to attack countries in Eastern Europe" in return for a ten-year colonial truce. This extraordinary plan "was first got into viable diplomatic shape at a party at the Astors' place at Cliveden on the week end of October 23rd–24th." There was no shadow of truth, not even of Cockburn's usual half-truth, in any of this. There was no "political" person present at the stated weekend other than Eden, who was generally, though mistakenly, considered to be opposed to the Halifax trip. In this instance the Astors had hoped to act as a bridge between Eden and the Prime Minister, a relationship already shaken by Chamberlain's increasing tendency to bypass his Foreign Secretary. Eden did in fact seek out Halifax, cautioning him to warn the Germans off Austria and Czechoslovakia. Halifax was in perfect agreement. His diary repudiated, in no uncertain terms, the Cockburn idea of a deal as "neither very moral nor very attractive."

Although Roosevelt had been persuaded by his "almost hysterical advisers" to give up the dramatic target date of November 11, he did approach Mr. Chamberlain again, on January 12, 1938. This time the Prime Minister did not delay. Instead he seized the opportunity given him by Eden's absence on a brief holiday to once again bypass his Foreign Secretary and shoot back to Washington a decisive and very revealing negative. He told the President that he was in the middle of negotiations with Italy through which he anticipated an "appeasement." He was prepared, he said, to recognize *de jure* Italian conquest of Abyssinia. In other words, he was willing to go very much more than halfway and to negotiate virtually on the dictator's terms. Even at this time he had gone beyond the sort of economic concessions the Astors and Lothian had in mind. In fact, Mr. Chamberlain was already more than halfway to Munich. There is no doubt that in his sublimely self-confident letter to the President he had thrown away England's greatest opportunity. Churchill, in his book *The Gathering Storm*, describes the situation well: "We must regard [America's] rejection—for such it was—as the loss of the last frail chance to save the world from tyranny otherwise than by war."

Later that month the Astors were again in America, having tea at the White House. (Nancy had informed Marvin McIntyre, "We don't take tea, but if it's all the President can do, we'll drink it.") At this meeting Waldorf, knowing nothing of the Chamberlain correspondence, anxiously asked Roosevelt if he thought there was anything the American people could do in the cause of peace.

"Not at this time," the President answered. He added that the initiative would be best received if it came from America. The presence of Mr. Chamberlain, like that of the Cheshire cat, can be felt rather than seen in the background of this scene.

Quite apart from Cockburn and the political disappointments of that year, 1937 had not been a happy time for Nancy. Her beloved Phyllis had died in January, and now Buck, Nancy knew in her heart, was also dying. She had sailed to America to be at his side. Buck, most purely happy and unselfish of mortals, the brother with whom "Nannie" never quarreled, was seriously ill with tuberculosis in the Blue Ridge Sanatorium in Charlottesville. Their last time together was as gay as ever—Buck, dying, was still Buck—but the family did sometimes wish that Nannie could be a little less of a militant Christian Scientist. Her last letter to him poured out a mixture of her religion and her human love. "Your spirit is free and God is spirit and no operation can touch the real you. . . . I do want to be with you—not because you need me, but because I love you so dearly. Buck Buck my darling brother. Get well."

Immediately after her return she was to be invested as a Companion of Honor. On the morning of the ceremony she had awakened, weeping, from a dream of Phyllis. Grieving, Mrs. Eddy said, is wrong, but perhaps Nancy's dream reflected her deepest need more accurately than did the teaching of Mrs. Eddy. Waldorf too was ill from time to time, but this could not be admitted. Nancy believed that whenever we are sick, or sinful, or unhappy, or even poor, it is only because we have forgotten that we are the sons of God. Waldorf, waking early and often breathing with difficulty, would start work at five in the morning, sitting propped up in bed and wearing his old blazer of the Eton pale blue. His secretary would find him there when she arrived in the morning. One day, feeling sorry, she brought him a bunch of violets. Waldorf was touched. It was the sort of thing Nancy did not do.

13

1938: The Fatal Year

In February Eden resigned as Foreign Secretary, an event which *The Week* attributed entirely to Cliveden's plots and strong-arm methods. This was a rather difficult feat as Cliveden had been closed, Philip had been in India, and the Astors in America during and for some months before the resignation. Actually Nancy had been shocked by the news. Interviewed by reporters on her return to England, she attributed it to Eden's being "young and overwrought, worn to a shadow by his work for peace." There was no truth, she said, to the rumor that he had been forced out. If he had been, his friends would have gone with him. She believed that he had resigned "upon a tiny issue." This was of course the government line, but Eden had encouraged it. His discretion had been absolute. No one, least of all the Astors, knew of Roosevelt's proposal and of Chamberlain's treatment of his Foreign Secretary.

At the time all this seemed more like an episode of domestic politics than the severe crisis of foreign policy it actually was. Hitler had been relatively quiet for two years, but how long would he remain so? His ambassador, the oily von Ribbentrop, remained a not very popular fixture of London society. This ex-champagne salesman combined Teutonic earnestness with an unpleasant slickness. Nancy had once demanded across the dinner table, "Aren't you a damn bad ambassador?" On his asking "Why?" she answered, "Because you have no sense of humor." Ribbentrop replied that not everyone could be as humorous as Lady Astor, but he just wished she could see the Führer and himself, and "how we both roar with laughter." He had once been taken to visit Blickling, and the awe which fell upon him as the great house came in view had never quite left him. Since then his assurances of the Führer's love of art and devotion to peace rose to great eloquence in his conversations with Lord Lothian. Philip had devoted some time to him, extracting earnest, if worthless, assurances that Hitler would never violate the territorial integrity of his neighbors.

On the morning of March 11 Ribbentrop was preparing to return to Berlin. T. J., Inskip, and Waldorf Astor breakfasted pleasantly at the embassy, where no sign appeared to disturb the early morning tranquillity. Waldorf left the company to go on to Plymouth, unaware, as apparently was von Ribbentrop himself, that German armor was preparing to move across the Austrian border. In Berlin Hitler, against the advice of his generals, moved with instant speed. The Anschluss was part of a long-range plan, but its exact timing was a move on a chessboard against his opponents in the army. It was all part of the German madness, of the incipient schizophrenia that left the logical British in a state of utter confusion. On the following day the Chamberlains were giving a farewell luncheon party for the von Ribbentrops at number 10 Downing Street when telegrams announcing the invasion were handed to the Prime Minister. Winston Churchill was among the guests and gives an entrancing description of the occasion.

> Sir Alexander Cadogan . . . got up, walked round to where the Prime Minister was sitting, and gave him the message. . . . The meal proceeded without the slightest interruption, but quite soon

Mrs. Chamberlain, who had received some signal from her husband, got up, saying, "Let us *all* have coffee in the drawing-room." We trooped in there, and it was evident to me and perhaps to some others that Mr. and Mrs. Chamberlain wished to bring the proceedings to an end. A kind of general restlessness pervaded the company, and everyone stood about ready to say good-bye to the guests of honour.

However Herr von Ribbentrop and his wife did not seem at all conscious of this atmosphere. On the contrary, they tarried for nearly half an hour engaging their host and hostess in voluble conversation. At one moment I came in contact with Frau von Ribbentrop, and in a valedictory vein I said, "I hope England and Germany will preserve their friendship." "Be careful you don't spoil it," was her graceful rejoinder. I am sure they both knew perfectly well what had happened, but thought it was a good manoeuvre to keep the Prime Minister away from his work and the telephone. At length Mr. Chamberlain said to the Ambassador, "I am sorry I have to go now to attend to urgent business," and without more ado he left the room. The Ribbentrops lingered on, so that most of us made our excuses and our way home. Eventually I suppose they left. This was the last time I saw Herr von Ribbentrop before he was hanged.

The Führer's blatant use of force was extremely embarrassing to the Prime Minister. It made him very unhappy, but he was still deeply convinced that war solved nothing. He was not about to fight, either for Austria or for Czechoslovakia. This he made perfectly clear, only a week after the unhappy luncheon party, in a letter to his sister Ida. "Czechoslovakia would simply be a pretext for going to war with Germany. That we could not think of unless we had a reasonable prospect of being able to beat her to her knees in a reasonable time, and of that I see no sign. *I have therefore abandoned any idea of giving guarantees to Czechoslovakia, or to France in connection with her obligations to that country* [italics added]." In his speech to the House on March 24 he made the explicit point: There would be no promise to come automatically to the aid of France if she were called upon to help Czechoslovakia.

The Prime Minister felt that he knew a better way, the way of personal diplomacy. He had experienced intense frustration with Eden, whose opposition, Chamberlain thought, had prevented *rapprochement* with Mussolini before the collapse of

Austria. It was Chamberlain himself who engineered the dismissal of Eden and substituted the temperate Halifax at the Foreign Office. As a result the Prime Minister now had the field to himself. No doubt a large part of Chamberlain's success in getting his own way was due to his skill in keeping his real policy under cover.

Like everyone else, Philip was ignorant of the President's offer. Speaking in the Lords in mid-February, almost a month before the Anschluss, he had made his position clear: "I am not an isolationist . . . nor am I a pacifist. . . . Unless the democracies are willing to face the obligations of war, they will be driven inexorably to retreat in face of the menaces we have seen applied to Austria."

After the Anschluss on March 11 an effort to organize defense was made at Cliveden. On March 26 a large party gathered there with the express purpose of encouraging Mr. Chamberlain to adopt positive measures. This in turn touched off the ire of *The Week*. "The creation of no less than three new ministerial offices is what has been under discussion—not least at Schloss Cliveden over the weekend. . . . A minister for the coordination of industrial defense, a minister for the coordination of military defense, another for the coordination of information. The presence of the Prime Minister at Cliveden was a political gesture directed at Berlin and Paris." For once the facts, if not the last inference, were correct. The difference was that to Cliveden these preparations meant strengthening the country against Hitler, while to *The Week* they appeared as a nefarious capitalist plot to conscript labor and control the working man. Although he was tactfully permitted to win at musical chairs, there seems to have been little other result of this effort to influence the Prime Minister. Mr. Chamberlain had already made up his mind; injury to trade, not German arms, was the threat from which he must protect his country.

By April Hitler was stamping with impatience. Although temporarily restrained by his generals and the condition of his armor, he issued a top-secret directive to all three services declaring his "unalterable decision to smash Czechoslovakia by military action in the near future." The atmosphere of crisis disturbed Chamberlain, who complained to his sister of "how utterly untrustworthy and dishonest the German Government is." Nevertheless he could not relinquish the idea of appeasement. This was the situation in May when the Astors, still hoping to sell the Prime Minister to America and America to the Prime Minister, arranged a luncheon for Mr. Chamberlain and the members of the transatlantic press.

On assuming office in 1937, Chamberlain had made it clear that he meant to be his own Foreign Secretary, and it is now generally agreed that he alone was the arbiter of British policy before Munich. He scarcely heeded his own cabinet and was certainly not affected by views expressed at Cliveden house parties.

The occasion of the press luncheon in May at 4 St. James's Square was typical of the Prime Minister's methods. Mr. Chamberlain, stiffly self-confident as usual, made a suggestion: Let the government of Czechoslovakia cede to the German Reich that part of her territory now occupied by the Sudeten Germans. No such demand had at that time been put forward by the Führer himself. Certainly the recommendation for an outright cession of territory bore no relation to the Astors' advocacy of "economic concessions" to Germany or to their long-held view that some autonomy for the Sudetens along Swiss cantonal lines was the answer to the problem of the German minority in Czechoslovakia. Less than two months before the Chamberlain statement, Waldorf had spelled out this policy in the Lords: "If it were possible to get the Czech majority government to grant to the German minority some measure of devolution and self-government, you would then have a situation in Czechoslovakia for which I believe nearly 100 per cent of the people in this country would be prepared to give a guarantee."

It should be possible at this time to identify three distinct positions held by Englishmen in regard to their foreign policy. One was Churchill's: unconditional containment of Germany and an all-out effort to rearm Britain. Another was the Astors' and Philip's view that economic concessions and possible constitutional reform on behalf of the German minorities might satisfy at least the moderate Germans and hence make war less likely. More important, it would satisfy the conscience of those English liberals who, like themselves, wished to see the injustices of Versailles rectified before drawing an absolute line against German expansion. They had not advocated the outright cession of Czech territory to Germany and were shocked when their old friend Geoffrey Dawson did so in his September 7 leader in the *Times*. They had supported defense expenditure and organization as strenuously and consistently as had Churchill himself. It was, in fact, their stand on defense that had incurred Cockburn's ire and been the original inspiration of the "Cliveden Set" conspiracy myth.

Chamberlain's position, also held consistently, was quite different. He believed that war might be averted by cession of territory, Abyssinia to Italy and the Sudetenland to Germany. He believed himself to be a "realist" and gave no sign, so far as I can detect, of any moral scruples regarding the justice of the arrangement. Both Chamberlain and the Astors were quite wrong in their appraisal of Germany's real intentions—neither form of appeasement had the slightest chance of success—but it is unfair to the Astors to equate their pre-Munich policy with the Prime Minister's.

Their efforts to influence Mr. Chamberlain were quite unavailing, and the attempt to introduce him to the ways of the American press ended in disaster. What had been planned simply as an opportunity for free discussion and exchange of views was turned by Mr. Chamberlain into an international incident. If he had swept all the crockery off the table onto the floor the crash could not have been louder. It was heard around the world, first in New York and Canada, and then in the House of Commons itself, and wherever these words of ill omen penetrated they were attributed to Astor influence.

Nowhere was the uproar louder or the reaction more unfair than in America. The *New York Times* came up with a particularly sweeping statement: "When men like . . . Lord Astor have political nightmares the ogre of their imagination is Russia, not Germany. Menace to their wealth, their social position, as they see it, is the creed of communism, and, in their minds, whatever endangers themselves endangers England." It would have been difficult indeed to substantiate this statement. If the editor of the *New York Times* had read the May–June issue of *International Affairs* he would have seen that Philip at that very moment was advocating a revived council of the League which should include Russia. Nancy herself did not like Stalin any better than she did Hitler, but when the pinch came she was not averse to a Russian alliance. Later on, when she gave a big luncheon party with Maisky, the Russian Ambassador, as guest of honor, she was heard to murmur: "I've got to be nice to that little man because he may become our ally in the war."

After the press luncheon Nancy did the best she could to gloss over the Prime Minister's shocking statement. In the House of Commons, under a storm of criticism, she tried to brazen out the whole episode by roundly declaring, "There is not a word of truth in it." When pressed she elaborated: The Prime Minister had indeed lunched with them, but he had not granted an interview. An interview "is a meeting arranged with a view of communication of information intended specifically to be made the subject of articles in the Press." The storm raised at this time was never quite to subside. Even the presence of the King and Queen dining with the Astors in order to confer upon them a sort of royal blessing failed to quell the Cliveden Set gossip. Later Nancy rather shrewdly pointed out that if they had been hatching a pro-Nazi plot they would hardly have invited American journalists to be present. But all was in vain. The Astors were never able to detach themselves from Mr. Chamberlain in the public mind. Like a great flapping black bird, he appeared to be tied around their necks forever.

The Week had succeeded beyond its wildest hopes. The Cliveden Set "was on every tongue; senators made speeches about it, and in those London cabarets where libel did not matter, songsters made songs about it." Photographers and reporters patrolled St. James's Square waiting to get shots of "The Set" going in or out of number 4. One day, when asked to give his name by a too-eager reporter, Geoffrey Dawson snapped out, "von Ribbentrop." It was the sort of sarcasm that did not endear him to those whose views differed from his own. Concerned friends wrote to Nancy from the States; that, and the *New York Times* piece, were the hardest to bear. To Felix Frankfurter she wrote: "I am neither a Communist [n]or a Fascist. . . . I loathe all Dictatorships whether of the Russian or the German type—They are all equally cruel." Always at her best when speaking directly to a friend, she stated the position clearly and simply: "As you know Philip Lothian and Waldorf have believed for about fifteen years that something should have been done in the reorganization of Europe, so as to rectify some of the mistakes of the Peace Treaties and remedy some of Germany's grievances. It was plainly impossible to keep Germany down. . . . Unfortunately by not making voluntarily certain concessions to Germany, we have made them feel that they can only get redress by force. A dangerous lesson or belief."

Frankfurter answered this letter by assuring her that he had written before the "silly chatter" about plots and conspiracies hatched at Cliveden had appeared in the American papers. It was not "conspiracy" but her rumored anti-Semitism that had distressed Frankfurter and roused his indignation, and the indignation of many others who now added anti-Semitism to the Astors' sins. A rather ambiguous statement ad-libbed by Nancy to a *New York Times* reporter was taken to be anti-Semitic. As quoted in the *Times*, she had "voiced a warning that the backers of anti-German feeling were overplaying their hands, and . . . if the Jews are behind it they are going too far, and they need to take heed. It will react against them." It was assumed by the American papers that she had meant to attribute anti-German feeling in America solely to Jewish propaganda, and that she had therefore condemned it. Actually she had meant to warn of the harm it would do to associate anti-German propaganda too closely with the Jews, as it would only strengthen the Nazi line that it was world Jewry and not the democracies *per se* that were against the Nazi abuses. This theory had been advanced by a German friend of her son David, Adam von Trott. Admittedly she had failed to make the point clear. It was a position later understood and adopted by Frankfurter himself in regard to American propaganda. He then made the point that Germans should not be encouraged to believe the Nazi myth that "this is a conflict . . . between Germans and Jews, not between Germany and the U.S. and the Allies of the U.S."

At the time of writing to Nancy, Frankfurter had not gone deeply into such subtle distinctions, but he did understand Nancy. He ended his letter to her with the purely personal conclusion: "People who do not know your warm qualities infer a sympathy on your part with Hitler's anti-Semitism which people like me, of course, know to be untrue." It was not her heart, he knew, but her unthinking statements that led her into trouble. As Mr. Sykes points out, she was not always able to make clear to others what seemed so obvious to herself, that is, that she was pro-Jew and at the same time pro-*Deutsch*, as she indiscreetly told Adam von Trott. But not pro-Nazi. It was perhaps not her fault that other people failed to make the distinction, so clear in her own mind, between the old liberty-loving, Protestant German culture and the Nazi aberration.

The promptings of her heart were certainly pro-Jewish. At the time of her letter to Frankfurter she had been busy getting after von Dircksen on behalf of Frankfurter's uncle. "I spoke to the German Ambassador. . . . and gave him, in no uncertain terms, our views of arresting aged scholars. He promised to do what he could. Three days afterwards, having heard no more, I talked to him again, and warned him that unless I received good news of Herr Frankfurter, I should go myself to Vienna." This, of course, was an individual case, and a human rather than a political reaction. Politically it would seem fair to say that she was pro-peace, peace with the pre-Nazi Germany, which, if she had only realized it, was now politically dead.

Frankfurter continued to believe that in Philip's case, at least, blindness to the threat of Hitlerism had been due to fear of the "bogey of Bolshevism." On a trip to Washington in December, 1938, Philip had met the famous jurist on the steps of the Justice Department and had raised his arm in a mock gesture of self-defense. They had a long conversation during which he convinced Frankfurter that he was, in Frankfurter's words, "as hot against Hitler as any of us." In a later letter to Frankfurter, Philip admitted that he had been blind, but insisted that the cause was not fear of Bolshevism but the desire to give Germany her rights as a sovereign nation. It was this that had caused many Englishmen, particularly liberals, to acquiesce in "Hitler's first successes, despite their dislike of his methods." He might have added that their friend Waldorf Astor, apparently alone among the Englishmen who had met Hitler, had had the courage to mention the mistreatment of the Jews.

During the summer of 1938 the atmosphere of crisis hardly disturbed the rhythms of daily life. Cliveden, ablaze with flowers, startled even Harold Nicolson with the splendor of the arrangements: "great groups of delphinium and tuberoses, great bowers of oleander." Cliveden parties continued to be lavish and political conversation to flourish. The Astors reposed less and less faith in their hope that Germany might be satisfied with what they thought of as her "legitimate demands." In February, 1938, Nancy had told her constituents, "The West Country knows that where there is Communism, Fascism, or Hitlerism freedom does not exist." Repeated envoys from German groups in opposition to Hitler were appearing in England during this period. Among them were Adam von Trott and Helmuth von Moltke, both known to Philip and the Astors. All these Germans bore the same message: England must take a stand, and then war might be prevented. British willingness to fight if pressed was a forthright position which Nancy was able to support without ambiguity. In 1938 she went to a conference of women in Copenhagen in order to tell them in no uncertain terms that Britons were not afraid to fight.

Chamberlain, on the other hand, still considered himself a realist in his desire to deal with those actually in power in Germany. Unfortunately he seemed to feel no doubt of his ability to do so. Beneath the surface events were moving far more quickly than anyone realized, for strangely enough it seemed to be the Prime Minister himself, confident of success, who wished to accelerate the process. In August Philip had been notified of his appointment as Ambassador-elect to Washington, but he had asked for leave to fulfill a previous commitment to lead the British delegation to a Commonwealth Conference on Foreign Affairs in Sydney. It was a natural move in a plan of long-term diplomacy, but events and Mr. Chamberlain outstripped him. "Beware of asking for time!" Mirabeau once exclaimed. "Disaster never gives it."

Disaster, prepared in greatest secrecy, was now approaching. Mr. Chamberlain had a "plan." In his private diary he described it as "so unconventional and daring that it rather took Halifax's breath away." This was, of course, a personal interview between the Prime Minister and Hitler. There was no doubt in his mind of what he meant to do there. He meant to capitulate. The Prime Minister reposed great faith in Hitler's view that Germany's greatest mistake had been the rejection by Bethmann-Hollweg of Joseph Chamberlain's earlier advances. "Old Joe" Chamberlain, father of Austen and Neville, had been a powerful political figure at the turn of the century. As Colonial Secretary he had worked assiduously behind the scenes ("in secret" is the phrase used by the *Encyclopaedia Britannica*) for an

Anglo-German alliance. He was convinced that this project held the key to world peace, and Neville was determined to repeat his father's offer.

Never, perhaps, has there been a sadder example of the legendary success of the younger son than in the case of Neville Chamberlain. Harold Nicolson, an observer of feline acuteness, remarked that Neville Chamberlain had "triumphed over the bullying of his father and the subtle hostility of his brother Austen." Their father had early decided that Austen was the heir apparent and that the lesser talents of his younger half-brother Neville should be devoted to the family business. In later years Neville was to repeat, in compulsive detail, a rather lack-luster version of his father's brilliant career. Joseph Chamberlain had made a fortune and a reputation for leadership in his native Birmingham; Neville made a respected place for himself in the same town. "Old Joe" had made protection and Empire preference a mighty Conservative crusade in 1903; Neville, in 1932, introduced import duties with a genuine surge of filial emotion. Now, six years later, he was to repeat another Chamberlain high point by offering Hitler an Anglo-German understanding.

Neville felt that he could not fail if he only let Hitler have his way in this little matter of Czechoslovakia. The Prime Minister was not unaware that there was an alternative—aligning Britain with France and together taking a strong stand against German aggression—but he never seriously considered it. In his case the threat of force would have been no more than a bluff, and when he considered, in the words of his biographer Macleod, that "it was not money but men with which we were gambling," he rejected the whole idea with a positive repulsion. These thoughts, crucial as they were, were Chamberlain's own. They were scarcely shared, much less discussed, even with the inner circle of the cabinet, now reduced to Simon, Halifax, and Hoare. Only his diary, and perhaps his sisters if they could read between the lines of his letters, was privy to the full inwardness of his "plan." Samuel Hoare, his agreeably pliant companion on early morning walks in St. James's Park, knew nothing in advance. As so often with the Chamberlains, it was a family affair.

On September 4 President Beneš, speaking for Czechoslovakia, upset the Führer by yielding to practically all the demands so far put forward by the Sudeten Germans. Only a hastily engineered incident could keep the Sudeten Czech battle alive. Any pretext would do. Actually Hitler was reduced to using an alleged blow from a riding whip by a Czech mounted policeman upon a Sudeten deputy. This was said to have occurred on September 7. All negotiations with the Czechs were immediately cut off from Berlin. Geoffrey Dawson, the erstwhile rebel of 1916, now showed himself to be almost mystically in tune with Mr. Chamberlain. Neither wished to wait for Hitler to spell out his demands. By anticipating them they no doubt felt that they would in some measure regularize what they no longer wished to prevent. The phrasing of the *Times* leader on the morning of September 7 had the maddening indirection and pomposity that were now characteristic of Dawson. "It might be worthwhile," he wrote, "for the Czechoslovak Government to consider whether they should exclude altogether the project, which has found favor in some quarters, of making Czechoslovakia a more homogeneous state by the cession of that fringe of alien population who are contiguous to the nation with which they are united by race." This should be contrasted with Garvin's leader of September 4, which supported "Lord Runciman's scheme of cantonal self-government" and roundly declared that the British government would stand against an armed onslaught on Czechoslovakia "like a block of steel."

The Prime Minister, like the rest of England, had now to wait anxiously upon Hitler's speech to the party rally at Nuremberg on September 12. This was to fall with different emphasis on different ears. Perhaps those understood Hitler best who caught only the tone and could not follow the sense of the words. Howling imprecations against the Czech people and their leaders alternated with the savage *Sieg Heil*'s of the faithful. A typical reaction took place in Sussex, where the Macmillans, Harold and Lady Dorothy, had been joined by a country neighbor as they prepared to tune in on Hitler. At the end of the speech Lord Cecil, who had been stretched at full length on the sofa, "slowly uncoiled himself from his recumbent position. He said, gravely and slowly, 'This means war.'" But in Downing Street, to Neville Chamberlain's strained attention, one thing alone was clear: Hitler had not asked for a transfer of territory, not even for a plebiscite. Vis-à-vis the other powers he was exercising caution. The Prime Minister of Great Britain heaved a sigh of relief. He could still feel himself a free agent, the voluntary bearer of an olive branch. The success of the traditional Chamberlain policy was almost within his grasp.

During these brief and fatal moments before the Berchtesgaden meeting consternation spread in high places, the sense of helplessness coming perhaps with greatest force upon those who, because they had continued to hope, were now the least prepared. Whether or not they had been whistling in the dark, the Astors had been genuinely convinced that Hitler was not going to march. But when Beneš had offered the Sudeten Germans in his country local autonomy—the whole, in fact, of that justice which Cliveden had so long considered the key to peace—they saw that it made not the slightest difference; Hitler was threatening to march just the same.

On the weekend of the tenth and eleventh, Parliament was in recess. Waldorf, Nancy, and T. J. retired to the long low house by the sea at Sandwich which had sheltered, in its time, so many of England's great. The Channel waters lapped at their doors, but no one knew what was transpiring on the other side. On Sunday morning newspapers, as usual, were being read all over the house. Lloyd George said in the *Sunday Express* that England was morally bound to support the Czech offer. All, in fact, were agreed. Garvin, in Waldorf's own *Observer*, had put it magnificently: "The frontier concessions remove every rag or shred of pretext for war. In these . . . circumstances an armed attack by the Greater Reich upon Czechoslovakia . . . would be without exception . . . the greatest crime that was ever committed in the world's history." Garvin went even further, making it quite clear that the *Observer* had no sympathy with Dawson's bland suggestion in the *Times* of September 7 that the Sudetenland be ceded to Germany. On the contrary, Garvin said: "Any diplomatic attempt to break up Czechoslovakia by surrendering the Sudetenlands to the Reich—lands which on three sides are the strategical keys to the whole—would mean world war as surely as the launching of armies." This was unequivocal. It underlined the divergence of the Astor line from Dawson's. At Sandwich they deplored the September 7 leader. T. J., for one, preferred to believe that Dawson himself could not have been responsible, a theory that was invalidated by the extant corrections in Dawson's handwriting.

Nothing was sure, all was rumor and opinion. First-hand information came to Sandwich at last, in the person of Bob Boothby, who arrived from London for tea. Boothby was a dissident Conservative who supported Eden and Churchill rather than the Prime Minister. He was also a good friend of the Astors. He now confirmed their worst fears. He described the cabinet as weakening in its opposition to the use of force by Germany; Nevile Henderson, the British Ambassador in Berlin, had not seen Hitler himself but only von Ribbentrop. Hoare and Kingsley Wood were against war in any circumstances. There was no certainty, therefore, that Hitler realized that if he used force against the Czechs and if France took action England would join in.

Boothby's statements did in fact reflect the position taken by most of the cabinet. The little group at Rest Harrow were indignant and struck by something like panic. Boothby and Nancy went to work on T. J., intermediary *par excellence.* They wanted him to go up to London to see what he could do with Horace Wilson of the Prime Minister's staff, known to be the one man Chamberlain listened to. T. J. and Waldorf left for London that evening, making their way through the returning Sunday traffic. This last-minute task force got no nearer to the Prime Minister than Inskip, who had no further news other than to report that the U.S.A. was very friendly, holding forth in "language of fervor, full of moral content." "Fine," said Waldorf. "For once there was a chance of British and American opinion coinciding and we should take the fullest advantage of it." It was all remote from the scene of action and intensely frustrating. Yet these two troubled and helpless men were popularly supposed to be manipulating the reins of government behind the scenes!

The last realistic chance of stopping Mr. Chamberlain had come and gone. It was in fact lost in the twenty-four hours after the Nuremberg speech. During that time Daladier had weakened, placing France's responsibility totally in the hands of the British. Chamberlain was now where he wanted to be: on his own, no longer forced to consider France, and virtually beyond the control of a shaken and unhappy cabinet. On the thirteenth he sent off a letter to Hitler proposing an immediate meeting between the Führer and himself. The tragic farce called Munich was about to go on the road.

14

Munich

On the morning of September 15 a gentleman in late middle age, accoutered in the formal black overcoat and furled umbrella of Britain's middle class, stepped aboard a British Airways plane at Heston Airport, bound for Munich. Could anyone have stopped him? Mr. Chamberlain himself was quite determined that no one should. High-handed as Hitler was, and high-handed and secretive as was Chamberlain, these two men could not have presided at the rape of Czechoslovakia if the moral climate of their two countries had not permitted it. It was in the Bendlerstrasse (war ministry) in Berlin and in Whitehall and Westminster and the City that the true drama of September, 1938, was played out.

Some, but certainly not all, Britons were aware of what was happening, but issues were carefully concealed from the average Englishman. His leaders, whether Conservative or Labour, simply had no heart to say to him, twenty years after the close of the most frightful war in history, "You must fight again." On the other side of the Channel there was no such possibility of mistaking the leader's purpose. Indeed, it was not any need to defer to Chamberlain but his own people who forced Hitler to forego even the tiniest fraction of the coming triumph. His generals were opposed to the attack, and even as Hitler was exclaiming in joy at the news of Chamberlain's coming they were plotting against him in the Bendlerstrasse. If there was one time more than any other in which Hitler came close to being checked this was it, and ironically the attempt was made from the German side. On the fourteenth there was a well-organized plot among high-ranking officers of the Wehrmacht to remove Hitler before he could give the order to march. Halder, Chief of the General Staff, and Witzleben, commander of the Berlin area, were actually in readiness, waiting only for Hitler's return to Berlin to launch the *coup*. Then the news of Chamberlain's surprise visit burst upon them. If the British Prime Minister could stop Hitler there was no further need for the generals to depose him. The *Generalität* were not revolutionaries; they were simply leaders of an elite group, the German Officer Corps, who felt themselves responsible in a way unknown to democratic armies for their country's future. If Mr. Chamberlain could prevent what they believed would be Germany's military ruin, they might continue to abominate Hitler the man but felt no imperative to destroy Hitler the leader. In fact the whole position would be reversed, and the moment would have become most inopportune. The *coup*, therefore, must wait upon the outcome of the meeting between the Führer and the Prime Minister.

In spite of his confidence, Hitler was justifiably a bit nervous at the beginning of the Berchtesgaden meeting. In due time, however, to Chamberlain's satisfaction, "they . . . got down to the crux of the matter," which was, precisely, Hitler's demand for the secession of the Sudeten German regions. To this Chamberlain replied that "he could state personally that he recognized the principle of ceding the Sudeten areas." As he later confided to his sister, he "didn't care two hoots whether the Sudetens were in the Reich or out of it." Everything, indeed, had occurred just as he had planned it. "On the way downstairs," he told his sister, Hitler "was much more cordial than on going up. . . . I had established a certain confidence. . . . Up to now"—and this is the key phrase in this whole letter, so full of self-congratulation—"things are going the way I want."

As the two men sparred at Berchtesgaden, crowds of silent supplicants kneeled in Westminster Abbey, praying for peace. In the City of London there was an upsurge of prices on the Stock Exchange, which did not, however, last out the day. In Sydney, Philip, sitting with the Commonwealth premiers, was concluding that "had the Czechoslovakian crisis ended in war, I have no doubt that Australia and New Zealand would have entered at once on the British side." While the conference in Sydney was still in session, Nancy wrote him a worried letter telling him how things were actually going at home. On the sixteenth he took time out to write her his personal view that Chamberlain's travels were "terribly likely to lead to another Hoare-Laval plan." His views on the subject are unequivocal:

> Hitler, I fancy, holds all the military cards unless we are prepared for a World War to stop Nazi expansion. He won't budge and therefore Neville will be forced to offer a compromise. That, if it is to suffice, will let down the Czechs and split the united country and world he now has behind him, or if it does not suffice to bring Hitler to abandon his designs on the Sudeten Germans in Czechoslovakia, will still leave us confronted with the necessity of world war if we are to stop him, in effect breaking up Czechoslovakia and bring[ing] all Eastern Europe not into a sphere of influence but under his control.
>
> It's a horrible dilemma. But having got so far as we have I'm inclined to think that rather than split the country and the democratic world by immoderate concessions we ought to say that if Hitler invades Czechoslovakia it means war.

Chamberlain was plunging into the very sort of intervention that Philip dreaded. As Philip was imparting these views to Nancy Astor, the Prime Minister, returning from Berchtesgaden, was responding graciously to the welcoming group at Heston. He expressed himself quite simply: he and Hitler now "fully understood what is in the mind of the other." Chamberlain had now to call together his cabinet and to consult with Daladier and Bonnet. In the inner cabinet, Simon, Hoare, and Halifax were all with Chamberlain, and the French soon made it clear that they intended to put on British shoulders the onus of France's abandonment of the ally to which she was bound by treaty. Mr. Chamberlain did not hesitate to take upon himself the leading role in negotiation. Indeed, he welcomed it. At his insistence the Anglo-French plan was drawn up, to be handed the next day to the Czech government on a take-it-or-leave-it basis. All areas containing over 50 per cent German population were to be immediately handed over to the Reich. Czechoslovakia's special relations with France and Russia, her treaties of mutual assistance, were to be given up in favor of a general guarantee of her new frontiers. Germany was to be included among the guarantors. Thus was the fly given over to the protection of the spider.

These decisions were taken on Sunday the eighteenth. A pall had settled over London. The service of unbroken intercession in the Abbey seemed to have reached its Gethsemane, and thereupon to have lost its way. The Dean, in his sermon, "found it impossible to believe that the world was going to literally peter out in the welter of chaos and confusion that now confronts us." "O Lord," he cried, "Hear our prayer," but the prayer that he offered was only that God should show "a way of escape for us from the calamity that threatens to overwhelm us." Few stronger voices were heard in England that day. Churchill did speak out in the press and in Parliament, when Parliament was at last recalled, but Eden's silence, from the Roosevelt peace move on to Munich, was all Mr. Chamberlain could have wished. "Since American opinion has not been asked," the *Times* remarked smugly, "it is assumed that an expression of opinion at this time would hardly be expected."

On this day of near paralysis in England, Roosevelt, the "impatient soul," as he had described himself to Felix Frankfurter, had called the British Ambassador, Sir Ronald Lindsay, for a very confidential talk at the White House. Once again Roosevelt put forward his idea of a world conference "for the purpose of reorganizing all unsatisfactory frontiers on rational lines. They should invite active heads of states to attend including Herr Hitler." The President himself would attend if the conference could be held outside Europe, in the Azores or some other Atlantic island. Assuming, however, that war became inevitable, he advocated a blockade in which he said America would be able to take part. In was almost inconceivable that American troops should be sent across the Atlantic, but "if Germany were able to invade Great Britain . . . such a wave of emotion might arise that an American Army might be sent overseas."

"I do not think," the Ambassador postscripted to this message, "he expects any particular answer."

If Philip instead of Sir Ronald had been sitting across from the President during this conversation, it is unlikely that he could have moved the Chamberlain government to action. However, it is quite certain that his report would not have included the extraordinary postscript, with its suggestion that the American offer be allowed to drop. Halifax received the message on September 20 and answered, with unshatterable aplomb, on the twenty-third. "It is of great encouragement to know that the President has been giving thought to these questions."

On the twentieth the Czechs, understandably, turned down the Anglo-French plan. In its place they proposed a solution that Philip had earlier recommended: an arbitral award. This Mr. Chamberlain found intolerable. The next morning the Czechs were informed that they must accept the Anglo-French plan forthwith and that Mr. Chamberlain was again flying to Germany. The Czechs yielded unconditionally, agreeing to cede the German areas.

Nancy was "very much worried." The Lindberghs, who were living in England at the time, were at Cliveden for the weekend. In default of another and wiser airman, T. E. Lawrence, the Astors had sought him out as the expert most qualified to give advice on Britain's rearmament in the air. Lindbergh was hardly reassuring.

On this day, the twenty-first, Churchill issued a statement to the press: "The partition of Czechoslovakia under pressure from England and France amounts to the complete surrender of the Western Democracies." At Stratford-on-Avon Mr. Eden told the English-Speaking Union that it was "not yet too late for a change in outlook."

But it was. The Prime Minister's plane was already out of its hangar, being gassed up for the morrow's flight. In Godesberg hundreds of little flags, Union Jacks and swastikas, were waving gaily on the terrace of the Hotel Dreesen, where Herr Hitler was to receive his guest. On the morning of the twenty-second the *Times* carried colorful pictures of this resort town on the Rhine. In Prague on this same morning people were buying the early editions. Some threw their papers down in the street, many wept. The headlines said "Tragic Chapter Ended." "Absolutely Forsaken."

Hitler took Chamberlain by the arm, leading him up the steps in the most friendly fashion. The Führer, however, had a grievous shock in store for the Prime Minister. Hitler at once, and with hardly an apology, rejected the whole Anglo-French plan, which had not been intended to include immediate occupation by German troops. Nothing less would now satisfy the Führer. Mr. Chamberlain returned sorrowfully to his hotel on the opposite side of the Rhine, but even now he would not give up. The next day he returned to the conference table and in effect agreed to all of Hitler's demands, although he did obtain from the Führer a promise to postpone the proposed date of the German occupation from September 29 to October 1. Unknown to the Prime Minister, this was no real concession, for October 1 was actually the target date already named in Hitler's instructions to his reluctant generals.

By this time the Prime Minister had become more German than the Germans. His farewell words as he left the Dreesen were warm and cordial. He spoke of mutual confidence and of "other problems" that he would be glad to discuss with the Führer "in the same spirit." He was, of course, tired, but, as he was fond of saying, pleasantly tired. Before retiring for the night he told a reporter: "It is up to the Czechs now." He, Neville Chamberlain, had played his part. There was, of course, still the return to London, but he felt no serious doubt that his cabinet would go along.

The cabinet met at once, on the afternoon of his arrival, on the twenty-fourth. At first all went well. As Sir Alexander Cadogan remarked in a state of horrified shock, Chamberlain "was quite calmly for total surrender," and he had carried the others with him. Then something quite unforeseen happened. Halifax, the second in command, the man who normally turned over all decisions to his chief, had spent a sleepless night. Never, since his association with Gandhi, had public affairs cut right down to the core of principle in this highly principled man. At the cabinet the next morning, when Chamberlain asked his Foreign Secretary to lead off, Halifax came out for refusal of Hitler's terms. This defection of his most trusted lieutenant was the most serious check Chamberlain had encountered. The Czechs were mobilizing, trenches were being dug in Green Park, even Daladier had partially mobilized the French and was now using the strongest language he had yet employed about French intentions. Whether or not the Prime Minister took time out to read the four-column spread under Garvin's byline, he must have known, had he in fact cared, that the Astors too were against him. "According to the Godesberg Plan," Garvin wrote, "barriers among the strongest in Europe would in effect be thrown down for the convenience of Germany by French and British hands."

On the evening of the twenty-sixth, Hitler was again to address one of his vast Nuremberg rallies. The Astors had the discouraging company of the Lindberghs, who arrived before dinner. Lindbergh had been on an inspection trip to France and Czechoslovakia and came loaded with gloomy prophecies and unfavorable comparisons of the French and Czech air strength to the German. He found the company at Cliveden "pretty depressed." He confided to his journal that "Lord Astor and Mr. Jones felt it was necessary for England to fight if Germany moves into Czechoslovakia. Lady Astor against war at this time."

Nancy had buried her head in the sand. On that day, before the Lindberghs' arrival, she had written to Virginia, to Buck's youngest son: "This is a very important day in the history of the world. Tonight [when Hitler speaks] I suppose we shall know whether or not there is to be another world war. I can't believe, I won't believe that there will be." Her son Bill was present that evening. As an M.P. and reserve officer in naval intelligence he had made a study of the situation in Europe, and he too was of the opinion that war could be avoided. If Philip's presence at that critical time might not have influenced the government, he surely would have opened Nancy's eyes to Hitler's intentions, which he had clearly recognized in his letter to her of the sixteenth. However, Nancy and Bill were alone in their optimism, and Lindbergh found the general atmosphere of Cliveden that night to be against him. He argued that it is necessary to take stock of armaments before jumping into a war. "There was no use talking" he sadly concluded; "the spirit of the 'Light Brigade' had taken hold. Again, the English are ready to fight for their principles, throwing all judgment to the winds." In the *Times* that morning Leo Amery, former cabinet minister and old friend of the Round Table, had put it clearly: "It is not Czechoslovakia but our own soul that is at stake."

Hitler spoke at eight o'clock that evening. Everyone at Cliveden adjourned to the parlor to hear him. The Führer started slowly but soon resorted to the usual howls and snarls, interrupted by the cheers of the faithful. Two young German refugees present that evening took notes and translated the substance of what was said. Hitler had given his pledge: "That area which in its people is German and has the wish to be German comes to Germany. . . . But now, and that immediately. . . . It is our holy will."

But German troops had not yet marched! This was what mattered to Chamberlain; the field was still open for British initiative. He sent Sir Horace Wilson as his emissary to Berlin with further assurances that England would make the Czechs carry out their promises "fairly and fully." Hitler would hardly listen to the hapless messenger. He edged to the door even as Sir Horace was speaking, muttering "*Ich werde die Tschechen geschlagen*" ("I will smash the Czechs").

It was a restless night at Cliveden. They all went up to London in the morning, to be as near as possible to the center of events. Unknown to them, a change was to occur on this day, September 27, in Berlin. Hitler had confidently told Sir Horace that the whole of Germany was behind him, but this was not the case. On the afternoon of the twenty-seventh the flower of his army paraded in Berlin for three hours. He had meant to review the troops from the chancellory, but the cold hostility of the Berliners first stunned, then enraged him. He sat down at once to compose the shrewdly conciliatory letter which he dispatched that night to Chamberlain.

Chamberlain had reached the nadir of his personal hopes. Yet even now, in a speech broadcast to inform his people that war might be on the way, he could speak of "a quarrel in a faraway country between people of whom we know nothing." He continued to resist demands that Parliament be recalled. In London the people were miles ahead of the Prime Minister. They were queuing up for gas masks only to find the supplies exhausted. Nothing was to be learned in London, and the

Astors, accompanied by the Lindberghs, returned to Cliveden for the night.

The next morning Nancy received the long-awaited notice: Parliament was called in special session for that afternoon. One knew that within a few hours England might be at war. Members approached the House through a crowd standing vigil outside the gate at Westminster. Some had placed flowers at the Cenotaph, others simply stood and stared. Nancy took her place, as ignorant of the course of events as the crowd outside. The Prime Minister was not above playing on the state of ignorance and suspense in which he had for so long kept the House; Members were unaware that a conciliatory letter from Hitler had been delivered to Mr. Chamberlain at 10:30 that morning.

Chamberlain began his speech with a chronological statement of events. He said that his first conversation with Herr Hitler had convinced him that the Führer was prepared to risk a world war. A shudder of horror went through the House. He then spoke of the personal shock that he had sustained at Godesberg. "We were all," Harold Nicolson wrote in his diary, "aware that some revelation was approaching." Chamberlain began to speak of his final appeal to Herr Hitler and Signor Mussolini. It was twelve minutes after four. At that moment a piece of Foreign Office paper was being rapidly passed along the government bench and was finally handed to the Prime Minister by Sir John Simon. According to Nicolson, Chamberlain "adjusted his pince-nez. . . . His whole face, his whole body seemed to change. He raised his face so that the light from the ceiling fell full upon it. All the lines of anxiety and weariness seemed suddenly to have been smoothed out, he appeared ten years younger and triumphant. 'Herr Hitler,' he said, 'has just agreed to postpone his mobilization for twenty-four hours and to meet me in conference with Signor Mussolini and Signor [*sic*] Daladier at Munich.' "

Pandemonium broke loose on the floor of the House. All, or almost all, stood, cheering and throwing their order papers in the air. Some wept with relief. Churchill sat silent, his head sunk between his shoulders. Eden got up and walked out of the Chamber. In the diplomatic gallery Jan Masaryk, Ambassador of Czechoslovakia, stood alone looking down at the weeping, cheering throng below.

The meeting at Munich was a mere formality. It ended with an agreement which extended very slightly (by ten days) the timetable for the German occupation. The terms, however, were no less brutal. As has often been pointed out, not a single cow was to be evacuated by the Czechs, who must flee their homes with nothing but the clothes in which they stood up.

One last thing remained to be done, the crowning act of Chamberlain's policy. The Prime Minister had yet to obtain, in writing and for all the world to see, evidence of what this unpleasant sacrifice of a small faraway people really meant. Privately, indeed secretly, with the aid of no one but young William Strang from the Foreign Office, whose role was that of a mere secretary, Neville Chamberlain produced the Anglo-German Agreement, at long last the fruition of his father's policy. Never again, the paper said, would the peoples of Germany and England go to war with one another. It was this pathetic scrap that Chamberlain, his face wreathed in smiles, waved aloft at Heston Airport.

A surge of relief swept the country. For the time being the cup had been taken from their lips. For Nancy this was Chamberlain's moment. He became, as she later wrote to Philip in dismayed retrospect, her "blue-eyed boy."

No one at that moment spoke of the Cliveden Set, and yet the question must be asked: How much, or how little, did the Astors contribute to the disaster of Munich?

The Cockburn-inspired legend of a pro-Nazi group of conspirators at Cliveden has been, one hopes, permanently exploded. There was no such thing. But there was a body of opinion held by the Astors and their friends that could be loosely described as Cliveden opinion. They favored moderate, mostly economic, and actually long-overdue concessions to Germany. No doubt their opinions were misrepresented to Hitler. Cliveden was assumed, falsely, to represent a peace-at-any-price party in England. There never was any such party. Hitler was completely ignorant of British society. He had a ridiculously inflated idea, surely encouraged by Claud Cockburn's diatribes, of the influence exercised on policy by what he believed to be a powerful nobility. If Waldorf and Philip had still been Mr. Astor and Mr. Kerr, the myth of Cliveden's power might never have been born, either in England or in

Germany. It *was* born, however, and was widely circulated. One must admit that it probably did do a certain amount of harm in both countries, although it cannot have had decisive influence in either. The Chamberlain policy, by itself, was the critical factor, and with Chamberlain the Astors patently had no influence at all. Their only close friend in the government was Lord Halifax, and it is significant that Halifax alone of the "inner cabinet" made a stand against the Chamberlain policy during the negotiations and before the final capitulation at Munich. Even this had made no difference. It was not the Cliveden Set but the whole trend of reaction in England, her retreat behind economic and national barriers, that brought England to Munich. The Astors, on the contrary, had wished to look out on a wider world. They were wrong about Hitler's Germany; there is no doubt about that. They underestimated first Hitler's own intentions, and then his power over the German people. They had wished to offer Germany, not the military dominance Hitler desired, but a legitimate place in an economically reformed Europe. They were wrong, yes—but wrong for the right reasons. Hitler was not in the least interested in their reasons. Theirs was a tragic miscalculation at a vital point in British history.

15

The Spark of Freedom

THE Member for Epping, Mr. Winston Churchill, rose in the House. "We have sustained a defeat," he said, "an unmitigated defeat. . . . The utmost the Prime Minister has been able to gain for Czechoslovakia has been that the German dictator, instead of snatching his victuals from the table, has been content to have them served to him course by course."

"Don't be rude to the Prime Minister," shouted Nancy.

"No doubt the Noble Lady has been receiving very recently a finishing course in manners."

"From von Ribbentrop," shouted a Labour Member.

Nancy was reduced to crying "Nonsense!" It was not her finest hour. But as Churchill himself described the occasion, hers was not the only interruption. "The storm which met me made it necessary to pause for a while before resuming. There was widespread and sincere admiration for Mr. Chamberlain."

Nancy's support of the Prime Minister was warm, but even in the beginning it was provisional. The Astors believed in giving Chamberlain a chance to enforce such conditions as had been retained, at least purportedly, in the Munich settlement. At this point Waldorf joined Runciman and Hoare on a commission to see whether "economic concessions" might still lead to arms stabilization and peace in southeast Europe. His attitude was the fatalistic one, "What do we have to lose?"

For Philip Godesberg was the point of no return. Even before Godesberg he had written from Sydney, after Chamberlain's first trip to Berchtesgaden, "If . . . we run away now and do something which is tantamount to 'selling the pass,' the prestige of the totalitarian methods and powers will be such, and the derision and depression of the democracies so acute, that it will go hard with the old British Empire." He had been back in England only two weeks when he led off with a resounding series of *Observer* articles, the first one headlined: "Britain Awake." It made perfectly clear his rejection of what he now realized to be the settled policy of the German nation. "The Czechoslovak crisis was not concerned merely with Germany's right to unity and self-defense. It was a bid, and a successful bid, for military dominance. . . . What was even more significant, Hitler wanted to achieve his ends . . . by violence, for violence is the instrument of his creed."

In the face of such clear danger, Chamberlain failed to reform his government, nor did he push rearmament effectively. Harold Macmillan places the "nadir of appeasement" at the end of January, 1939. The Cliveden Set story had lain dormant for a time but was now revived vigorously by the press. At a meeting of a private club, the Romney Street Group, to which the Astors did not belong, Lindbergh had made some exaggerated claims for the German air force, which he appeared to think could annihilate Britain at will. Having no legitimate copy to use concerning Cliveden, the press simply adopted Lindbergh as a full-fledged member of the Set, describing his defeatist statements made at the meeting of the Romney Street Group as representing opinion at Cliveden.

The story, since it concerned two of their countrymen, was

given wide coverage in the American press. The Astors' helpless frustration may be imagined. Nancy, as she had formed the habit of doing in time of trouble, turned to GBS for advice. He agreed that something should be done to destroy once and for all the perennial myth of the Cliveden Set. Contrary to all Shavian custom, he sent an article for which he received no pay to the American magazine *Liberty*. "Machiavellian plots for the subjection of the German race to Fascist control!" Shaw scoffed at the idea. Lady Astor, he said, has no political philosophy at all. She "dashes at any kindly social work which presents itself, whether it is an installment of socialism or a relic of feudal patriarchalism." As to these so-called plots, he would as soon suspect President Roosevelt "of conspiring to revoke the Declaration of Independence."

Nancy followed this up by "interviewing herself," as the *Saturday Evening Post* put it, in one of their March issues. This was the last occasion on which the Astors responded publicly to the grotesqueries of the "Set" stories.

In the meantime Philip had pinned his hopes on American support. In December of 1939 he wrote to Lloyd George and Tom Jones from America: "If the President can get his ten thousand front-line planes into production in time there will be no war." The difficulty, as he admitted to Lloyd George, was "that public suggestions that the U.S. should get ready to help Great Britain do more harm than good. The only effective method is private conversation." Garvin's editorials during these months were very much in line with the Astors' views. He had hoped after Munich that Hitler might be contained, but by January he too doubted that the Chamberlain policy of "business as usual" could lead to anything but "progressive surrender."

It was not until the Nazi armies actually marched into Prague on March 15 that Nancy and Waldorf finally realized how futile their hopes had been. The next day Nancy rose boldly in the House to demand that the "Prime Minister lose no time in letting the German government know with what horror the whole of this country regards Germany's action." Some people thought it was rather late in the day. Speaking in the Lords in April, Waldorf made a formal confession of error. He had believed, or at least hoped, that economic concessions to Germany might prevent war. Now he saw that the only hope lay in a far stronger line:

> I believe that a declaration by His Majesty's government in the near future that it was their intention to call upon their country to give the whole of that which we possess, the whole of that which industry possesses, the whole of the manpower and wealth of this country, would have an enormous psychological effect, and would probably be the last chance, or one of the last chances, of preventing the outbreak of . . . war.

No one really in a position to know ever accused the Astors of lack of patriotism or of zeal to prosecute the war. Even so, although the Cliveden Set chatter may be disregarded, it is true that by 1938 Cliveden's heyday had passed. In its great period Cliveden had been what the Astors intended it to be, an open forum where all shades of opinion met, and where men of good will from all the nations of the world might talk to one another. It was a remarkable effort, an exercise in bridge building between nations. But all that was doomed by 1938, doomed to be swept away by the totalitarian flood.

Perhaps none of Cliveden's past successes is more worthy of praise than the abortive effort made there and at Blickling in 1939 to encourage the "other Germany." England at that time was a natural refuge for Germans fleeing from Hitler, and even more significantly for men opposed to the Nazis who might be expected to return to their homeland to defy Hitler on their own soil. Helmuth von Moltke and Adam von Trott, both at that time in England, were young Germans of this sort. The Astors and Philip believed in these young men. After all it was the Nazis, not all Germans, who must be crushed. They believed, and were ahead of their times in believing, that the crushing of bodies is not the only way to win a war. Minds must be won as well. The Round Table method of encouraging small groups in different countries dedicated to international cooperation was a tool ready to hand. It should not surprise us to learn that even in Nazi Germany in the midst of war, under daily threat of discovery, torture and death, such a group took shape.

The Kreisau Circle was one of many small isolated groups

of opposition to Hitler within Germany. Its leader, Helmuth James von Moltke, had had legal training both in Berlin and at the Inner Temple in London. He was an intimate friend of Lionel Curtis and spent much time at the Curtises' house at Kidlington, where conversations on federalism went on far into the night. Federalism was no alien concept to a German student of his nation's history, for until 1870 Germany had been simply a collection of autonomous states. As Hitler's determination to bring all Eastern Europe under a single rule of iron became clear to Moltke, he faced a choice: to stay in England or to return to Germany to work against the spreading evil at home. In the event he was trapped in Germany by the outbreak of war. In due time he became the leading spirit of the opposition group known as the Kreisau Circle. The large meetings of opposition figures at Kreisau, the Moltke family estate in Silesia, resembled nothing more than the South African moots of the Kindergarten or the Round Table meetings in England in the vigorous years. They were in fact a shadow constitutional convention which set itself the task of creating a federal constitution for a future Germany, to take effect after the fall of Hitler. The authors of the Kreisau documents, which survived the war, have been accused of living in a dream world, of pursuing, in their exquisitely dangerous games, a form of psychiatric therapy rather than serious political activity. Actually, it was Moltke's efforts to unite the opposition groups and to build a broad political base for the attempt to eliminate Hitler that resulted in their downfall and the mass slaughter of the opposition in Germany. Both Trott and Moltke, with virtually the whole Kreisau group, were executed after the attempt to assassinate Hitler in July, 1944.

It would be difficult to say now what good was done by Moltke, Trott, and their friends. They kept alive the values of Christianity and the image of human decency against appalling odds. It may not be too far-fetched to ask what more any martyr does, Socrates or even Jesus. It is certain that there will be a place for Moltke in the great tradition of those who have died to preserve and enhance the human spirit.

What did the Astors have to do with these young Germans? They knew some of them personally, they knew that the movement existed, and, contrary to the prevailing Foreign Office view, they felt that this resistance movement in Germany might have a part to play in political warfare.

Unlike Moltke, who cherished no illusions about his native land, Adam von Trott displayed a certain ambivalence, attempting to combine German patriotism and respect for freedom, attitudes which were, to say the least, incompatible in 1939. Nancy had known Trott since 1936, when, after several "long and serious conversations," Philip had recommended the young man for a traveling fellowship to China. What Trott sought there appears to have been deeply personal, some sense of a single identity dependent on his own proper relationship to a totalitarian regime. Hitler's state and the ancient Chinese Empire were both totalitarian, he told a traveling companion, "but while one was founded on a religious ideology, the other was racialist and pseudo-religious. What bearing did this have on the question 'Why do subjects obey?' " It was a question it took the rest of his brief life to solve.

Nancy liked this romantic young man. When he was ready to leave for the East she gave him a down-to-earth sendoff by asking if he had riding boots. He didn't! Naturally she swept him off to the right shops and bought him an outfit without which, she inferred, he could hardly make it across China. On this journey one thing at least came clear to Trott: the answer to both his personal and political problems lay in Germany. He was to find his fate (and his death) in his homeland. He returned there to fight for the reign of law and for European federalism with the Kreisau Circle, but he never renounced his Germanism. "When I come back," he told a friend in China, "I will stay [in Germany], and lead a double life."

Leading a double life was exactly what he was doing in England in June of 1939. He returned there as a representative of the German Foreign Ministry. Before Munich, all emissaries to England from the German opposition had carried the single message: "Stand firm." If Hitler had then launched his war, the "generals' plot" to overturn him would have gone into action, whether successfully or not we cannot know. The plan that Trott came to England to promote took a quite different line, although the object, the removal of Hitler, remained the same. According to Trott, "A continuation of Chamberlainite appeasement would in the end . . . take away Hitler's political *raison d'être*, and he would be followed by men capable of being appeased." The plan was to restore the independence of Czechoslovakia, excluding the Sudetenland, in exchange for readjustment of the Polish Corridor. If England would agree to this, then, in Trott's view, Hitler would have to go along, or he would be removed by the German moderates.

Adam's first move on reaching England was to ring up David Astor, who invited him to Cliveden for a few days. Not only the Astors themselves but Lothian, Lord Halifax, and Inskip were to be present, a typical Cliveden weekend and one most fruitful for Adam's purpose. At dinner on that June evening Nancy had seated Philip on her left, Halifax on her right, and the young German on Philip's other side. She made it difficult for him, as he said in his report, "with her aggressive and mocking manner." In other words, she enjoyed putting him on in the familiar Chilliesque style and clearly was not sympathetic with his views. After dinner he warmed to his task and felt that he succeeded in making an impression.

The three older men were sympathetic but firm in their handling of Trott. Halifax told him that feeling in Britain had hardened against Germany since the occupation of Prague in March. People were asking who was going to be attacked next. Britain's guarantee of Poland, which had immediately followed the occupation of Prague, was an act of sheer self-defense. Waldorf pointed out that even after Munich he had "advocated concrete concessions to Germany's right to live," but now that Hitler had destroyed the vital rights of another independent nation he could no longer defend "the first steps in a German policy which must inevitably lead to the destruction of all Germany's neighbors and ultimately to the annihilation of Britain herself." Philip was equally emphatic. He saw the "liquidation of an independent nation [as] going beyond the limits of strategic requirement. . . ." He spoke of the readiness for war and death of the average Britain, who was as moved by Prague today as he had been by "Belgium," and all that this word stood for, in 1914.

In his report to his home ministry Trott naturally represented himself as being completely unaffected by these remarks. This report to his Nazi superiors at home was meant as a cover. Its true object was not to influence Hitler, which was recognized to be hopeless, but to represent Trott's plan as coming directly from a British source. This, he believed, would be the most effective approach to those more moderate men connected with the regime who might thereby be encouraged to revolt. To this end Trott attributed the whole plan to Philip, apparently without scruple putting his own words in Philip's mouth.

The report can have had little influence of any kind in Germany, its course to Ribbentrop's wastebasket seems to have been short and direct, and there was no sign of response from the German moderates.

On a weekend at Blickling at the end of June, a more realistic voice was heard. Dr. Bruening, ex-Chancellor in exile, spoke sadly but unequivocally: War was inevitable. It was at this Blickling weekend that the Europe Study Group was formed. David and Waldorf Astor attended the first meeting, as did Philip, Lionel Curtis, Tom Jones, and a few others. One of its objects was to help opposition Germans formulate a constitution for a new, post-Hitler Germany. The relation to the work at Kreisau was implicit in this meeting. Trott and Moltke returned to Germany to work and plot underground against the Nazis, until they met death at the hands of Hitler's executioners in Ploentsee prison.

Sandbags filled by schoolboys fortified the Embankment, rows of balloons punctuated the skyline above London; for the second August in succession Europe was on the edge of war. Writing home to Virginia, Nancy tried to collect her thoughts, but it was "like walking on the extreme edge of a very dangerous precipice and trying to make light conversation on the way." She had come up from Sandwich for a special session of the House. On September 1 the House was darkened against air attack, but somehow the suspense of the Munich period was lacking. Perhaps one had been there too often before. Again negotiations were understood to be taking place, this time between Hitler and Poland. At the session of September 1, Chamberlain revealed to the House that the demands that Hitler now claimed had been rejected by the Poles had never even been submitted to them. A gasp of astonishment met this announcement; Nancy exclaimed in ringing tones, "Well, I never *did!*" Mr. Chamberlain fumbled with his papers for some time and then produced a document, the British ultimatum to Germany, which he read very slowly.

Two days elapsed before the government moved, but at last the formal declaration came: England was at war. Mr. Chamberlain, although he had brought himself to commit his country to a war, could not bring himself to fight one. "What I hope for," he said sincerely, "is not a military victory—*I very much doubt the feasibility of that*—but a collapse of the German home front." It was not a very likely hope or a very inspiring attitude from the leader of a nation at war.

Nancy put her own feelings quite simply in a letter to her family in Virginia: "If Hitler and Stalin win, death would be better." By October Waldorf, dining with like-minded members of the so-called Eden group, expressed his conviction in strong words: "The Prime Minister should be removed and Winston Churchill should take his place." In a later letter to Philip he described Chamberlain as "an egotist, a mediocrity, honestly obstinate." It was one of Nancy's cardinal political principles that the public good must supersede private friendship. "Duds must be got rid of," she told the House of Commons, "even if they are one's dearest friends." In April, she was calling for new blood in the Chamberlain cabinet. "When there is a sweep it must be a clean sweep, and not musical chairs." Garvin, also impatient with the leader of the phony war, congratulated her in the *Observer*: "Two women [Nancy had been supported by Eleanor Rathbone] had the pluck in Thursday's debate to express the smothered conviction of the House." Clearly, long before Chamberlain fell, the Astors had wanted a change. Their personal differences with Churchill were no longer important. They knew that he, like Lloyd George in 1916, was the man to win the war.

Philip, as Ambassador to Washington, was as impatient as anyone with Chamberlain's methods. He took up his task a few days before the outbreak of war. It was to be the climactic point in his life; now, for the third time, he found himself at the center of great affairs, this time wielding what was to be a decisive influence. He went to Washington with a liberated spirit, knowing that he was to serve in the field in which he was most at home. Nancy was immensely proud.

"When I met him," she said, "he knew nothing of America." Now he was to carry the things they both cared for most back to the land of her birth.

Philip's first impulse was to write to the old soldier in South Africa who had shared the dreams and visions of the past, to explain the opening he now saw ahead. "If things get worse for us, as I think they will," he told Smuts in April, "I do not think it is inconceivable that the democracies should this time knit themselves into an integral union which will prove to be a nucleus of world federation." Sir Ronald Lindsay and such American observers as Abraham Flexner had sent him solemn warnings against talking world government to the Americans. In this letter to Smuts we can hear the echo of Lloyd George in 1917—"Mr. Kerr, young and of a naturally hopeful disposition." But perhaps Philip was wiser than his critics. It could be that this was an essential part of the great strength of his ambassadorship. His mixture of the down-to-earth horsetrading of diplomacy with a mind open to the new idea, the creative innovation, was more American than British. It was the fuel that stoked his enormous output of energy in the months ahead. As Philip himself might have said, it worked.

Smuts sent his blessing from Pretoria in a letter which, as usual, went straight to the heart of the issues: "Your mission, the greatest any man can have today, is ultimately to carry our dear friends into the war. Western civilization may hang on this issue." Smuts did not exaggerate. The fate of Western civilization did hang on American aid, which was, in effect, in the hands of one man. The valor of Britain's flyers, the magic of Churchill's oratory, all would have been of no avail without American production, and without the Squire of Hyde Park, American production would never have got off the ground. The birth of the Grand Alliance was as simple and as decisive as that. Churchill and Roosevelt were its architects, Lothian the indispensable craftsman whose supreme task it was to bring the two concepts, British and American, into one.

The hour was indeed late. Churchill, speaking of Chamberlain's rejection of FDR's overtures, said that it left him "breathless with amazement" that "Mr. Chamberlain, with his limited outlook and inexperience of the European scene, should have possessed the self-sufficiency to wave away the proffered hand stretched out across the Atlantic." Now Chamberlain was paying a bitter price. It was too late for England to build her own armament industry. The Prime Minister, who had for so long avoided gearing his own country's economy to the production of arms, must now strip her to the bone, mortgage her future, and commit her to financial ruin in order to buy abroad what he had failed to produce at home—assuming, that is, that the Americans would go along. And this was a sizable and risky assumption. Roosevelt had problems with the military, with industry itself, and with the Congress. Naturally enough, there were many men both in the army and in Congress who could not immediately grasp the advantage of selling American plans and equipment to a foreign country, even if such sales would result in greatly expanding our own output at foreign expense. Industry was frankly fearful of overexpansion. Another difficulty was the disposition of the British Exchequer to talk to J. P. Morgan & Company. Morgenthau, Roosevelt's Secretary of the Treasury, felt impelled to warn the British that the house of Morgan had become a national myth, its purported evil machinations used to scare school children; it was widely charged with responsibility for the last war. Roosevelt, convinced as he was that the United States must support the British, was highly sensitive to considerations such as these.

In his first speeches Philip was exceedingly cautious. He delighted his American audience by quoting a Midwestern editor who had warned his countrymen of the subtlety of this new envoy from perfidious Albion: "In short," said the editor, "a dangerous man." Philip wrote rather wryly to Nancy that one newspaper said he looked "more like an American businessman than a British aristocrat," and that, said Philip, "after I had put on my store clothes!"

When he spoke to the legislature in Nancy's own Virginia, he let himself go. First he described that great moment, her introduction as the first woman Member of Parliament: "I shall not soon forget the sight of Lady Astor's trim little figure dressed in appropriate black, advancing from the bar of the House of Commons flanked by Mr. Balfour and Mr. Lloyd George. . . . I am afraid that the other six hundred and fourteen male members of the House . . . were not quite happy at the portent of that solitary and unaccustomedly demure figure. That was your second conquest of Britain." Virginians are nothing if not gallant, and the applause was thunderous.

Then Philip called the roll of the great Virginia names: Washington, Jefferson, Madison, Monroe, John Marshall. He said:

> It is always easy to strike for liberty. What is difficult is to create the institutions which ensure and protect it in a revolutionary age. . . . Thanks to [the great Virginians] the revolution here did not lead to the devastation and militarism to which it led in Europe. . . . Our political international structure of over seventy sovereign states. . . . is as much an anachronism as would be an attempt to turn the United States back into an anarchy of forty-eight states. . . . Why should not the Virginians of today aspire to emulate, if not excel, the achievements of their ancestors? For like them we live in an age when we must create something greater and nobler than has ever been seen before, or see liberty perish from our midst.

So, he had said it, and if the new world was not immediately ushered in, neither did the heavens fall. At home Nancy was even bolder. Supporting evacuation of British children to America she said: "It may be an aid to the possible union of the two nations in future."

A rather greater test of ambassadorial tact was the arrival in the United States of Adam von Trott, now equipped with a British accent and a Balliol tie. Unfortunately, his outspoken pro-Germanism had raised suspicions in England which were reflected in the States. David Astor had prepared the way for his friend by a series of letters to Philip, which appear to have mystified their recipient. In a letter to Bill Astor Philip spoke of "David, who seems to be conducting intrigues the nature of which I, at any rate, cannot follow." Trott's mission on this visit was to extract advance pledges of Allied cooperation should the German moderates succeed in overturning Hitler. He felt, rightly or wrongly, that the German resistance to Hitler could not be asked to risk their lives if they were immediately to be treated as defeated enemies by the Allies. He wished to be assured, in the event of any opposition *coup*, of an equal place for Germany as a "good European" in a new Europe. In this enterprise he was completely unsuccessful. Along with obvious sincerity and considerable charm, Trott carried with him a certain cloak-and-dagger aura which did not always inspire confidence. There was the suspicion that he was enjoying himself, and there was also the undoubted fact that his suggestions were not very appealing to combatants in an all-out war. There was a fear that acquiescence in Trott's plan might weaken the Allies' will to fight and might even encourage them to arrange a truce on the basis of a putative revolution in Germany that might never take place or, worse, might be only a cover for the old regime.

Philip, of course, knew that Trott represented a genuine, if not necessarily a strong, opposition movement. He had one elaborately arranged "secret" meeting with Trott at the Mayflower Hotel. How secret this meeting was may be open to question; however, any meeting at all in wartime between the representative of His Majesty's government in Washington and a German from the Foreign Ministry must be considered extraordinary. Philip soon turned Trott over to his assistant, John Wheeler-Bennett, who maintained contact through the fall and winter. Roosevelt was fully informed and mildly entertained by this contact with intrigue and derring-do in the person of Trott. "For heaven's sake," he wrote to Felix Frankfurter after Trott had finally left for home. "Surely you did not let your Trott friend get trotted out of the country without having him searched by Edgar Hoover. Think of the battleship plans and other secrets he may be carrying back. . . ." While FDR, who knew very well what Trott was about, was simply amused by the suspicions of the FBI, poor Trott was sweating it out. He was convinced that the men tailing him were Gestapo agents.

It would be hard to say what precisely were the results of this mission, undertaken at such deadly risk to Trott himself. There was no official response, no declaration of policy such as Trott desired. He did apparently enlist the support of Philip's old friend Walter Lippmann. In October, 1939, this most respected of American commentators called upon the Allies "to state their war aims with a view to making clear to the German nation that the siege can be lifted whenever they have a government with which it is possible to negotiate. . . . They can declare that they are not committed to the 1919 or to the 1939 frontiers in Central Europe, but to the liberation of the Czech and Polish peoples." All this and more had been said before—it had not brought results then, and it seems extremely unlikely that it would have brought results in October, 1939.

Perhaps Sumner Welles's exploratory mission to Europe in the following spring was in effect a response to Trott's efforts. Philip alerted Nancy to Welles's coming; he often used Cliveden in this way, as a sort of English branch of the Washington Embassy, sending her Welles and many other Americans who wished to make useful contacts in England.

Unfortunately Welles found no hard evidence in Berlin of an approaching *coup* or of any significant interest in an acceptable peace. What, then, did Trott accomplish? Nothing more, perhaps, than keeping open the very fragile thread of communication between the German opposition and the free world. Trott could have stayed in America—David Astor begged Philip to use all his powers of persuasion to keep him there—but he would not abandon the "other Germany." He was like a man reaching out for air from a dark prison of the spirit. The distance was too great to span, but the spark continued to burn in little scattered groups throughout the years of darkness. One must believe that it survived, that the spark of freedom in Germany was not extinguished in Ploentsee jail nor the memory of men such as Trott and Moltke lost in the maelstrom of our modern world.

16

Fifty Destroyers

THE phony war came to an abrupt end in May, 1940, with Hitler's successful invasion of Norway. The spectacle of British ships retreating before German air power shook England to her foundations. The Navy was no longer enough. "One plane now is worth a hundred in August," Nancy wrote to Philip, and well she might, for England was defenseless as she had not been since Drake had sailed out to meet the Armada some three hundred and fifty years before. Only Neville Chamberlain seemed oblivious to the tidal wave of feeling that was about to sweep him out of office. The Astors, almost in desperation, had turned to Lloyd George, wishing to restore the spirit of 1916. The Great Man, a nearly extinct volcano at 77, came to lunch at 4 St. James's Square on the day of the debate on Norway in the House. Nancy informed him at once that "he had been produced for inspection and to be tested for his fitness to return to the helm." Garvin, himself close to an unwilling retirement, pronounced Lloyd George "still good for six hours a day, and it would be six hours of radium," but the old lion preferred to rumble quietly offstage—except for one last time, when Nancy, sitting in the House, was to hear once more that full-throated roar.

That afternoon in the House Leo Amery led the attack on the Prime Minister. Rising to a Cromwellian climax, he quoted the Protector's famous words: "Depart, I say, and let us have done with you. In the name of God, go." On the next day, May 8, before the vote of confidence or no confidence was taken in the House, Chamberlain put the challenge on a personal basis: "I call upon my friends to support us in the Lobby tonight." It was then that Lloyd George rose to his feet. Standing with his legs apart and his mane of white hair thrown back, he looked at the man he had despised these many years. "It is not a question of who are the Prime Minister's friends. It is a far bigger issue. . . . He has appealed for sacrifice. The nation is prepared for every sacrifice so long as it has leadership." His voice deepened, the note of the Welsh preacher once more ringing through the House. "I say solemnly that the Prime Minister should give an example of sacrifice, because there is nothing which can contribute more to victory in this war than that he should sacrifice the seals of office."

When the division vote was taken Nancy filed out with the opposition, one of the forty whose vote removed Chamberlain from office. Waldorf was triumphant. He wrote to Philip, "What overthrew him was actually the adverse vote of the serving back bench M.P.s." Unlike Lloyd George, Churchill had no need to seize the first office in the state; almost by popular acclaim it fell into his lap.

After voting in the House Nancy would hurry back to Plymouth, where she and Waldorf had their own war to fight. For thirty years the Astors had been an integral part of the life of the city, and now the Plymouthers turned to them in their hour of need. The Lord Mayor of Plymouth usually served for one year, but in November, 1939, Waldorf was elected to the office he was to hold for five years. He was re-elected yearly until the end of the war. It was to this port town that the Yanks were to come as they had in the first war, only this time in far greater numbers and fighting force. Here, in and around Plymouth, the invasion forces assembled, and it was here that they suffered their first casualties. For a time England itself was to be the democracies' front line, and Plymouth was as hard hit as any city in England. Nancy, either at Waldorf's side or on her own, rallied the home defense. "Plymouth," she had said, "is my Virginia in England." There could be no stronger expression of devotion.

In May, 1940, Britain for the first time looked straight into her future. It was apparent that the Churchill government, unlike its predecessor, was ready to pawn all its assets to buy arms. On the other hand, Churchill had not realized, as Philip did on his side of the Atlantic, how much military prestige and autonomy it would be necessary to yield to the United States. On the occasion of the King's visit to America in the previous June, Roosevelt had opened the subject of an American naval patrol operating from British bases. Churchill had been enthusiastic, apparently without realizing that the American Navy meant to be free agents, in command of any facilities so employed. In May, 1940, Philip reopened the question from Washington. Churchill countered with his first appeal for destroyers, but he was far from ready to meet the President's terms. He was willing to make free with Britain's treasure, but her prestige and her territorial possessions were quite a different matter.

Philip, in close touch with the President, was well aware of the need for a solid *quid pro quo* to show to the Congress and the nation. Nevertheless he felt that the flight of the Prime Minister's oratory went rather further than was necessary to meet the case. After the rout of the British forces in France and its famous evacuation at Dunkirk, Churchill made the first of his great fighting speeches. He hurled defiance at the victorious enemy and swore that even if England herself went down her fleet would "carry on the struggle, until, in God's good time, the New World . . . steps forth to the rescue and liberation of the old." Philip, who had spent years convincing America of the terrible consequences to herself of the loss of the British fleet, was concerned that these words might undo his work. Churchill, who had directed this speech at Germany rather than at the United States, immediately instructed his Ambassador to "discourage any complacent assumption on United States' part that they will pick up the debris of the British Empire by their present policy." And so the matter rested, until the terrible speed of the Blitzkrieg, culminating in the fall of France, began to carry its own message to America.

It was England's and Churchill's great gift to the world that, in 1940, when Britain could have made peace at the expense of Europe, she chose to fight on alone, until Hitler should yield up utterly his bloody conquests and ill-gotten gains. Cliveden was wholly behind the Prime Minister in this resolve. Philip, in Washington, received one of the German peace offers of July. He was approached by the Quaker Malcolm Lovell acting as intermediary between the German Embassy and the British Ambassador. The offer submitted by Lovell took the form of a telegram, which Philip duly transmitted to Halifax by telephone. He quoted: "The German Government would welcome a fair peace and one that Britain could properly accept." Harold Nicolson described Philip as telephoning "wildly," saying that he found the German terms "most satisfactory."*

At this moment of pause and reassessment Mussolini's reaction was typical. With France out of the way, he dashed out bravely to claim the jackal's share of the spoils. Roosevelt responded on that same evening, when he happened to be speaking to his son's graduating class at the University of Virginia. Now at last the President took off the wraps and gave the nation the full force of his own conviction about the war: "We as a nation . . . are convinced that military and naval victory for the gods of force and hate would endanger the institution of democracy in the Western world." He drew a picture of an isolated America, "lodged in prison, handcuffed, hungry, and fed through the bars from day to day by the contemptuous unpitying masters of other continents."

After this speech Philip could tell himself that it was only a matter of time. America would fight, he had said, "when her own vital interests are menaced, and these interests include her ideals." On July 5–6 Philip telegraphed Churchill that

> . . . informed American opinion was at last beginning to realize that they were in danger of losing the British fleet altogether if

* It would appear that the phrasing of the German telegram was attributed to Philip by Nicolson's unnamed informant. The evidence of the intermediary points to this conclusion, for Lovell reported that Philip was "extremely discouraging" throughout, before as well as after he had talked to London. His only sin appears to have been in transmitting the German telegram, which was surely part of his ambassadorial duty.

the war went against us and if they remained neutral. It would, however, be extremely difficult to get American public opinion to consider letting us have American destroyers unless it could be assured that in the event of the United States entering the war the British Fleet or such of it that was afloat would cross the Atlantic if Great Britain were over-run.

At the end of July Churchill came through with a really rousing letter to the President, again stressing his need for the destroyers, but saying nothing about the fleet. "We could not sustain the present rate of [destroyer] casualties for long, and if we cannot get a substantial reenforcement the whole fate of the war may be decided by this minor and easily remediable factor. . . . Mr. President, with great respect I must tell you that in the long history of the world this is a thing to do *now*." Altogether, in the long history of the world, there have been few more persuasive letter writers. But eloquence was not enough. There was still, as Philip on the spot was well aware, the President's need for a *quid pro quo*, which Churchill continued to ignore.

In the skies over London the Battle of Britain was under way. No one but the cabinet and the fighter command knew how thin the margin was to be. Luckily no one, least of all the Germans, was quite aware of the "fewness of the few." England's pilots went up four or five times a night, returning, if they did return, to fall asleep in chairs or wherever they happened to be. The night came when the RAF had put its last fighter in the air. If one more bomber had come across the Channel the little Tiger Moth training planes were on the line, warmed up to go. If such stories cannot be verified they were near enough to the truth as to make no difference. In Washington William Knudsen, director of defense production, was unable to meet the British order for aircraft engines. He was moved to tell Arthur Purvis, chief of the Allied Purchasing Commission, that if the British "were going to lose the war on account of a three-day delay they were really up against it." Purvis told him, in effect, that the war could be lost in three hours. The navy was Britain's lifeline; all the fighter planes in the world could not help unless they had safe passage across the Atlantic. She was just keeping her head above water; without more destroyers she would go down.

On the evening of August 1 Philip reached Frank Knox, the new Secretary of the Navy, on the telphone and asked him to come over to the embassy. The two men talked for a long time. Philip made the supreme effort of his life. He told Knox that Britain must have the destroyers, and that he wanted Knox to exhaust every means he could think of before saying no. Unless they got these fifty destroyers he did not know what would happen to the British Isles. Knox was genuinely moved. He asked whether it would hurt the British government if this desperate situation were made public, and Philip replied that they would have to take the chance. Knox then asked whether his government would consider selling a part of the British islands in the Western Hemisphere in exchange for the destroyers. Philip gladly agreed to forward a suggestion, so much in line with his own thinking, to Churchill.

This conversation took place on Thursday evening. At a cabinet meeting on Friday afternoon, Roosevelt for the first time got down to serious work on the destroyer deal. His first move was to ask the British, through Philip, for further assurance that in the event of German success in Great Britain their Navy would sail for North America or British Empire ports. Philip relayed Churchill's answer directly to the President on August 5, enumerating the bases, which ran from Newfoundland to British Guiana, where facilities would be granted to the United States in return for the destroyers. Three days later, on August 8, he took up the assurances concerning the fleet with Sumner Welles, Roosevelt's Under Secretary of State. Churchill, that Former Naval Person, now authorized Philip to quote the splendid fighting words which he had previously instructed him to suppress. Now he wished the Americans, as well as the Germans and the Italians, to know that "We shall defend our island whatever the cost may be, we shall fight on the beaches, we shall fight on the landing grounds, we shall fight in the fields and in the streets, we shall fight in the hills," ending with the promise that "our Empire beyond the seas, armed and guarded by the British Fleet, would carry on the struggle." In London, when repeating this speech for broadcast, he had made an interpolation for the benefit of Edward R. Murrow that is not in the official text: "And we shall hit them over the head with beer bottles, which is all we shall have to hit them with."

Sumner Welles seems not to have been impressed by Churchill's rhetorical assurances, which both the Americans and Churchill himself knew were beyond the power of any present British government to guarantee. On top of this, from the British point of view, fifty over-age destroyers hardly made a very brilliant showing in return for the bases, much less a possible fleet. Nevertheless, after much consultation and many exchanges of cables, principally drafted by Philip himself, a suitable form was devised, so worded that neither British pride nor American self-interest would appear to have suffered in the deal. The finishing touches were, as the President said, a mapping operation. This was the sort of thing that FDR enjoyed most, the moving of pins about on a map, after weighing considerations of global strategy. Philip was in daily consultation with the President and with the American Army and Navy—a great experience for him, watching his most cherished ideas worked out in action. He never paused to count the cost to himself of the intense strain and heat of that August. As the end drew into view, the strain lessened; nevertheless, Norman Davis noticed that Philip would often fall asleep in the car on their way to their weekly golf game at Burning Tree. Then he would rouse himself. Flashes of his old great game would remind Davis of their Sandwich weekends and of Blickling.

Before the deal was closed, Philip advised Churchill to have British destroyer crews at Halifax and Bermuda ready to take over the ships. It would create the worst possible impression, he told the Prime Minister, if the ships were ready and there were no men to receive them. On September 2 he and Hull signed the final papers. The announcement came on the Presidential special train at an informal press conference on September 3.

The President: "In twenty minutes there is going to the Congress the following message—it is probably the most important thing that has come for American defense since the Louisiana Purchase. . . . [Reading:]

"To the Congress of the United States:

I transmit herewith for the information of the Congress notes exchanged between the British Ambassador at Washington and the Secretary of State on September 2, 1940,—

"in other words, that is yesterday—[reading:]

"—under which this Government has acquired the right to lease naval and air bases in Newfoundland, and in the islands of Bermuda, the Bahamas, Jamaica, St. Lucia,—"

Q. (interposing): "What is that last one?"

The President: "St. Lucia."

Q.: "How do you spell it?"

The President: "S-t, period, L-u-c-i-a, period. Now, I am not fooling on those. These are real places." (*Laughter.*) The President continued reading: "—Trinidad, and Antigua, and in British Guiana—"

Thus casually was the Western world changed forever.

"Expect me Thursday, Philip Kerr." Nancy had been waiting a long time for this message. "Thursday" was October 16, 1940. He had been away over a year, working at full stretch, a year which, on both sides of the Atlantic, had seemed more like ten by any normal reckoning. But neither Nancy nor Philip quite realized the effect the sight of destruction would have on him. He had been working with the facts and figures of disaster, but until he saw London and Plymouth, he could not know. Those at home had gradually gotten used to a new world. One slept in basement purlieus; the camaraderie of the sponge bag (toilet kit) and the dressing gown in unfamiliar cellars had taken over London. A raid shattered the night into a thousand pieces, "shrieking and jabbering," said Nicolson, "like an African jungle." Nancy, who was never afraid in Plymouth because she had too much to do there, did succumb one night in London. Walking in Bond Street she had suddenly felt afraid to be alone. She caught up with a New Zealand soldier and asked if she might walk with him. "My mother," he said coldly, "warned me to beware of women like you."

In Plymouth things were quite different. Nancy regularly made the rounds of the shelters during raids. Once, sensing morale at a low ebb, she said not a word but simply made a tour of the room turning cartwheels and somersaults. "Are we downhearted?" "No," shouted everyone. The shock treatment had worked once again, and Nancy left the shelter feeling the better for it. If more of our leaders would stand on their heads . . . ! But perhaps the thought is subversive.

For Philip, the modern man *par excellence*, nothing was stranger than the blackout. The sound of footsteps, not heard in the Western world since the coming of the combustion engine, now echoed in empty streets. Medieval London had been like that. Opening a door in the blackout into a pub or private party would suddenly reveal a pool of light, a burst of talk. People were more important than they had ever been, but not all one's friends were there to greet one. Bobbie Shaw, Nancy's little Bobbie, now turned forty, had been badly hurt, and 4 St. James's Square had lost half its rooms. Nothing serious, Nancy said; she had much to be grateful for.

She soon saw that Philip was not only reacting to the Blitz but that he was physically ill. They both recognized it, and although Christian Science forbade his seeing a doctor they both knew that he should rest and take time off to do the "healing work" of his church. Of course there was no time for it, only for interviews, briefings, conferences. During his first week at home he made his way through the blackout for a major press conference. It was a night of dark fog, where stars and shell bursts glimmered almost interchangeably in a dim sky. Philip was exhilarated, an effect that the blitz, once accepted, sometimes produced. He gave a fine talk, reported Harold Nicolson. "He sits there quite placidly under the glare of arc lamps and the barrage of questions. He manages the thing with consummate ease."

The effects of uremia are intermittent; at times Philip was his old self and must have thought himself well again. There were other times, as those nearest him knew, when only the force of a trained will carried him through his multitudinous tasks. It is the submissiveness of this will that strikes one. Paradoxically, it was the source of his great strength, surely the mark of religious development of the highest order. For a long time Philip had recognized that his hopes for federalism and an expanded world order were not to be realized in his lifetime. One evening at Blickling a friend, quoting from Tennyson's *In Memoriam*, had referred to Arthur Hallam as "a noble type/Appearing ere the times were ripe." "No, not so," said Philip. "Of course no man, in reality, lives before his time—especially reformers. A man may die, as many do, without seeing the result of his work with his mortal eyes. But so long as he plays the part allotted to him on this world's stage, and, in the doing of it demonstrates what there is in him to reveal, he's done his job—for the time being—whether he dies early or late." Philip very rarely spoke of religion; he did not need to, he lived it. His last days in England and in Washington were luminous with this very pragmatic faith.

What he did speak of, and what was in the forefront of his mind during this visit, was money. No one knew better than Philip the Yankee contempt for a sucker and his disposition to look on the ability to make a good deal as the *sine qua non* of manhood. He believed that once Americans knew the real facts of England's plight this concept of a deal would disappear, to be replaced by the instinctive generosity of a pioneer stock, rushing to help a neighbor in a tight place. This was the simile Roosevelt himself was to use: the man who lends a length of garden hose to put out a neighbor's fire does not want $15—he wants the hose back. But there were still people in America who suspected the British of having a supply of hose stashed away unused in their own tool shed. Churchill's eloquence and the matter-of-fact courage of his countrymen were gradually coming home to Americans. They were deeply stirring to Philip himself, but he knew that they were not enough. Absolute honesty was needed to effect the necessary change of heart in the United States. Nothing could be done until after the Presidential election coming up in November. In a letter to Virginia telling of the damage to 4 St. James's Square, Nancy added, "I do hope Roosevelt wins." On November 5 they hung over the radio until the news was in: FDR was to lead the American people for another four years.

On November 15 Philip met Churchill at Ditchley. Twenty-two years before, there had been the same ultimate need and the same desperate call to America for help. Now, once more, the day of reckoning had come for Britain. In Churchill's words, "Even if we divested ourselves of all our gold and foreign assets, we could not pay for half we had ordered, and the extension of the war made it necessary for us to have ten times as much."

That was the simple truth, clearer now than ever to Philip, but not yet clear in the United States.

The setting in which the great decisions were made was a country house. It was not deemed wise for the Prime Minister to be always at Chequers, which was too logical a target for the German bombers. Their hostess at Ditchley was Nancy Tree, Nancy Astor's niece and namesake, now married to her second husband, Ronald Tree. Churchill referred to Ditchley as "a large and charming house" whose comforts and appointments he found most congenial. He had always considered Philip rather a lightweight. Now he found "an earnest, deeply stirred man," urging him with utter conviction to lay Britain's cards upon the table. Until then the Prime Minister, in his own words, had been leaving "future financial problems on the lap of the eternal Gods." Philip now put it to Churchill nearly as strongly as he had to Knox. He urged him to make a full and frank statement; without it their strongest supporters, even Morgenthau and the President himself, would be forced to retreat. He wanted Churchill to put the whole situation into American hands. That, and that only, would enable Roosevelt to cancel the bill that Britain could not pay. Churchill was convinced. In consultation with Philip, he drew up a personal letter to the President, "one of the most important I ever wrote." When he recognized the need, Churchill went the whole way. His letter to the President was far-ranging, lucid, and absolutely open. It crossed the Atlantic like an arrow, straight to the heart of that other naval person on the far side of the sea.

While the exhaustive review of the facts contained in this letter were being checked out by the British Chiefs of Staff and the Treasury, and while it was being read and approved by the War cabinet, Philip's brief time at home came to an end. He had been to Blickling, where he told a cousin that after the war he wanted nothing more than to settle down on the border and lead the life of a shepherd. All his life he had been detached from place, a man without physical heirs; yet he felt, in his weariness, this last pull of the native earth. His spiritual home and his mental heirs were at Cliveden, and to those he returned for his last weekend. There was a full moot, in which he could tell what he had seen and helped to bring about in America. It was the old vision, first seen in South African days, adapted to the new reality. "The fundamental new fact . . . was the mutual recognition of interdependence of the United States of America and the British Commonwealth. . . . In peace there should be some kind of Amphictyonic Council. . . . The position of the Dominions was inseparable from that of the United States [which] must share in the *whole* strategic framework of the British Empire. . . . What was needed was a Pan-American British Empire Conference for political and economic cooperation in war and peace." Cliveden had always been the place to dream dreams; now, between the British Embassy and the White House, fragments of a dream were becoming reality.

On Philip's last afternoon in England Nancy fretted. She wanted him to herself, and he would go off with Waldorf, Lionel Curtis, and Arnold Toynbee to talk about the World Order papers being sponsored at Chatham House. At last she caught him up in her car and drove him down to Oxford, where they had a hilarious evening with his friends the Allens at Rhodes House. Nancy entertained them all with a description of how her new motor bicycle at Cliveden had run away with her. The Allens nearly succumbed with laughter. Philip was in top form, taking in deep draughts of vicarious vitality. Later that evening they left, Philip to catch the bomber that was to fly him back to America.

In Lisbon the plane was held over for a week. Philip, during this enforced rest, let his mind flow back into those wide channels explored at the last moot. It was time, he thought, and perhaps he knew that his time would not be long, to bring some such message to America. But when he was met by the usual crowd of reporters at La Guardia, plans for the future had to give way to the pressure of the present. Churchill's letter had not yet reached the President, and his Ambassador gave the press his own nine-word version of it: "Well, boys, Britain's broke. It's your money we want!" Few ambassadors can have dropped a calculated bombshell in more casual fashion.

Churchill's letter arrived on December 9. It reached the President as he cruised the Caribbean in the battleship *Tuscaloosa*. Roosevelt later told Morgenthau that he hadn't looked at a single report brought from Washington. He had sat in his deck chair, reading and rereading the letter from London. "For two whole days he was plunged in intense thought, and brooded silently." There, on the sparkling blue seas, the concept of Lend Lease was born.

On December 11 Philip was to address the Federation of American Farm Bureaus in Baltimore, his first full-scale speech since he himself had seen the blitz. It was his duty to touch the imagination of America as surely as it had been to reach Roosevelt, Stimson, Knox, Marshall, and the others at the top. He felt himself to be England's messenger and not only that, but a spokesman for "all whose ideals and principles are similar." He was not to give this speech himself; it was read for him, but this hardly mattered. At last passion and necessity came together; his ideas, once directed toward the future, now assumed the weight and density of present time.

First he gave them the blitz.

Hour after hour the bombers came back, guided by the fires already lit. There was no flinching, no crying for peace. All London fought; rescued and tended the wounded, beat down the flames. "And finally had come the gradual petering out of the much heralded invasion of Britain . . . every day it is made more difficult as our armies increase . . . and as our squadrons multiply." He proclaimed the magnitude of that victory: "Without the conquest of Britain Hitler cannot win the war."

> Nazism is . . . war, total war, war without limit, without mercy, with its concommitants, propaganda and fraud, as a means of total subjugation of other nations to serve the Nazi will. . . . This war is not a war between nations like the last war. . . . It is a revolutionary war waged by Hitler and his military totalitarian machine against all other nations and the free world in which we have lived, so as to make them military, political and economic satellites in a totalitarian world empire.
>
> Then Hitler will have given the world peace—the peace of death—and employment—the employment of the slave.

Under the rain of fire Philip had become a harder man. The world he now offered the Federation of American Farmers was more limited and much more immediate than the world federation that he had described so often in the past. Strategically it was conceived as a ring of fortress bases*: Britain itself, Gibraltar, Capetown, Egypt, the Suez Canal, Singapore, Australia, New Zealand, Hawaii, and Panama, behind which "political and industrial freedom [would] be secure." The fatal policies pursued after the last war—prohibitive tariffs, reparations, reckless lending to compensate—all must disappear. Markets and employment for all must be the goal. Philip had not abandoned the vision; it was simply that the dictator countries were not ready. The present brought a nearer test, from which there could be no escape.

"I have done," he said. "Since May there is no challenge we have evaded, no challenge we have refused. . . . The issue now depends largely on what you decide to do. . . . It is the great strength of democracy that it brings responsibility down squarely on every citizen and every nation. And before the judgment seat of God each must answer for his own actions."

This was the reckoning, the hard truth that lies at the bottom of the cup.

On the eighth of December Philip was acutely ill. He had lunched at the State Department and had planned to have dinner with Norman Davis at his home, but Davis came instead to have supper with him in his bedroom at the embassy. Philip, in evident pain, worked that evening on a long dispatch to his government. It was the final draft of Churchill's personal letter to the President. That finished, he told his friend not to worry, that he would "straighten himself out" as Davis had seen him do before. Mrs. Fowler, a Christian Scientist, was his attendant during these days and nights. On Monday morning, the tenth, after a terrible night, Philip turned to her with a smile and said, "Well, it's all over." She thought he meant the crisis of his illness. He meant life, so full, so various, still for him at high tide. He heard on Tuesday night that his speech to the Farm Bureau had been read in Baltimore. In the early hours of Wednesday morning he died.

* We must remember that he was speaking in the prenuclear age. His choice of bases today might not, indeed could not, correspond with the list of 1940, but the principle of a peripheral ring of defense would still be applicable. He believed the United States, like Great Britain, to be a sea-air power, and that it should hold aloof from continental involvements.

17

Virginia in England

FROM the *Tuscaloosa* at sea the President of the United States cabled to the King of England: "I am shocked beyond measure to hear of the sudden passing of my old friend your Ambassador the Marquis of Lothian. Through nearly a quarter of a century we had come to understand and trust each other."

To those at home who loved him Norman Davis wrote a full account of Philip's last days. Nancy answered: "I can't mourn for Philip," but she did. She comforted herself by remembering his words: "He always told me when I mourned for Phyllis [it was] wrong and this life was the dream not the reality. I feel he's alright [*sic*] and happy. I can't think of him as dead. . . . He and I had an unbroken friendship of nearly thirty years, and I never even realized [what it would be] to be without him or Phyllis. Now they have both gone. Well—I still thank God for his goodness and that I could think that I helped Philip to a religion which gave him peace and health and that he understood America. . . . He made Winston see."

She sent Norman Davis the program of Philip's memorial service in Westminster Abbey. The lesson, John 15:1–12, closed with the words "This is my commandment. That ye love one another, as I have loved you." Then the hymn was sung which Philip himself had loved, and used most often,

> Rejoice. . . .
> That God has given you, for a priceless dower,
> To live in these great times and have your part
> In Freedom's crowning hour!

closing with the words he had quoted to the American pilgrims:

> I saw the powers of darkness put to flight!
> I saw the morning break!

On the back of the program Nancy had written: "Oh, Norman, if only I could have been there! I know it's foolish, but I wish I had been."

She wrote impulsively to Eleanor Roosevelt offering to come over to speak. "I could go west or south or where they were lukewarm about the war. But only if it would do good." In the New Year, Lindbergh did not help matters by testifying before the House Foreign Affairs Committee. He told the congressmen that the "United States and Britain together cannot defeat Germany." Nancy was indignant, "positively appalled and deeply hurt." His wrong-headed view of the situation made her all the more aware of the need for good advice in America. However, her offer to come over was not taken up. She was not to go to America; America, actually, was to come to her.

The Astors knew Plymouth intimately, its streets and its people. Waldorf's talent as an administrator, never used to the full, now came into its own. Where before he had often been in the supporting role, now he was "king in Plymouth," as Nancy wrote Norman Davis. "It's the best organized place in England. He's raised over $130,000 for his Welfare Fund."

Waldorf had started the relief fund in his first month in office. Next had come the North Road Canteen. From February,

1940, through February, 1944, this famous canteen had served hot food twenty-four hours a day, every day but one, after the first blitz in March, 1941. That first night Nancy had stood for a moment watching Plymouth going up in flames. Her eyes filled with tears, but her next reaction was typical: "We'll build it again." The Lord Mayor's office and a primitive little office on the top floor of number 3 Elliot Terrace were the nerve centers of a resistance as great as any in England. The full strength of the blitz hit, strangely enough, on the night of one of Plymouth's proudest days, the day of the visit of the King and Queen. Nancy's maid, the indomitable Rosina Harrison, wrote an account to friends in Virginia.

> We all missed Lord Astor. He was ill at Cliveden, but never mind, Lady Astor made up for it and it all went off grand. . . . Lady Astor got Florie, her house maid, and I . . . their Majesties' signatures. . . . Well, at 8:30 P.M. the sirens went and the raid got bad so I told Lady Astor I had a sailor boy friend in to see me and I couldn't send him home in a raid and so that was all right. . . . Well, Lady Astor came upstairs, changed into her air raid clothes and put her tin hat on and took the old fur coat, gas mask, etc., and went [out] the front door. . . . I saw a bomb drop on the Hoe and up the lot went, so later hearing glass crashing all around I flew to the basement and we all went in to the shelter.
>
> Lady Astor and Mr. Jim [Brand] came in and I heard the front door glass broke and Lady Astor got some splinters in her hair and the powder glass was on her shoulders. I picked the splinters out of her hair.

Rosina Harrison, always called Rose, was a Yorkshire woman whose stalwart temperament was a perfect match for Nancy's. Michael Astor gives us a typical scene: "One of the points about Rose was that she talked nearly as much as my mother and, in her broad Yorkshire accent, always answered back. 'It's no good your going on like that, m'lady. You told me last night to give you the yellow print, and now that you've got it you're not *satisfied*.' Rose always emphasized the last word in her sentences. But Rose's words would probably be lost to my mother, who by this time would be telling her to do something quite different." The two women understood and respected each other. Nancy once told a reporter: "Nobody would keep Rose but me, and nobody would stay with me but Rose." Through the alarums and excursions of thirty-five years Nancy and Rose remained together.

After the March blitz the raids came nightly. One simply improvised. The Lord Mayor's Parlour (office) had vanished and was set up again on a small wooden table in a corner of the library (undamaged) on Tavistock Road. Rows of beds were placed in Virginia House to take care of the homeless. In the blackout, the bombers often mistook the town for the harbor, where the great ships lay. At night the fires bloomed one after another, until there were waves and curtains of fire all over the city. Wherever the sky remained clear there was a garden of rockets and shells, and searching beams. Once, without a sound, a column of white water rose to an enormous height in the harbor, but in the morning the ships were still there, like ships in a painting, as though nothing had happened. Old Smeaton Tower, brought in from the sea after a hundred and thirty years on Eddystone Reef, glowed rosy red from the fires, then stark white under a magnesium flare—like a giant phallus pointing at the sky.

On mornings after the raids Nancy walked out among the rubble. One morning she came upon a girl of twenty-two standing silent as a stone in the place where her home had been the night before. Her baby, her mother, and her grandmother had vanished from sight. Nancy put her arm around the girl's shoulders and after a while they moved away together. Over and over she was to find people standing like that, lost souls among the rubble; somehow she brought them back to life again.

When Waldorf was ill, as he often was that spring, it delighted her to discover that she could make a good Lord Mayor herself. She wrote to Norman Davis, "Since my work down here I feel competent to take on any job, go to the Admiralty, War Office, or even the Foreign Office, but I've a sneaking feeling I shan't be asked." She was proud now that Philip had once likened her to Lloyd George. Although she had resented it at the time, she now saw that he meant that like Lloyd George she could do disagreeable things and do them quickly. When there was incompetence in Plymouth she would not have mistakes covered up, no matter whose toes got trod upon.

Perhaps it was harder when Waldorf was there; although he

was always a support to her, the waiting role was more difficult. One night she had stood in the street below while he went into a house that had been hit by fire bombs to bring down an old woman from the top floor. It was the latest German custom to drop oil mines that would reach the cellar, explode, and in a moment send up the whole house in flames. She and a Red Cross friend had tried to get a fire pump, but a warden had made them leave it in its proper place. There was nothing for it; she, like so many others, had to wait out those moments that determine one's fate. Would that bomb go off or not?

When the Churchills visited the ruins that had been Plymouth, Winston wept. Nancy turned to him. "It's all very well to cry, Winston, but you got to do somethin'." She meant that he must step up the inadequate fire-fighting services, a need that she had been pointing out, until then fruitlessly, in the House.

Both these master politicians knew that Clemmie Churchill's popularity was a political asset, and Nancy had accordingly arranged some appearances for herself with Mrs. Churchill alone, without the Prime Minister's presence to steal her thunder. Faced with this maneuver Churchill drew a few paces aside and stood with his back to the ladies, apparently sunk in deep thought; then, turning to face them, he pronounced with the utmost gravity: "In time of war the supreme decisions must rest with the Prime Minister and with him alone. Mrs. Churchill will come with me." This time victory in their recurring duel was plainly with the male champion.

But it was a minor victory. Nancy didn't really need Clemmie. In those days she *was* Plymouth. In April she had written to Davis: "We have had three raids since Monday. . . . There is no Plymouth. I never imagined I should see such destruction. I am working all day and all night. This is just to tell you that blitzes don't break our spirits, but only our hearts."

The Hoe, now pockmarked with bomb craters, faced the great oceans: Plymouthers have always watched there for the foe. They had danced there in the Napoleonic wars. From the days when she had gone "eefing" in the streets of Richmond with blind Willy, Nancy had loved to dance, and now it was her inspiration that once again there should be dancing on the Hoe. There was a military band, and that first night Nancy led the dance. Every evening in the twilight hour, before the bombers came over, the people came. The writer Clemence Dane described the scene in a poem:

> Who dances?
> Oh—sailors—girls from the canteen
> Men at a Warden's post—
> A smiling couple from a ravaged home—
> And others who lost everything,
>   They come
>
> . . . every night sedately
> Most innocent and stately
> The boys and girls are dancing,
> Are dancing on the Hoe.

Privately Waldorf and Nancy made the ultimate gesture; they changed their wills to specify that if they should be killed in a raid they were to be buried in the common grave at Plymouth. Waldorf had a wooden board placed over the portal of the ruined church of St. Andrews bearing the single inscription: Resurgam.

Few saw the other side of Nancy's courage. She wrote to Davis: "I am giving my life's blood, which is running thin." And, "Oh, how I miss Philip." Cliveden was still a place of refuge, but there they seemed to miss Philip most of all. "Cliveden talks," said Nancy, "are no longer Cliveden talks."

The Astor boys were all on active duty. Jakie and Michael were in a home-based liaison unit. Jakie had inherited his mother's gift for the unexpected phrase. On the first day of the war he remarked, "Everything looks the same but feels different." There was a special bond between the two youngest boys, who had been in the nursery together ("like Phyllis and me," Nancy said), and now the two were together again, "careening about the country in their little tanks," according to their mother. As the danger of invasion lessened, both were sent overseas with their regiments, Michael serving as liaison officer between the British and American forces.

"Little Bobbie" Shaw, now forty, was severly wounded in a bombing raid. He had attempted to join a cavalry outfit but finally had to settle for home defense. Bill Astor was a naval intelligence officer stationed in the Near East. Until 1940, David had devoted himself to propaganda work and to the Europe Study Group, which remained active through the first year of the war. He had hoped for a special appointment that might lead him somehow to Adam von Trott on the other side. Sir Stafford Cripps, now Lord President of the Privy Council and leader of the House, was sympathetic, but the Foreign Office turned a consistently deaf ear. After Dunkirk, David gave up his rather frustrating activities in the propaganda field to join the shooting war as a Marine.

At Cliveden the Canadian hospital had been reinstated for its second war, and Nancy worked there as hard as ever. The motor bicycle described to the Allens at Rhodes House had not been a joke but a serious mode of transportation, for Nancy's constant shuttling back and forth, from the House of Commons, to Plymouth, to Cliveden, and back to London, soon exhausted her gas ration. Although she did not look it or feel it or act it, Nancy was at this time over sixty, and Waldorf was perhaps right in making her give up her motor bike. GBS, ever concerned to keep Nancy out of trouble, cautioned her seriously: "Be very careful not to use the Red Cross car for private visits." Later in the war she was fined £50 and costs for ordering unrationed clothing from the States, an event that caused Jakie to remark to GBS that his mother was working much too hard and a year in the clink would do her a world of good!

All through the war years emissaries and messages continued to arrive from the underground resistance in Germany. In June of 1941 Waldorf took up the cudgels for political propaganda aimed at these resistance groups. He spoke twice on the subject in the Lords. He was not afraid of demanding a comprehensive statement of war aims, and of making a leap into future planning. "One alternative to Hitler is union between freedom-loving nations. . . . We have to do for Europe what Abraham Lincoln did for United States of America, and I believe we can do it." It was Philip's old theme. Reflecting the Trott memo from Washington, which David had fruitlessly passed on to the Foreign Office, Waldorf spoke of "thousands of anti-Hitler Germans in Germany as well as out of Germany . . . and of many downtrodden Belgians, Dutch, and Norwegians who cannot be expected to risk their lives just to save England" but who would presumably be ready to do so for the future of

Europe. He wanted British propaganda to make a positive appeal to all freedom-loving groups, not excluding those in Germany, who might rise against the Nazi tyranny.

In February, 1942, disturbed by the current hardening propaganda line of the overseas broadcasts, Nancy spoke to the same theme in the Commons. It was un-English, she said, to appeal to hate. If she had only stuck to her subject she might have put across a vital and forward-looking new approach to this field of propaganda and political warfare. Instead she wandered into digressions and worse, into using phrases loosely and exposing prejudices that obscured the real meaning of her speech. She began directly enough:

"When we talk about foreign propaganda, we have to remember that all over Europe there are millions of people like the people in this country who really want a new world and who did not want this war. They are living under dictatorships and it is not easy for them to get from under those dictatorships, but we have not, so far, appealed to that particular strata. . . . There are people who hate Naziism, but still like the people of Germany. Those are the people who should appeal to the Germans and who would get a response from them. . . . I know a great many . . . people who loathed Naziism long before any of us did in this House. They understood it and dreaded it, but they are never asked to Broadcast. There ought to be a little more idealism and vision in the BBC. I am rather frightened of the sort of Foreign Office touch that we are getting. If there is one thing true about this country it is that it is strongly protestant. We are a protesting people. If we were not . . . we should be like Europe. We should not have loved freedom of thought. The BBC ought to be very careful of the kind of people they are putting at the head of their talks."

Brendan Bracken (the Minister of Information): "Will the Noble Lady tell us exactly what she means?"

Nancy: "You must have what I might call a protestant point of view. . . . Look at Italy, France, Spain and all those countries. They are living in a sort of ecclesiastical despotism. . . . We want free thought, protestant thought . . . and I feel that a lot of us have thought that the Foreign Office is far too unprotestant to represent the country. . . .

"An Hon. Member has said that the world is fighting to go back to where it was. You cannot go back. Even God cannot bring back the past, and I do not think many people want it back. We want a new world, a world built not on speeches and not on sham, because we have had enough sham, we have been led up the garden path for years by people talking about brotherhood when they did not know what it was."

The Deputy Chairman: "The Noble Lady is talking of affairs at home. The Vote is for Broadcasting abroad."

Nancy: "I was talking about things I wanted to happen, and the world the BBC is trying to build up abroad. We want a new kind of world and we are fighting for it. I believe it will appeal to thousands of people abroad. Do not let us put out hate. Do not let us be afraid to tell the people abroad that we are fighting as much for them as for the people at home. So far you have not done that, and I believe the reason is that you have not got the right kind of people to do it. Words without feeling are clouds without rain."

Sir Irving Albery: "I want to deal only with the question of finance. . . ."

Mr. Bracken: ". . . the Noble Lady the Member for the Sutton Division of Plymouth made a speech which I thought in a way was deplorable. Religious bigotry is un-English, undemocratic and wholly harmful. To bring religious prejudice to bear against anyone occupying a high position at the BBC is a monstrous injury to our public life."

Nancy: "I did not say that. I said it was a point of view which was un-English. I said I thought that the BBC was getting too much of the tone of the Foreign Office. . . ."

Mr. Bracken: "I am sorry that I cannot accept criticisms of the Foreign Office. I have very little time left."

She had tried to convey the idea of a common humanity in Europe to which Britian might appeal. Like Waldorf she had wished to invoke the vision of a new Europe, a rallying point for all who loved freedom and who could combine for peace, the vision in fact of which she had first spoken on the American tour of 1922. Times had changed, bitterly and for the worse. Now the all-powerful Minister of Information, the man at Churchill's right hand, seized upon her prejudices, her old and now thoroughly outdated belief that only those of the Protestant faith could really believe in freedom. There were now many impatient men in the House who were all for the hard line, for total victory, "unconditional surrender," and all that implied, and who preferred to ignore what the Member for the Sutton Division of Plymouth had to say.

It may be that we are having second thoughts on this subject and that we are now more willing to take into account what Nancy was rather ineptly trying to convey to the House in 1942. George Kennan, writing in the *New York Review of Books* in 1973, attributes the lack of interest in the German resistance to the fact that its members came so largely from the formerly conservative classes in Germany. Trott and Moltke, for example, were members of the old Prussian aristocracy, the group most distrusted by many people in authority in England and America. It was the old story of the tendency to fight a current war still burdened by the concepts of the war that had immediately preceded it. According to Mr. Kennan, both Churchill and Roosevelt "believed themselves to be still fighting in the second World War the Prussian Junkerdom they had conceived themselves to be fighting in the first." They simply did not believe that any conservative group in Germany could genuinely wish to turn power over to the people.

Actually, the Kreisau documents were conceived on advanced democratic principles, including even the principle of participatory democracy which Jefferson had wished, but had failed to establish in America. These Germans today are still not given their due. "One gains the impression," says Kennan, "of a certain real irritation, as though the persons in question had had the ill grace, before dying in their various forms of agony, to confuse the issue by disturbing an otherwise tidy pattern of unadulterated Germany iniquity."

It was this tidy pattern that Nancy had in mind when she spoke of the Foreign Office point of view. Her reference to the Catholicism of certain members of the BBC was uncalled for and most unwise; unhappily it obscured her real point. She wished to tell the House that there were people in Germany far more dedicated to the defeat of Hitler than anyone in England, and that these people should be considered in directing propaganda to Germany. It was a sound point, and does her more credit than Brendan Bracken's summary "I cannot accept criticism of the Foreign Office."

Waldorf heard all this with deep concern. Nancy had been put down in the House before, but never before with contempt, and, even though she may not have realized it, never before had she seemed so helpless before attack. It occurred to him that they must see the war out together, and that then the team of Astor and Astor, so long in public life, might honorably retire.

At this time Waldorf was making major changes in the *Observer.* He had long been concerned about Garvin's drinking. The editor had never been a teetotaler, but now, to Waldorf's mind, his drinking was going too far. This trouble came at a time when the two men were growing apart politically; as Waldorf moved to the Left, closer to David's views, Garvin was growing more conservative. The issue came to a head with Garvin's vigorous support of Churchill's move to take personal charge of the Ministry of Defence, which Waldorf had publicly opposed. The editor was not the man to give way easily, but Waldorf's mind was made up. Under the terms of the original contract he brought the matter up before an agreed tribunal, who found against the editor. To put it bluntly, Garvin was fired. He was replaced by Ivor Brown, who was to act until David should take over. Nancy agreed to these changes at the time, but as the paper moved further to the Left she often regretted the good old (prewar) days.

In 1942, with the war in the forefront of everyone's mind, it would appear that the Cliveden Set story had been laid to rest. Unfortunately President Roosevelt himself casually, almost inadvertently, used the phrase in an effort to stir up some of his own lagging patriots at home. Any reference at all from such a source cut Nancy to the quick, and she made no effort to suppress her feelings. She wrote at once, in a letter delivered by the Ambassador.

Dear Franklin,

I thought that Philip Lothian had laid the Communist lie about the Cliveden Set. Waldorf and I were distressed that you should have used that term in referring to isolationists, defeatists, etc. As you knew Philip and realized that his was the leadership of the so-called Cliveden Set, I really am distressed that you as a friend should have given such widespread publicity to a really cruel lie. Forgive my feeling so strongly, but as a politician like yourself, I *do* feel strongly—I've never believed lies about you or Eleanor, and fought your battles in and out. Mr. Pegler was the man who must have widely spread the lie! Your mother would not have believed it.

May we meet soon.

Yours,

Nancy Astor.

Roosevelt was troubled by this letter. As he explained to Sumner Welles, he had used the expression "Cliveden Set" in a general sense, without wishing any reference to Nancy or Waldorf personally. "They were not subversive, but they were proved wrong by hindsight." Most people, right or wrong, believed that they had belonged to the Chamberlain school in England. "The term 'Cliveden Set' became a symbol of not just appeasement, but of a failure to evaluate the world situation as it really was." There were still people in Washington who subscribed to the same theory. "They have been proved wrong but have continued in their wrong headedness, while Waldorf and Nancy didn't."

All very well, as far as it went, although the identification with the Chamberlain school was not entirely accurate. Apart from that it was a very fair statement. Rather sadly Sumner Welles memoed back that "he did not like the tone" of Nancy's letter and recommended that no answer be made. It was finally agreed that Mrs. Roosevelt should answer, using, if she liked, the words of FDR's memo.

In the fall the *Daily Worker* again took up the attack, but Waldorf decided that there should be no public response. No responsible person on either side of the Atlantic doubted their patriotism, and the time had come to ignore these attacks. "Newspapers," said Nancy, "can't make a bad man good, or a good man bad." In 1942 one had no time to worry about "The Set."

When General C. H. Gerhard, U.S. Army, arrived in England in July, 1943, to take over the command of the 29th Division in

Plymouth he was given three directives, one of which was "to get along with Lady Astor." The General drove in at once to call on the Lady Mayoress. "My mother was Richmond," he began. They were off to the beginning of a natural partnership, the best Nancy had had since she and Colonel Newborne had worked together in the Canadian hospital during World War I. The arrival of the 29th gave her a tremendous lift. "To hear that Southern accent on every corner of a Plymouth street is almost Heaven." Still, human nature being what it is, there were times when some of the boys needed straightening out. She told them "When you're good, tell them you're from Virginia. But when you're drunk or disorderly, say you're from New York." In far-gone cases she would bring the boy in to sleep it off on the couch at 3 Elliot Terrace. One such unconscious body awoke and stumbled into Waldorf's study, demanding that the Lord Mayor give him a drink.

There were service clubs on either side of the Lord Mayor's house, and Nancy was constantly in and out of one or the other. Some of the American officers were billeted in number 3, among them a black who was always included, even when pressure of guests sometimes made Nancy ask others to go out in order to make room at the table. They were one household; the segregation mores of a Virginia girlhood had happily been outgrown.

One day the Lord Mayor of London came to visit, and Waldorf took him into the Red Cross Club next door. The staff was rather afraid that its American clients might take the two Lord Mayors, all resplendent in robes, plumed hats, and gold chains, to be characters from a traveling circus. Nancy came upstairs to report to the staff that all was well and to take over the canteen so that the Englishwomen might go to shake the hand of the Lord Mayor of London. This was an experience to be recounted to future generations, equivalent to that of the old ladies of Nancy's childhood who boasted that they had been kissed by Robert E. Lee.

That fall Nancy was made a Pfc at a ceremony held at division headquarters. Later on she was promoted to corporal. One of Corporal Astor's cherished privileges was occasional attendance at mess. In World War I she had written to Mr. Neve, "Don't speak to *me* of sausages," as though the very thought caused her agonies of hunger. In this war she was not above taking home from the mess hall a drumstick or a piece of chicken breast wrapped in a napkin. With increasing rank, her ambition, and her greed, rose higher; she wanted nothing less than a whole pig. She had previously gone down with Gerhard to a camp in Cornwall to speak to the men and had regaled them with Cornish dialect stories. Later on, at a division concert and variety show, the general invited her on stage and introduced her to the audience. If she would tell her Cornish stories he promised her a splendid prize. Nothing loath, Nancy obliged, bringing down the house, but the applause became absolutely deafening when a beautiful pig, all perfumed and pink-beribboned, was led forth for the formal presentation. As though this were not glory enough, after the capture of St. Lô she was given a battlefield commission as second lieutenant. She wanted to be flown to Normandy, and an official request was made that Corporal N. Astor be allowed to rejoin the division, thereby throwing the U. S. Army record office into considerable disarray.

After St. Lô, victory could only be a matter of time. In Plymouth the rebuilding was well under way. This was Waldorf's special concern. He had started the Plymouth Improvement Plan in 1941, while the bombs, literally, were still falling on the city. Advanced ideas of city planning were employed in the rebuilding, under the direction of Professor Patrick Abercrombie. Waldorf was tireless and successful in raising funds from private, municipal, and government sources. Some of the new ideas really shocked Nancy—she had loved the old Plymouth, now gone forever—but as the war drew to an end her mind was not on Plymouth. It was on the elections to come.

18

Some Carry a Light

It had become almost impossible to think of a world without Hitler, without Roosevelt, without Churchill; yet all, in 1945, vanished from the scene—Hitler by his own hand, Roosevelt by death after more than twelve years in office, and Churchill by the ballot. A whole world was abruptly swept away, and with it went the career of the first woman Member of Parliament.

The end of the war for Nancy was the beginning of the most serious struggle of her personal life. Never before in thirty-nine years of marriage had she and Waldorf come to an irreconcilable difference on a point vital to them both. In the last months of 1944 it was obvious that the war would soon be over. To Waldorf, shattered in health at sixty-five and bone-tired, it seemed that their work was done. More clearly than Nancy, he saw the new world coming in. She had never fought an election alone, and the time had come when he could no longer help her. Even if he could, where in that new world would she take her place? He told her that she should not contest the next election. Nancy was equally determined that she should. She felt no diminution of her physical powers; mentally she was as alert and quick as ever, and as committed to the things that she and Waldorf had always worked for. Deeper than this, she felt that he belittled her as a person, as a woman, in taking from her the career that she had worked so long and so hard to win. He had always supported her, and his withdrawal now simply bewildered her. Well, she would not go down without a fight.

Shaw innocently entered the lists by asking her how she was going to run in the coming election, "as a Churchillian, or a Beveridgean or a Communist or (which I recommend) as Nancy Astor?" Nancy now called on her old friend for advice and help in her battle with Waldorf. Shaw was a bit floored at first and then responded to her request with a serious Shavian look into the political future.

> How am I to know what is in the mind of Waldorf and your serpent brood if they really want to hound you out of public life? . . . Obviously you have twenty years work left in you yet, and are getting deeper instead of being merely quick-witted and inconsecutive.
>
> Both you and your mate are in a false position as members of the Conservative Party, or indeed of any party . . . When Hitler and Mussolini are finally steam-rollered, there will be only three parties: the Die Hards, the Fascists, and the Communists. The regime will be Fascist, as Fascism, which is Capitalism established and endowed by the state, is too firmly established here, and too acceptable to the Trade Unions, to be shaken. The Opposition will be Communists trying continually to substitute State ownership for Capitalist ownership, and State enterprise for Capitalist enterprise. National banking and transport, municipalization of urban land, and collective farming will be the Opposition programs in the rest of the century. Waldorf will be an Urban Land municipalizer or he will be nothing. That is to say, he will be a Communist, whether his party calls itself so or not. You in the Commons cannot go on voting with the Die Hards against him. You will both be against the Fascists and for the Communists on every important division. You will both find yourselves in embittered conflict with your Cliveden guests, just as old Lady

Carlisle . . . found her social circle broken up when the Liberal Party split over Home Rule. This monstrous caravanserai in which you and Waldorf live will be deserted by its rabble of Tory subalterns and public school boys and their relatives as the Carlisle mansion in Kensington Palace Gardens was deserted by the Chamberlain Whigs. . . . It may end in your living sensibly in a twelve-room villa as Charlotte and I did.

A very sensible letter, although Shaw ignored the Astor skill in combining the use of state and private capital. He was well aware of Waldorf's approach to the planning and rebuilding of Plymouth, and he naturally approved of Waldorf's increasing inclination toward the Left. Plymouth was rising from the ashes under what Shaw referred to as "dual control," and of which he only partly approved. He suggested that Nancy might profitably take over Plymouth Improvement, although he must have known that city planning was not her cup of tea.

Altogether it was a discouraging reply; he seemed to share Waldorf's doubts and fears. She had once represented the future, but was not the future already past? Both Waldorf and Shaw feared that she might increasingly vote with the diehards, falling back on prejudices now completely outworn. Even in wartime she had opposed Sunday opening for theaters and allowances for the "unmarried wives" of men overseas. Small things that can perhaps be defended, but the legislator out of step in the small things may find himself alone, and the big things will escape him too. Once Nancy had belonged in the strange new world that followed a war. Now she no longer did.

She tried to put the battle on a domestic basis, but Shaw would have none of that:

The question of your contesting Plymouth again is not a domestic one. It goes far beyond that. No man has a right to make his wife give up a public career to look after his grown-up and married family. No woman has a right to throw over her public work merely to make things comfortable for herself at home. So you twain must fight it out on other lines.

If your retirement would secure the parliamentary seat for a woman younger and abler than yourself, then I should say that the twenty-fifth anniversary would be a good opportunity for retirement. But if it would reduce the number of women in the

House by one, and substitute some ordinary male duffer, I should say hold on like grim death.

And as for Waldorf, Shaw asked:

What the devil is Waldorf to do with you if you have no Parliament to go to, and no children to bring up? You would be a grandmother and spoil your grandchildren; but you certainly wouldn't spoil Waldorf. He ought to thank God for Westminster.

That was Nancy's view, but in the end her decision was a domestic one. She decided, not, as Shaw might have had her do, as a woman, or as Nancy Astor, but as a wife. The formal announcement, made on the day of her twenty-fifth anniversary in the House, simply stated that "Lord Astor informed Lady Astor that he did not at his age feel physically able to go through the heavy strain and stress of another contested election. . . . Lady Astor and he have fought seven elections together, and including the period when he was M.P. for Plymouth, have supported each other actively in the political arena for thirty-five years. It would be difficult for Lady Astor to stand again without his help."

Nancy put it a bit more vigorously. "Today," she said, "I have done one of the hardest things I have ever done in my life, but a thing that every man in the world will approve of. I have said that I will not fight the election because my husband does not want me to. I have had twenty-five years in the House of Commons and I am bound to obey. Is that not a triumph for men?"

There were fitting celebrations. In November, the Bishop of Plymouth conducted a service of thanksgiving for her twenty-five years of service. On December 1, 1944, the anniversary of that short but famous walk from the Bar of the House to the Speaker's table, the Sutton Division of Plymouth sent twenty-five red roses and the women Members of the House gave a luncheon in her honor. That night there was a dinner attended by delegates from women's organizations all over the country. Waldorf, despite their differences, rose to the occasion: "When I married Nancy, I hitched my wagon to a star and when I got into the House of Commons in 1910, I found that I had hitched my wagon to a shooting star. In 1919 when she got into the

House, I found that I had hitched my wagon to a sort of V-2 rocket. But the star which is represented by Nancy Astor will, I am sure, remain a beacon light for all with high ideals."

It was a far cry from the days when Members had drawn aside "as though," as she said, "I were Lady Godiva." There were many Members that day to wring her hand. Still Nancy vacillated. She had announced her intention to retire, but the decision need not be irrevocable until after the July election. Even at this late date it seemed that to yield gracefully was beyond her power. Yielding gracefully had never been a Langhorne trait. Shaw, a true friend, pulled no punches. He pointed out that one of her speeches at the beginning of the New Year had been "virtually an appeal to the public" for their support. She could not leave the question hanging; either she must defy Waldorf and declare her candidacy now or else she must retire. She must face facts: "If a Conservative candidate is chosen . . . or a Labour candidate with Waldorf's support . . . the situation created would be intolerable if you then resolved, too late, to split the vote against Waldorf and your own party."

There was no turning back. She did not actually have to yield her seat until June, but finally the last day came. She had never depended on eloquence in the House but rather on "a shameful audacity much needed in that place." But this day was different. Her true feelings came out, and in a simple way her comment on the occasion was eloquent: "I am heart-broken about going, and I shall miss the House. But the House won't miss me. It never misses anybody. I've seen them all go—Lloyd George, Asquith, Baldwin, Snowden, MacDonald and the rest—and not one of them was missed. The House is like the sea, and M.P.'s like little ships that sail across it and disappear over the horizon. Some of them carry a light and others don't. That's the only difference."

It was now time for Nancy to devote herself to Waldorf and her "serpent brood." It was not in her nature to hold a grudge, but she never in what remained of her life was to admit that Waldorf had been right. Fifteen years later she wrote that her beloved Waldorf had been ill when he made her give up Parliament and "ill men don't make good judgments." In another letter written at the same time she expressed the same thought with less tact: "Waldorf made me leave Parliament after he was feeble minded. *He* didn't gain by it, *I* didn't gain by it, and neither did Parliament."

There may have been some element of self-deception in Nancy's view of these events. Waldorf was terribly distressed by her reaction against him. On their next trip to Virginia he took Nancy's dear friend, Ella (Mrs. Gordon) Smith, aside and begged her to make Nancy understand. He insisted that he had not "forbidden" or "prevented" her from standing for the 1945 election. He had told her that his health would prevent his campaigning with her, and that he thought in any case, as a Conservative, *she would lose the postwar election.* Ella Smith tried, but without effect. In her illogical way Nancy knew that without his certainly very strong discouragement she would have stood, and, in her own view, would have won the seat. This was equivalent, in her mind, to being made to retire, and she clung to this unfair view in the face of all his protests. Some of the total unreason of her attitude may have been due to the Christian Science doctrine, so often misapplied by Nancy, that all disability is "unreal" and therefore can be overcome.

A stronger, younger man than Waldorf might have weathered the storm. Even Waldorf might have, if something rather sad had not been coming between them. The cherished views, the mutual political goals that for so long had made them a splendid team, were diverging. Nancy, as so often happens as one grows older, was leaning to the Right, while Waldorf, with his far greater sensitivity to political trends, was moving to the Left. The new status of the *Observer* helped to point up these differences. Waldorf was in sympathy with his leftist son David, soon to be editor under a newly organized *Observer* trust, while Nancy regretted Garvin and the good old days, when Waldorf and she and the *Observer* had been all of one mind.

The drifting apart, the virtual estrangement of these years, was not entirely Nancy's fault. In 1941 Waldorf had suffered a slight stroke or heart attack, or possibly both; with failing health, he was becoming increasingly critical of his wife's unpredictable ways. It was an almost superhuman adjustment that he expected of her at the end of the war. Nancy had thrived on the frenetic activity of the war years; now the abrupt end of all that was, in effect, a physical shock. At such a time of stress she would have turned to Philip, not only her dearest friend but the source of support in trouble through many years. But Philip was no longer there. Waldorf's defection, as it seemed to her, his withdrawal from their common activities, came at a time when she needed him most. There were times at which he seemed almost to add to her burdens. In his attempt to simplify his life, Waldorf sold 4 St. James's Square and Nancy was reduced to a flat at 35 Hill Street. The St. James's Square house was a symbol; its passing was a sign that the great days were over. Her family, too, was drastically reduced. All four of the Astor boys had married during the war: Michael in 1942, Jakie and David in 1944, and Bill in June, 1945, the same month that saw Nancy's departure from Parliament. Without children, without a career, almost without Waldorf—was it any wonder that these were difficult years?

During the war GBS had been a pillar of strength, "Now that the old Round Table are all gone," he said, "I shall have to take it upon myself to act as the Cliveden Set." The job was bigger than he realized. Charlotte Shaw died in 1944. Nancy, riding with him to the crematorium, was shocked by his levity. He explained that his real farewell to Charlotte had been said at home, sitting alone and playing over the records of classical music that they had loved and played together. Shaw, constantly absorbed in his work, was not built for heavy emotional burdens. The relationship to Nancy remained close, but after the war he found it necessary to back away.

"I want you to forget and drop me because I am an old and dying man (actually I am dead and considerably decomposed) and you must find a Sunday husband young enough to last your time."

Not unexpectedly, even the violence of the Shavian language failed to check a friendship that was perhaps necessary to them both. They had too much in common. One day, talking of the ever-fascinating if reputedly vulgar subject of money, Nancy and GBS discovered that both now were allowed to keep only sixpence out of every pound of income. A melancholy distinction. Nancy declared that he must leave her all his money in his will, so that the world would know that she was the love of his life. The sage did not commit himself, perhaps already toying with his secret passion for phonetic spelling. He came less frequently to Cliveden, complaining of the "fearfully miscellaneous crowd of nobodies whom your Virginian hospitality tolerates." Rather pathetically, Nancy welcomed them all. Like Chillie, she invited in all passersby. She wrote to her old friends Barbara Brown and Bessie Hobson, "If any Virginians are planning a trip to England, tell them I want to see them. Whether I like them or not."

Unquestionably it was a lonely time. "All my children," she said, "have country houses," and her grandchildren rarely came to London. The children were occupied with their own lives. Bill had taken over the family business interests in New York in addition to his chores as an M.P. Although Bill was the only one of her sons who was seriously interested in a parliamentary career, Michael and Jakie both served briefly in the House.

All three of the boys were contesting seats in the 1950 election when Waldorf, in an effort to offer Nancy at least a peripheral role, asked each of them to have her speak for him once during his campaign. In his book *Tribal Feeling*, Michael describes a previous occasion when his mother had appeared on his platform. The candidate had been billed to speak first. Nancy's was the supporting role. When Michael had resumed his seat amid the usual polite applause she had turned to him, remarking in a voice audible throughout the hall, "Where did you learn to do this? I feel like Balaam when the ass spoke."

On the later occasion Michael awaited the moment of his mother's speech "with mixed feelings of curiosity and apprehension." Apprehension perhaps prevailed. He went round to visit her beforehand, to discuss the speech and to suggest that restraint should be the order of the day.

"The women of England," began Nancy, "need rousing." As a married man, said Michael, this was not quite the line that he wanted her to take. "Well, then, I'll talk about the humbug of the Labour Party." Michael thought that this was more like it, but he made the mistake of telling her "whatever else you do, omit all reference to me."

Nancy's response was instantaneous: "You've given me a good idea. I'm going to make my speech about *you*. I'll pay you out, Michael, I'll tell the meeting that politics bore you stiff, and that all you really like is painting. I'll tell them you're just a

Lothario, an artist, and not a very good husband; and that you make fun of them all behind their backs and that they shouldn't vote for you. How would you like that?" And then, in the tones of a Virginian Negro, she went on: "I'll tell 'em you don't know nothin'. I'll tell 'em you're crazy. I'll tell 'em I got a son who's crazy. That ought to rouse them if nothing else will. Or," she added, holding her head very erect, looking down her nose and assuming a haughty English accent, "I might tell them how *privileged* they are to have the opportunity of voting for my distinguished son, how *privileged* they are to be addressed by his distinguished mother. That wouldn't rouse them; that would put 'em to sleep." She finished in her normal tone of voice: "Now get on with you. I must work on this. Oh dear, oh dear, I never knew that I could ever miss anything as much as the House of Commons."

When the moment actually came for her speech she was pathetically eager to do well for Michael's sake. She arrived sitting in the back of a car reading, not her notes, but the Ninety-first Psalm. Michael described the scene in his diary:

> At the start a youth of about eighteen heckled and shouted at her. She . . . told him he must first learn manners and then would be the time for him to find out about politics. . . . "Young man, don't you dare be impertinent!" then, looking him straight in the eye, she gave him a smile almost of recognition, "He's only a boy," and shaking her finger she finished with "Now just you shut *up*." Which he did.

Once Nancy was launched on her speech Michael admitted that she spoke like a political veteran, driving a wedge into both the Socialist and the Liberal vote. She used all the old techniques: "laughing, scolding, giving them the benefit of the doubt, and [then] giving it to them straight from the shoulder. . . . They cheered and called for more." On a later occasion, speaking for Bill, she was interrupted by an old man who shouted: "When your party was in power I was in the workhouse." "I wish to heavens," she told him, "you were there now." It was the old recipe, and on the platform, at least, it still worked.

But life was not all campaigning. The children still loved her, but none of them really needed her now. Young people seemed altogether less satisfactory than they had been in the past. She had forgotten her own dictum that "Old people have always thought that the young were going to the devil. They ought to know; they've been there themselves."

It was not perhaps so much the young who baffled her as the world they lived in, where they married and unmarried casually and *never answered letters*. They were not going to the devil in the way she was used to. Even royalty was not the same as it had been. Mrs. Simpson had been defeated, but for what? For Margaret Rose! Having working men to meet the King and Queen at 4 St. James's Square, yes; but a party in Nancy Lancaster's decorating shop, attended by Princess Margaret for no other purpose than to enjoy herself, that was something else. Nancy Lancaster's younger son Jeremy had been pub-crawling with the Princess a few nights previously until 4 A.M., and Margaret, as princesses must do if they want to go anywhere, had invited herself to the party in the (very superior) shop. Bohemia, even Mayfair Bohemia of the mildest sort, was not Nancy's cup of tea, but something, maybe tribal feeling, drew her to the party. After all, Nancy Lancaster was her eldest sister Lizzie's child.

Somewhere along the way to her niece's party, Nancy had acquired a companion. When two other young members of the tribe, Virginia Brand and Douglas Langhorne, arrived together, they saw their Aunt Nancy seated with another woman on a sofa. Waving casually, they had started for the bar when they were arrested by a familiar voice aimed unerringly in their direction: "Ma'am, may I present my niece and nephew. . . . Her Majesty, the Queen of Rumania." The result was utter confusion. Virginia made a deep curtsy to her aunt, then turned halfway up and made a very shaky one to the Queen. Douglas shook hands, but "forgot," as he later said, to take his other hand out of his pocket. "The look Aunt Nancy gave me was worth preserving . . . in fact anyone less immune to dirty looks from Lady Astor might have turned to stone on the spot."

The party threatened to become, as Nancy Mitford would have said, a case of Ma'am and Super Ma'am, with two royal ladies under one roof. Who should take precedence, an ex-Queen or a very current Princess? This nice question was discussed at the bar. Nancy, displaying a tact the young rarely gave her credit for, removed herself and Her Majesty before the arrival of Margaret Rose.

Her Virginia family offered little more satisfaction. "The more you try to help them," she complained to a nephew, "the less they like you," and indeed she did find it difficult to regulate all their lives in the course of a brief visit every year or two. A regular Virginia stop was with "my nephew the farmer" and his family, who lived on a working dairy farm in Albemarle County. When their noble relative was expected everyone turned to in an effort to make the place look a little more civilized. Lunch would be no problem as old family servants reappeared for the day to put on an old-time Virginia feast for "Miss Nannie." But advance preparations could be hectic. A sister-in-law once complained that an otherwise pleasant visit had been ruined by her being put to work cleaning up the "yard," removing cow pies with a pitchfork. The visit, as usual, was a rousing success. When invited to inspect the dairy "Aunt Nannie" declined: "A cow, you know, doesn't like to be looked at. A cow doesn't think she is interesting. [In some fantastic way she contrived to look like a cow, bridling.] I wish more people were like her. You, for instance" [pointing at a delighted child]. "That one," she announced triumphantly, "is the spitting image of my father." Spying a tricycle left out on the newly fragrant lawn, she threatened to spank the culprit herself, who was by this time so dissolved in laughter that he did not believe a word of it. As her large black car ("Only queens, corpses, Lady Benger and I still ride in Rolls Royces") receded down the farm road she leaned out, calling "Goodbye, goodbye, you awful people." With a somewhat lighter heart her young relatives resumed life among the cows and the tricycles. It remained, however, an occasion. There were few left, and they were getting fewer, those people with whom she could just be part of the every day.

Old friends, with whom she could feel really at home, were vanishing on both sides of the Atlantic. GBS was to die in 1950 at ninety-four. When he was still only ninety-three she had taken Douglas Langhorne to see him. "Don't corrupt my nephew. He's already infatuated, but he'll soon get over that," etc. The sage performed amiably for the young admirer, even going so far as to refer to "Poor Ellen [Terry]. You know she was something of a prima donna." "It was what you had in common," said Nancy. Shaw answered with the understatement of all time: "I don't go about with the modest cough of a minor poet; I know I'm a capable writer." Now the old man had only a very short time left. In the last weeks of his life Nancy and his niece, Mrs. Musters, were the only persons he wanted to see. On the day before he died he told Nancy: "Oh, Nancy, what I want is to sleep, sleep." It was Nancy who gave the death notice to the newsmen waiting at the door, speaking with the simple eloquence that was hers when she chose. "From the coffers of his genius," she said, "he enriched the world."

In 1948 her old friend Mr. Neve had died. Only a month before she had written him for the last time, signing herself "with love and always gratitude for your inspiration which you gave me over fifty years ago." True friendship, Nancy said, never fades, and indeed with her it never did. Almost at once she was to find a new spiritual counselor, or, perhaps more accurately, a correspondent with whom she exchanged counsel. He was not, as might have been expected, someone from her own church, but a young man then engaged in carrying on Mr. Neve's work in the Blue Ridge Mountains near her old home. The Reverend Douglas Pitt was an Episcopal clergyman, equally at home with mountain people and at a country weekend in a great English house. He was, like Nancy herself, a Virginian, and Virginians, as she said, were not like other folk. Like her he "followed a light," and like her too he could admit to discouragement and frustration. He visited her in England, and she saw him occasionally on her visits home. He was near, but not too near. In her letters to him she opened her heart perhaps more freely than to anyone else in these last years. If Douglas Pitt could not be quite the guide that Mr. Neve had been, still he was a true friend. He filled a critical need in her life.

In the summer of 1950 Waldorf suffered a stroke. He now withdrew from the hurly-burly into his own wing at Cliveden, or into a little sheltered grove on the grounds which he could visit in a wheel chair. "It keeps me sane," he told a friend. He had decorated his retreat with some little leprechaun figures, a pathetic outreach, the friend obviously thought, for some aesthetic that life had denied him. Perhaps he had once found it in Nancy. Then for some time it had failed him.

It was not an easy time for Nancy. She wrote Douglas Pitt, "I have to pray and work . . . over many problems." They included her strained relations with Waldorf, her struggle with loneliness, and the healing work for Waldorf's health. In the last year of his life they grew closer together again. She had tried to keep herself available when, as sometimes happened, he called for her. In June of 1952 she wrote, "He is better . . . sticks to his Bible. Is happy." In the last days the warmth of their old love revived. Then, in October, this fine, gentle, and good man died.

Again Nancy tried not to mourn. After his death she wrote to Douglas Pitt, "I wish I had you here tonight. I know Life is Eternal and Waldorf alright. It's just the shock of parting. . . . God never seems nearer than in trials. I get great comfort—and I need it."

After his death true loneliness struck her down. They had been often apart in the past years but had depended on one another just the same. Bill, the heir, would not have hurried her out of Cliveden, but it was now impossible for her to stay. She left Cliveden and all its glory to the new Lord and Lady Astor and departed to 35 Hill Street without complaint, although not without remarking, some time later, "I never got used to living in a flat."

Travel is the usual anodyne recommended to the new widow, but in Nancy's case her family did not encourage it, and as the years went on Nancy herself was not very keen. In 1953 she had contemplated a tour of Africa but at family urging settled for a visit with friends in Rhodesia, a trip so successful that one wonders why something of the sort was not attempted again. (She had greeted the Governor of Southern Rhodesia, Sir Stewart Gore-Browne, with "Welcome to you, as one slave holder to another!") But her contacts were not with whites alone. A meeting was arranged for her with a group of African intellectuals; if one had not known Nancy one might have feared disaster from this confrontation of old-fashioned Virginia and the black avant-garde. Questions and answers started to fly back and forth: "If your daughter had to choose between marrying an Indian with a very Eastern background and a Rhodesian African with an English culture, which would she choose?" It was certainly a carefully loaded question. Nancy answered without a moment's hesitation, "The Rhodesian African, of course, and God forbid she should marry either." Marriage was hard enough anyway, she said, there was no point in making it harder. Another man asked her did she think her son better than his. "Which are you talking of? I have five sons. One I would trust to run the Empire. Another I wouldn't trust to take me across Berkeley Square."

Once they were laughing she had them eating out of her hand. "Avant-garde" the Africans might be in their own country, they were nearer to Nancy than one might suspect. She certainly spoke to them without any crippling sense of "them" and "us." Her family seems sometimes to have feared that without Waldorf she might become a traveling clown, but, after all, was not that what she really was, a traveling player with the gift of going straight to the point, and then delivering it with a comic twist? Waldorf had given her direction and the larger stage, but Nancy would have been Nancy in any setting.

After this visit she sent most of her collection of Confederate books to friends in Rhodesia. She then wrote to Douglas Pitt for replacements and for work by new writers, but it was not altogether a happy idea. The Confederacy revisited simply upset her. These books, she wrote Douglas, "stir me up and make me hate." She still tried to subdue the Old Nick, who was still there just below the surface and ready to fly out.

In 1954 Irene, Nancy's last surviving sister, fell ill in Virginia. Mirador had been sold in 1950, and Irene spent her last year in a cottage on her son's place in Greenwood. Into her visits with Irene, bedridden and almost in a coma, Nancy threw the whole force of her personality and of her healing faith. For Nannie alone Irene would open her eyes, smile, and sometimes speak. It was after one visit that Nancy wrote, "I must face up to the rather human longing for the past. I was a regular Lot's wife." How could she help it, when the mountains looked the same, but there were no Langhornes left at Mirador?

She played the "I" game with Douglas Pitt as she had used to do with T. E. Lawrence, underlining the wicked pronoun in her letter. "Look in *Science and Health*," she told him, "where the real 'I' is." But her exhortations to look in *Science and Health* became fewer, as age and loneliness gained on her. "I am ashamed of being lonely and missing Waldorf and Cliveden.

I should rejoice and get to work and heal. Well, we must try. . . ." A kinder faith might have told her that as God's child she need not have felt ashamed of her creature feelings.

Bill was good to her. On her visits she observed, like Jakie, that Cliveden "looked the same but felt different." Nancy wrote to Douglas Pitt: "It seems so strange to see another Lady Astor sitting at the head of Cliveden. She's very nice and it's natural. What is not natural is how long I live. I am 81. My family all died before 80–." Bitterest of all came the cry: "Oh, how I miss my Waldorf, my Phyllis, and my whole family who have gone. . . . Where do we go? No one knows–and no one has come back." Perhaps her friend Ella Smith best explains these doubts and the sadness of Nancy's last years. "Nannie," said Mrs. Smith, "was a devout Christian Scientist, but not a good one. She kept confusing herself with God. She didn't know when to step aside and give God a chance." If this is a true judgment, and I believe it is, it was Nancy herself who suffered most. In her desperate honesty she had outlived the new faith and could not recapture the old. She could not go gently into that good night.

Little Bobbie Shaw was now "an old gentleman with a bay window," as his mother described him. But age had not mellowed their relationship, always embattled, nor dulled the painful acuteness of their love. Wissie, as was perhaps natural in a daughter, was closest to her mother in the last years. Nancy never lost the faculty of gratitude. "A marvelous daughter," she said. Nancy Lancaster kept a room ready for her aunt at her home, Hasely Court, a far more luxurious room than she had known at Cliveden. But Nancy did not want luxury. She wanted Cliveden and Waldorf. Nor did her real feeling, even for Wissie, become sentimental with age. She liked to describe Wissie's houses: "twice the size of Cliveden and she's a splendid housekeeper. One of her houses caught on fire and *she* put the fire out! I told her she had made a mistake."

Then there was the marvelous occasion after her eightieth birthday when her beloved Plymouth honored her with the freedom of the city. Here she and Waldorf had ridden in an open carriage festooned with red, white, and blue ribbons, how many years ago it seemed now! Here the young Jim Brand and herself had gone out in the blitz, and Rose had brushed the shattered glass from her hair. Here they had danced on the Hoe. There was Mt. Batten, where she had mounted T. E. Lawrence's motor bike and ridden wildly over the moors. Many were gone, but nevertheless, on this occasion, Nancy was home. Plymouth's wide avenues were new, laid out on plans drawn in the Lord Mayor's office during the war, but Virginia House was still there, and the Astor Institute, and the little park that Waldorf had set aside in the heart of the old city. Since Nancy had entered politics, peace had certainly not come to the nations, but life was better for the working man and woman and for their children. The evidence was all around her. "I am happy to say," she declared, "we have no juvenile delinquency in Plymouth."

As she rose to speak that evening in the Grand Hotel on the Hoe, the sight of a Plymouth audience fired her heart. First she spoke seriously of what she and Waldorf had cared for. She was "very pleased that my husband was the first to recognize the power women ought to have." (Perhaps she had forgotten who had first pointed it out to *him*.) Very soon she was back to telling the old stories, in that accent straight from Greenwood, Virginia. There was the one about little Maybelle and the Negro preacher. Extolling the joys of purity to his flock, he had called upon all the virgins present to stand and praise the Lord. Only one woman had stood, and she held an infant in her arms. "Sister," he remonstrated, "I said virgins." "Amen, Brother, but little Maybelle is too young to stand!" After that there was very little left to say except at the end, "I have never been happier than I have been today." Nor braver, one would like to add.

Mr. Sykes suggests that Nancy from the time of her retirement suffered from a form of premature senility. This would explain her unreasonableness and her persistent quarrel with the husband she really loved. Those who knew her well during those years do not agree. In 1944 Shaw had written her: "You are getting deeper, instead of being merely quick-witted and inconsecutive." Shaw was not often wrong about people, nor was he given to flattering Nancy. Mrs. Gordon Smith, her closest friend in Virgina in the last years, agrees with my own observation that she did not deteriorate mentally to any marked degree until she was past eighty. When I visited her in 1957 she was her old self, moralizing at one moment, serious, alert, and curious about the world at another, and then, most often at the dinner table, telling stories and clowning at the top of her bent. She was a mixture, someone has said, of Joan of Arc and Gracie Fields, and inevitably her family saw her in both parts, neither one of which could have been sustained had she been prematurely senile.

By 1963 all this had changed. Her stories were as good as ever, but they might be, and usually were, repeated word for word five minutes later. But surely at eighty-four one has a right to be senile. Actually senility was a blessing at this time, for it insulated her from the Profumo–Christine Keeler uproar then shattering the peace of Cliveden. This rather inflated political scandal centered on John Profumo, Secretary of State for War. Bill had rented the boathouse at Cliveden to a certain Dr. Ward, who, it later appeared, occasionally entertained call girls in this cottage. Profumo attended swimming-pool parties at Cliveden, and it was believed that he may have betrayed military secrets to one of the girls, Christine Keeler, who was also at that time having an affair with a Russian suspected of being an agent. How much substance there was to this charge is still open to question, but there is no doubt that Profumo lied about his relations with Christine Keeler when questioned in the House of Commons. This the House never forgives, and Profumo was driven out of office to the accompaniment of relentless newspaper publicity.

So long as Nancy stayed at Sandwich she could be kept in ignorance of the whole sorry affair. The newspapers were confiscated and the television set was always said to be broken. "Tell Dean [the butler] to have it fixed," she would say. The whole performance would be repeated the next evening without disturbing her in the least. When finally a dental appointment took her to London, her eyes, keen as ever, caught the name Astor on the newsboy's billboards. "We must tell Bill, we must telephone Bill at once!" she cried—as though Bill had been able to think of anything else for weeks! She was not able to reach him that night, but later on she went to him at Cliveden. She was quoted by Nancy Lancaster as saying, "Fancy Bill having a pool full of prostitutes and not knowing what they were!" but it seems probable that this is what Nancy Lancaster thought her aunt would have said if she had been capable of grasping such alien concepts as swimming pools and prostitutes. Had she not always asked Bill, "Why do you need a swimming pool at Cliveden?" *She* had swum in the river. It is doubtful whether Nancy ever understood the few details that were allowed to reach her; in any case it is immaterial. She stood by Bill, as she would have done if her mind had been perfectly clear.

As the end came nearer it seemed not to Heaven that her thoughts turned, but to Virginia. "Are the Goodloes all gone?" she asked Douglas Pitt. "I can see Afton clearly. Oh, how I hope I can see you all once more." Her children would no longer let her take the long trip. "It's six to one ag'in it; five boys and one girl."

In her last months there were successive blows. Timothy d'Eresby, Wissie's boy, was lost at sea, and then her own dear friend and contemporary, Bob Brand, died. In March a still more painful blow fell: Bobbie Shaw attempted suicide. She was told only that he had suffered a stroke, but once she was with him it seemed that some instinct told her the truth. After her return from the hospital it appeared to Wissie and to others that something physical within her had given way. At any rate, the "awful vitality" of which she and Shaw had both complained in old age left her that day.

There were still flashes. Michael, who was with her on her return from the hospital, remarked on how lovely she looked. She was wearing a mauve dress trimmed with fur. "Do you still buy new clothes?" he asked her. "I like your cheek," she said. "What do you think I do? Buy old ones?"

After this she and Wissie went to the Ancaster place in Lincolnshire (one of Wissie's houses). On the afternoon of her arrival she suffered her first stroke. Regaining consciousness, she had opened her eyes on an unaccustomed scene; all her children were gathered at her bedside. "Am I dying," she asked, "or is this my birthday?" A doctor was brought in to whom she did not seem particularly to object. "Considering that I am dying," she told him in a friendly fashion, "I am very well." She was going quietly, at her own pace. Michael described her as "dying in the same way as she (particularly as a young woman) must have done most of her living, unevenly, at different paces. Dying, gliding, reviving, trying, submitting."

Late in the afternoon of May 1 she lifted her hands and cried, "Waldorf." There was nothing more. Early on the morning of May 2 she died.

The memorial service in the Abbey was held on May 13. Many plain people were there, people known to no one in particular. Somewhere, at some time, Nancy had touched them. The Prime Minister of the day, Sir Alec Douglas Home, and his predecessor, Harold Macmillan, were there. *Her* Prime Ministers, Lloyd George and Mr. Balfour, were long gone. There were the American Ambassador and the representatives of the royal family. The Right Reverend Norman Clarke gave the address, but it seems more natural to think of her in fragments, in the short phrases of her friends and enemies. Even Harold Nicholson had said, "There is something about her, a flame somewhere." And laughter. If there is laughter in Heaven, Nancy will be there.

Notes on Sources

The principal sources consulted in preparing each chapter are listed below. Full reference for the published works cited is given in the Bibliography, beginning on page 269.

Chapter 1

Principal sources for this chapter are NA's privately printed autobiographical memoir, *The Astor Story*, and conversations with her girlhood friends and relatives—especially the late Mrs. Saunders Hobson; the late Mrs. William Abbot, NA's first cousin; the late Mrs. Douglas Forsyth; Mrs. Tucker Brown—and, above all, with NA herself. Other sources consulted are *Tears and Laughter*, a memoir by Ella Williams Smith; an article by Barbara Trigg (Mrs. Tucker) Brown, published in the *Richmond Times Dispatch*, October 9, 1966; *A History of Emmanuel Church, Greenwood*, by Langhorne Gibson; and *The Church of the Living Waters*, by Frederick William Neve. For further information concerning Mr. Neve, I am indebted to the Reverend Dennis Whittle. I am grateful to Mrs. Natalie Blanton for information concerning Miss Jennie Ellett and for the opportunity to consult the Virginia Ellett papers. For Langhorne family history, I have consulted *Reminiscences*, by the Reverend W. H. Langhorne, and, among books of local history, *Campbell Chronicles and Family Sketches*, by A. H. Early. *The Astors*, by Harvey O'Connor, has been a principal source for this and the following chapter. It is quite impossible to note all the sources of information, all the kindnesses and fascinating reminiscences that my interest in NA's Virginia girlhood has elicited over the years, but those mentioned above have been major contributors.

Chapter 2

For this chapter I am again indebted to NA's memoir as well as to *Nancy*, by Christopher Sykes, and *The Astors*, by Harvey O'Connor. A principal source for NA's courtship and marriage has been family letters.

Chapter 3

My main sources for this chapter are NA's letters to her father at the time of her engagement and marriage. Also, I have again relied on her own memoir. Descriptions of Cliveden I owe partly to observation and conversations with the Cliveden staff and partly to *Tribal Feeling*, by Michael Astor. The quotation from Hilaire Belloc may be found in Mr. Sykes's biography.

Chapter 4

Material used in this chapter was drawn from *The Public Career of Lady Astor*, by Phyllis Laverne Ayers, an unpublished paper on file in the Library of Congress. For information concerning Plymouth, I am most deeply indebted to NA's Plymouth secretary, Miss Joyce Knight. *The Astors*, by Harvey O'Connor, has been of use in tracing the Astor-Roosevelt connection. The best general source for the Kindergarten period is *The Unification of South Africa*, by L. M. Thompson. For information about the personal background of the Kindergarten group in South Africa and in the early Round Table, I am most indebted to the late Lord Brand and, to some extent, to *Geoffrey Dawson and Our Times*, by Evelyn Wrench. A principal source for the early life of Philip Kerr is *Lord Lothian*, by J. R. M. Butler. I would also recommend the delightful memoir *Cecil: Marchioness of Lothian*, by Lady Anne Cecil Kerr.

Chapter 5

For the Asquith correspondence in this chapter, see *Nancy*, by Christopher Sykes. I am indebted to several conversations with the late Lord Brand for information concerning the early relationship between NA and Philip Kerr. Her conversion to Christian Science is taken mostly from her own memoir, and here, too, I owe something to Mr. Sykes. Information concerning the *Observer* and Waldorf Astor's relations with Garvin may be found in *The "Observer" and J. L. Garvin*, by A. M. Gollin. For a general impression of talk at Cliveden, I am indebted to *Tribal Feeling*, by Michael Astor, and to conversations with NA's youngest son, the Hon. J. J. Astor.

Chapter 6

A great many books were consulted for this chapter. Among the most important were *Memoirs of the Peace Conference*, by David Lloyd George; *The "Observer" and J. L. Garvin* and *Proconsul in Politics*, both by A. M. Gollin. *The Diaries of Lord Riddell*, all volumes, are an invaluable source for these years. Quotations from Harold Nicolson may be found in *Peace Making, 1919*. I have again used NA's memoir, and some material from her American speeches published in *My Two Countries*. Articles by Philip Kerr in the *Round Table* and the signed leading articles in the *Observer* by J. L. Garvin have been consulted. Relevant issues continue to be consulted throughout later chapters. For a detailed day-to-day coverage of the peace conference, see Arno J. Mayer's *Policy and Diplomacy of Peace Making*.

Chapter 7

The principal sources for this chapter are *The Public Career of Lady Astor*, by Phyllis Laverne Ayers, unpublished thesis on file in the Library of Congress; Lord Riddell's *Intimate Diary of the Peace Conference and After;* J. R. M. Butler's *Lord Lothian;* and *The Prevention of War*, by Philip Kerr and Lionel Curtis. For this chapter, as for all subsequent chapters, I have also made frequent use of a scrapbook of newspaper clippings in the possession of the Langhorne family. Quotations from Waldorf's diary describing Nancy's American speaking tour are from Mr. Sykes's *Nancy*. NA's speeches quoted in this chapter are from *My Two Countries.*

Chapter 8

For Nancy's views on foreign policy, see Phyllis Laverne Ayers, *The Public Career of Lady Astor*. Descriptions of family life have been taken from Michael Astor's *Tribal Feeling* and from conversations with the late Lord Brand. Again, I have consulted the Virginia Ellett papers. The factual description of Wissie's accident is taken from Mr. Sykes's book and from NA's memoir but I must say that I do not agree with Mr. Sykes's suggestion that NA's later account of Wissie's cure was a "noble lie." Surely it was a question of emphasis, not a "distortion of facts."

Chapter 9

I have used the Lothian papers in Register House, Edinburgh, extensively in connection with the naval conferences, the Kellogg pact, the Russian trip, and NA's speeches. For the account of the Russian trip, I am also indebted to conversations with Miss Gertrude Ely and to *Bernard Shaw*, by Hesketh Pearson. For the discussion of economic theory, I have consulted *The Life of John Maynard Keynes*, by R. F. Harrod; *The Age of Keynes*, by Robert Lekachman; *The Return to Gold, 1925*, by D. E. Moggridge; and *The Economic Consequences of Mr. Churchill*, by J. M. Keynes. The four articles by Keynes sent to the President by Waldorf Astor appeared in the *Times* (London), on March 13, 14, 15, and 16, 1933.

Chapter 10

A principal source for the first part of this chapter is *A Diary with Letters*, by Thomas Jones. There are numerous books on Lawrence, and I have consulted most of them. The material used in this chapter is taken from *The Letters of T. E. Lawrence*, edited by David Garnett; *Private Shaw and Public Shaw*, by Stanley Weintraub; *T. E. Lawrence by His Friends*, edited by A. W. Lawrençe; and *Letters to T. E. Lawrence*, edited by A. W. Lawrence. The description of Lawrence's funeral may be found in *The Secret Lives of Lawrence of Arabia*, by Philip Knightley and Colin Simpson.

Chapter 11

The Chaplin visit is described in *Charlie Chaplin*, by Theodore Huff. A few chance remarks by NA herself gave the clue to her attitude toward him. Other sources for this chapter are letters in the possession of the Langhorne family and among the Lothian papers in Edinburgh. The Roosevelt papers at Hyde Park were also used, as were relevant files of the *Times* (London) and the *Observer*. Philip's interview with Hitler has been published as an appendix to J. R. M. Butler's *Lord Lothian.* For the period of the occupation of the Rhineland, see *A Diary with Letters,* by Thomas Jones. I have used extensive quotations from the April, 1936, supplement to *International Affairs,* published by the RIIA. The quotations from Claud Cockburn are taken from *The Week,* June, 1936–December, 1938. His own explanation of the genesis of the "Cliveden Set" pieces appears in his autobiography, *Crossing the Line.* For the account of his father's interview with Hitler, I am indebted to the Hon. David Astor.

Chapter 12

See Hansard, *Debates–House of Commons,* vol. 308, for the passages on the Education Bill. I have again used family letters and NA's letters to Mr. Neve. The Roosevelt-Chamberlain correspondence is in the Roosevelt papers at Hyde Park. I have again used Jones's *Diary with Letters,* and the Lothian papers. Details of Roosevelt's peace plan may be found in *A Time for Decision,* by Sumner Welles. The Lothian-Cecil debate in the House of Lords is from Hansard (Lords), vol. 104.

Chapter 13

A principal source has again been Jones's *Diary with Letters.* The description of the Chamberlains' farewell luncheon for the von Ribbentrops is from *The Gathering Storm,* by Churchill. A most useful source for letters and documents of the Munich period is *Peace or Appeasement,* by Francis L. Loewenheim.

I have also consulted Anthony Eden's *Facing the Dictators; The Nemesis of Power,* by John Wheeler-Bennett; *Roosevelt and Frankfurter,* edited by Max Freedman; *The Winds of Change,* by Harold Macmillan; *Lord Halifax,* by the Earl of Birkenhead; and others. Starting with 1938, *The Diaries of Sir Alexander Cadogan* is a useful source.

Chapter 14

The Munich literature is, of course, very extensive. I have consulted *The Life of Neville Chamberlain,* by Keith Feiling; *Neville Chamberlain,* by Iain Macleod; and *Munich,* by John Wheeler-Bennett. Loewenheim has again been most useful. For details behind the scenes in Germany, see Christopher Sykes's *Troubled Loyalty* and, again, Wheeler-Bennett's *Nemesis of Power.* The Roosevelt-Lindsay interview is from *Documents on British Foreign Policy.* The London background of the Munich crisis is taken from files of date of the *Times.* Chamberlain's remarks on leaving the Hotel Dreesen at Godesberg are from *The Rise and Fall of the Third Reich,* by William Shirer.

For the scene in the House of Commons on September 28, I am indebted to Harold Nicolson's *Diaries and Letters,* vol. 1. Philip Lothian's letter to NA of September 16 is quoted from Mr. Sykes's *Nancy.* The last sentence in this chapter is a paraphrase of a statement made to the author by David Astor.

Chapter 15

Churchill's speech in the House after Munich and NA's interruptions may be found in Hansard. Philip's leading articles after Munich in the *Observer* appeared on November 13, 20, and 27, 1938. His letters of the period may be found in Butler's *Lord Lothian* and in Jones's *Diary with Letters,* as well as in the Lothian papers. The Cliveden Set rebuttals may be found in *Liberty* for January 1, 1939, and in the March 4, 1939, *Saturday Evening Post.* The quotation from NA in the Commons after the occupation of Prague is from

Hansard (Commons), vol. 345. Waldorf's speech in the Lords may be found in Hansard (Lords), vol. 112. For information concerning the Europe study group, see Thomas Jones. For further information concerning Moltke in England, I am indebted to a conversation with Mrs. Lionel Curtis and to many conversations with Moltke's widow, Freya von Moltke, to whom I wish to express here my most particular gratitude. Mr. Sykes's *Troubled Loyalty* and *Helmuth von Moltke: A Leader Against Hitler*, by Michael Balfour and Julian Frisby, are principal sources for this chapter. For Trott's report to the German Foreign Ministry, see *Documents on German Foreign Policy*, Series D, vol. 6, Doc. 497, p. 674. A detailed account of Trott's visit to Cliveden may be found in *Troubled Loyalty*, pp. 240–48.

Hansard continues to be my source for NA's remarks in the Commons. The Lothian-Smuts letters are from the Lothian papers. The quotation from Churchill concerning Chamberlain and FDR may be found in *The Gathering Storm*. Philip's speeches are quoted from *The American Speeches of Lord Lothian*.

Chapter 16

The principal sources for this chapter have been *The Years of Urgency*, from the Morgenthau diaries, edited by John Morton Blum, and Churchill's *Their Finest Hour*. A full account of the Malcolm Lovell incident may be found in *1940*, by Laurence Thompson. The account of Philip's last trip to England has been taken from various sources, among them a conversation with Miss Heather Harvey, Nicolson's *Diaries and Letters*, and *Sunshine and Shadow*, by Dorothy Allen. The description of his death may be found in the Norman Davis papers at the Library of Congress.

Chapter 17

The Norman Davis papers have been a principal source for this chapter, as have the Roosevelt papers at Hyde Park. The quotation from Rose Harrison is taken from a copy of her letter of March, 1941, to the late Mrs. Saunders Hobson in Richmond. Further descriptions of NA's part in the Plymouth blitz are from a letter from Miss Adelaide Massey to the author and from the very kind and extensive reminiscences of Miss Joyce Knight, NA's long-time secretary in Plymouth. Letters from Bernard Shaw to Nancy have also been quoted. Literature on the German opposition to Hitler is extensive but perhaps little known. Again, the recent biography by Michael Balfour and Julian Frisby of Moltke and *Troubled Loyalty*, by Christopher Sykes, are principal sources. A vivid account of NA's relations with the 29th Division in Plymouth was furnished to the author in a letter from General C. H. Gerhard, USA, retired.

Chapter 18

For this chapter, I am indebted to the Shaw correspondence and to NA's letters to the Reverend Douglas Pitt. Family letters have again been used, particularly those from Douglas Langhorne and NA's letters to me. Conversations with Mrs. Gordon Smith have been most helpful; so were visits with NA at Mrs. Smith's home in Greenwood. For NA's trip to Rhodesia, I am indebted to Mr. Sykes's biography and to a conversation with Mr. Pitt. My impression of her last years is drawn largely from meetings with NA as they occurred during the 1940s, 1950s, and early 1960s. Our last meeting was in 1963. The description of her final illness is taken mainly from Mr. Sykes's account.

Selected Bibliography

Books and Pamphlets

ADDISON, CHRISTOPHER, *Four and a Half Years* (London: Hutchinson, 1934).

ALLEN, DOROTHY FRANCES, *Sunlight and Shadow* (London: Oxford University Press, 1960).

ASTOR, MICHAEL, *Tribal Feeling* (London: John Murray, 1963).

ASTOR, NANCY, *My Two Countries* (New York: Doubleday, Page, 1923).

———, *The Astor Story* (Baltimore: Emmanuel Church, 1951). Referred to as NA's memoir.

BALFOUR, MICHAEL, and JULIAN FRISBY, *Helmuth von Moltke: A Leader Against Hitler* (London: Macmillan, 1972).

BIRKENHEAD, EARL OF, *Halifax: The Life of Lord Halifax* (Boston: Houghton Mifflin, 1966).

BLUM, JOHN MORTON, *Years of Urgency, 1938–1941: From the Morgenthau Diaries* (Boston: Houghton Mifflin, 1965).

BULLOCK, ALAN, *Hitler: A Study in Tyranny* (New York: Harper Torchbook, 1962).

BUTLER, J. R. M., *Lord Lothian* (New York: St. Martin's Press, 1960).

CADOGAN, SIR ALEXANDER, *The Diaries of Sir Alexander Cadogan* (New York: G. P. Putnam's Sons, 1972).

CHURCHILL, WINSTON S., *The Aftermath* (New York: Charles Scribner's Sons, 1929).
———, *The Gathering Storm* (Boston: Houghton Mifflin, 1948).
———, *Their Finest Hour* (Boston: Houghton Mifflin, 1949).
COCKBURN, CLAUD, *Crossing the Line* (New York: Monthly Review Press, 1969).
DAVIES, JOSEPH A., *The Prime Minister's Secretariat, 1916–1920* (Newport, Mon.: R. H. Johns, 1951).
EARLY, R. H., *Campbell Chronicles and Family Sketches* (Lynchburg, Va.: J. P. Bell, 1927).
EDDY, MARY BAKER G., *Rudimental Divine Science*, published by Allison V. Stewart (Boston, 1909).
———, *Science and Health, with Key to the Scriptures*, published by the Trustees under the will of Mary Baker G. Eddy (Boston, 1934).
EDEN, ANTHONY, *Facing the Dictators* (Boston: Houghton Mifflin, 1962).
FEILING, KEITH, *The Life of Neville Chamberlain* (London: Macmillan, 1946).
FREEDMAN, MAX (ed.), *Roosevelt and Frankfurter: Correspondence* (Boston: Atlantic Monthly Press, 1967).
GARNETT, DAVID (ed.), *The Letters of T. E. Lawrence* (New York: Doubleday Doran, 1939).
GIBSON, LANGHORNE, *A History of Emmanuel Church, Greenwood, Va.*, 1960.
GOLLIN, A. M. *Proconsul in Politics: A Study of Lord Milner in Opposition and in Power* (New York: Macmillan, 1964).
———, *The "Observer" and J. L. Garvin* (London: Oxford University Press, 1960).
GRAVES, ROBERT, and BASIL LIDDELL-HART, *T. E. Lawrence to His Biographers* (London: Hart, Cassell, 1963).
HALIFAX, LORD, *Fullness of Days* (New York: Dodd, Mead, 1957).
———, *Speeches on Foreign Policy* (London: Oxford University Press, 1940).
HANKEY, LORD, *The Supreme Control of the Paris Peace Conference, 1919* (London: George Allen and Unwin, 1963).
HARROD, R. F., *The Life of John Maynard Keynes* (New York: Harcourt, Brace, 1951).
HOARE, SIR SAMUEL, *Nine Troubled Years* (London: Collins, 1954).
JONES, THOMAS, *A Diary with Letters* (London: Oxford University Press, 1954).
KERR, LADY ANNE CECIL, *Cecil: Marchioness of Lothian* (London: Sands & Co., 1922).
KERR, PHILIP, and LIONEL CURTIS, *The Prevention of War* (New Haven, Conn.: Yale University Press, 1923).
KEYNES, J. M., *The Economic Consequence of Mr. Churchill* (London: L. and V. Woolf, 1925).
KNIGHTLY, PHILIP, and COLIN SIMPSON, *The Secret Lives of Lawrence of Arabia* (New York: McGraw-Hill, 1970).
LANGHORNE, REVEREND W. H., *Reminiscenses* (Edinburgh, 1893).
LAWRENCE, A. W. (ed.), *Letters to T. E. Lawrence* (London: Jonathan Cape, 1962).
——— (ed.), *T. E. Lawrence by His Friends* (London: Jonathan Cape, 1937).

LEKACHMAN, ROBERT, *The Age of Keynes* (New York: Random House, 1966).

LINDBERGH, CHARLES, *The Wartime Journals of Charles Lindbergh* (New York: Harcourt Brace Jovanovich, 1970).

LLOYD GEORGE, DAVID, *Memoirs of the Peace Conference*, vol. I (New Haven, Conn.: Yale University Press, 1939).

———, *War Memoirs*, vol. III (Boston: Little, Brown, 1934).

LOEWENHEIM, FRANCIS L., *Peace or Appeasement* (Boston: Houghton Mifflin, 1965).

LOTHIAN, LORD, *Pacifism Is Not Enough, Nor Patriotism Either*, The Burge Memorial Lecture (London: Oxford University Press, 1941).

———, *The American Speeches of Lord Lothian* (London: Oxford University Press, 1941).

———, "The Demonic Influence of National Sovereignty," in *The Universal Church and the World of Nations* (London: George Allen and Unwin, 1938).

MACLEOD, IAN, *Neville Chamberlain* (London: Frederick Mueller, 1961).

MACMILLAN, HAROLD, *The Winds of Change* (New York: Harper and Row, 1966).

MAYER, ARNO J., *Politics and Diplomacy of Peacemaking* (New York: Alfred A. Knopf, 1967).

MOGGRIDGE, D. E., *The Return to Gold, 1925* (London: Cambridge University Press, 1969).

MOWAT, C. L., *Britain Between the Wars* (Chicago: University of Chicago Press, 1955).

NEVE, FREDERICK, *The Church of the Living Waters* (Hobart, Ind.: Parish Leaflet, 1920).

NICOLSON, HAROLD, *Diaries and Letters*, vols. I and II (New York: Atheneum, 1966 and 1967).

———, *Peace Making, 1919* (London: Constable, 1933).

O'CONNOR, HARVEY, *The Astors* (New York: Alfred A. Knopf, 1941).

PEARSON, HESKETH, *Bernard Shaw* (London: Four Square Edition, 1964).

RIDDELL, LORD, *Lord Riddell's Intimate Diary of the Peace Conference and After* (New York: Reynal and Hitchcock, 1934).

SHIRER, WILLIAM, *The Rise and Fall of the Third Reich* (New York: Simon and Schuster, 1960).

SMITH, ELLA WILLIAMS, *Tears and Laughter* (Richmond, Va.: McClure Press, 1972).

SMUTS, JAN CHRISTIAAN, *Holism and Evolution* (New York: Viking Press, 1961).

SYKES, CHRISTOPHER, *Nancy: The Life of Nancy Astor* (New York: Harper and Row, 1972).

———, *Troubled Loyalty: A Biography of Adam von Trott* (London: Collins, 1968).

THOMPSON, LAURENCE, *1940* (New York: William Morrow, 1966).

———, *The Unification of South Africa* (Oxford: Clarendon Press, 1959).

TOYNBEE, ARNOLD J., *Acquaintances* (London: Oxford University Press, 1967).

VIERECK, PETER, *Metapolitics: The Roots of the Nazi Mind* (New York: Capricorn Books, 1965).

WEINTRAUB, STANLEY, *Private Shaw and Public Shaw* (New York: George Braziller, 1968).
WELLES, SUMNER, *A Time for Decision* (New York: Harper and Brothers, 1944).
WHEELER-BENNETT, SIR JOHN W., *Munich: Prologue to Tragedy* (New York: Viking Press, 1964).
———, *The Nemesis of Power* (New York: Viking Press, 1967).
WILSON, TREVOR, *The Downfall of the Liberal Party* (Ithaca, N.Y.: Cornell University Press, 1966).
WRENCH, SIR EVELYN, *Geoffrey Dawson and Our Times* (London: Hutchinson, 1955).

Periodicals and Documents

Documents on British Foreign Policy, 3d Series, vol. 7, January 14, 1938; September 20, 1938.
Documents on German Foreign Policy, Series D, vol. 6, pp. 674–685, June 1–8, 1939.
Foreign Relations of the United States, vol. II, 1937.
Liberty, January 1, 1939.
New York Herald Tribune, October 10, 1939, Walter Lippmann.
New York Review of Books, "Noble Man," George Kennan (review of *Helmuth von Moltke*, by Balfour and Frisby), March 22, 1973.
New York Times, May, 1938.
New York Times Book Review, September 28, 1969.
Observer, London. Editorials by Garvin; articles by Philip Kerr, September 22, 1929; November 18, 1934; October 24, 1937; November 13, 1938.
Parliamentary Debates (Commons), Hansard: vols. 125 (February 24, 1920), 215 (March 21, 1928), 299 (March 11, 1935), 308 (February 13, 1937), 345 (March 16, 1938), and 377 (February 17, 1942).
Parliamentary Debates (Lords), Hansard: vols. 104 (March 2, 1937); 112 (April 13, 1939); 119 (July 16, 1941).
Punch, January 2, 1929.
Richmond Times Dispatch, October 9, 1966. Feature story by Barbara Trigg Brown.
Round Table, 1910–1939. Numerous articles by Philip Kerr are listed in an appendix to *Lord Lothian*, by J. R. M. Butler.
Royal Institute of International Affairs (RIIA), *Bulletins and Special Supplements*.
Saturday Evening Post, March 4, 1939.
The Week, ed. Claud Cockburn, June, 1936–December, 1938.
Times, London, December 4, 1916; March, 1933; November 13, 1934; September, 1938; December 2, 1944.
Western Morning News, Plymouth.

Unpublished Sources

Chiswell Dabney Langhorne, by his grandson, Langhorne Gibson.
Langhorne family letters.
NA's letters to Mr. Neve, in the possession of his daughter, Mrs. Allen White.
NA's speeches: *A Problem for Women*, NA's maiden speech in pam-

phlet form, 1920. Radio Broadcast to the United States, 1922, typescript. *Free But Not Lawless*, 1937, typescript. (See also NA's *My Two Countries*, Hansard; and Ayer, *The Public Career of Lady Astor*.)

The Franklin D. Roosevelt Papers, Hyde Park, N.Y.

The Lothian Papers, Register House, Edinburgh.

The Norman Davis Papers, Library of Congress.

The Public Career of Lady Astor, Phyllis Laverne Ayers (University of Pittsburg, 1958). Unpublished thesis on file in the Library of Congress.

The Virginia Ellett Papers, Richmond, Va.

Index